DAILY

366 Poems from the World's Most Popular Poetry Website

Diane Boller, Don Selby, and Chryss Yost
editors

Rita Dove and Dana Gioia
advisory editors

SOURCEBOOKS, INC.
NAPERVILLE, ILLINOIS

Published by Sourcebooks, Inc.
P.O. Box 4410, Naperville, Illinois 60567-4410
(630) 961-3900
FAX: (630) 961-2168
www.sourcebooks.com

Library of Congress Cataloging-in-Publication Data

Poetry daily : poems from the world's most popular website / edited by
Diane Boller, Don Selby, and Chryss Yost.
    p. cm.
 ISBN 1-4022-0151-6 (alk. paper)
 1. American poetry—21st century. I. Boller, Diane. II. Selby, Don.
III. Yost, Chryss.
 PS617.P63 2003
 811'.608—dc21
                              2003008843

Printed and bound in the United States of America
ED 10 9 8 7 6 5 4 3 2 1

ABOUT THE EDITORS

Don Selby cofounded Poetry Daily with Diane Boller and Rob Anderson following a twenty-year career in the law-publishing industry. He is a graduate of Swarthmore College and the University of Virginia School of Law. He lives in Charlottesville, Virginia.

In addition to her work with Poetry Daily, **Diane Boller** maintains a career in law and publishing. She is a graduate of the University of Virginia and the George Mason University School of Law. She lives in Charlottesville, Virginia.

Chryss Yost is an award-winning poet, writer, and web designer. She works at the University of California and is an editor of *SOLO: A Journal of Poetry*. With Dana Gioia and Jack Hicks, she coedited *California Poetry: From the Gold Rush to the Present*. She lives in Santa Barbara, California, with her daughter, Cassidy.

Rita Dove served as Poet Laureate of the United States and Consultant to the Library of Congress from 1993 to 1995. She has received numerous literary and academic honors, among them the 1987 Pulitzer Prize in Poetry and, most recently, the 2001 Duke Ellington Lifetime Achievement Award, the 1997 Sara Lee Frontrunner Award, the 1997 Barnes & Noble Writers for Writers Award, the 1996 Heinz Award in the Arts and Humanities, and the 1996 National Humanities Medal. Her latest poetry collection, *On the Bus with Rosa Parks*, was published in 1999. Editor of *The Best American Poetry 2000*, she is Commonwealth Professor of English at the University of Virginia in Charlottesville.

Dana Gioia was born in Los Angeles in 1950. He received his B.A. and M.B.A. degrees from Stanford University. He also has an M.A. in Comparative Literature from Harvard University. For fifteen years, he worked as a business executive in New York before quitting in 1992 to write full-time. Gioia is the author of three volumes of poetry, *Daily Horoscope, The Gods of Winter*, and *Interrogations at Noon*. which won the American Book Award in 2002, as well as an opera libretto, *Nosferatu*. Gioia's critical collection, *Can Poetry Matter?* was a finalist for the National Book Critics Circle Award. He is chairman of the National Endowment for the Arts.

table of contents

January

February

March

october

november

december

Acknowledgments

After six years online, the poets, editors, publishers, and friends to whom we owe our gratitude are too numerous to list here. Support and encouragement have come from poets, who have so generously offered the gift of their poems as well as their time and energy for a growing variety of special editorial features at Poetry Daily; from editors and publishers, whose position to our editorial windward has insured our clear sailing; and from friends, some of whom we see every day and many more we have met only online, all of whose encouragement has been daily. Here, to stand for these many friends (and family), are just a few of our early stalwarts: Barbie Selby, Rob Anderson, Joseph Parisi, Helen Lothrop Klaviter, Stephen Young, Jill Bialosky, Peter Davison, Wen Stephenson, R. T. Smith, Lynn Leech, Judith Moore, Jim Gibson, Laura Horn, Jeff Coughter, Ed Lowry, Luther Gore, Angelo Verga, Dana Gioia, Rita Dove, Marion K. Stocking, Barbara Hamby, David Kirby, Billy Collins, Robert Pinsky, Don Lee, Steve Turner, Bob Hicok, Susan Hahn, Peg Peoples, April Ossmann, Albert Goldbarth, David Lehman, James Reiss, J. D. McClatchy, Peter Johnson, Brian Henry, Jeffrey Levine, Martha Rhodes, Richard Foerster, Sarah Gorham, David Graham, Michael Chitwood, Laure-Anne Bosselaar, David Yezzi, Roger Lathrop, C. Dale Young, A. E. Stallings, David Baker, David H. Lynn, Jeffrey Shotts, Rebecca Wolff, Jessie Lendennie, Dick Allen, Steve Boller. Heartfelt thanks to these and so many more.

introduction

Are you reading this while standing in front of the poetry shelf of your local bookstore or library, wondering what contemporary poetry might be worth exploring? Have you had the experience of coming upon forgotten poems you'd clipped from *The New Yorker* or *The Atlantic*, and of wishing that poetry could be a part of your life *every* day? Or have you ever left the magazine section of your bookstore after looking there in vain for the one or two literary journals you've heard of, in the hope of finding at least a small sample of what's new in contemporary poetry?

If any of these things are true, or if you are looking for a window from which you can see for yourself the variety of what is happening in contemporary poetry, this book is for you. And, if you are a poet yourself, in need of a means to refresh your sense of the heartening diversity and vitality of contemporary poetry, *Poetry Daily* is for you too.

In 1997, when we launched Poetry Daily (www.poems.com), our anthology of contemporary poetry published every day on the Web, it sometimes seemed to us that secret handshakes were the only way to find other readers of contemporary poetry, and that praying for a rare miracle—the appearance of a review of a book of poetry (certainly by a poet both still alive and not carrying the seal of approval of the Nobel Committee) in a newspaper or magazine—was the only chance of discovering new poetry. But from the first day, Poetry Daily has been proof that the late, lamented "literate reading public" is not just part of a legendary past, but is real, active, very large, and *growing*: at this writing as many as thirty thousand readers visit Poetry Daily on a given day to read a poem selected from a newly released book or magazine or to catch up on the latest news and reviews from the world of poetry. And the ranks of our readers grow *daily*.

It has been more than ten years since Dana Gioia, poet, critic, and current Chairman of the National Endowment for the Arts, in his now famous *Atlantic* essay "Can Poetry Matter?" issued his challenge to the poetry community to reclaim its ancient position in society, not by "dumbing down" poetry, but by making it literally more accessible; not by draining the art from poetry so as to make it somehow "easier," but simply by making the art available to everyone—a part, once again, of everyday life.

This is the challenge we took up in launching Poetry Daily online—to help make contemporary poetry available to anyone, anywhere, every day. The Internet has become a complex place since we began, but its greatest virtue is still the same one promised at the outset: free, democratic *access*. The goal of our website is to help you make poetry a vital part of your daily life by providing you with a new poem each day selected from the latest books and journal issues published in English. Rather than attempt to supplant the work of our betters in poetry publishing, our purpose is to lead you to them. Our poems come from large publishers and small—you'll find selections from well known commercial publishers like W. W. Norton & Company and Houghton Mifflin, and long-established university presses like the University of Chicago Press and LSU Press; but you'll also find poems selected from new, independent presses, such as Tupelo Press and even chapbook publishers, like Slapering Hol Press. You'll find the oldest poetry and literary journals represented, like *Poetry* magazine, *The Kenyon Review*, and *Shenandoah*, but also the most recent (and sometimes ephemeral) magazines and journals, such as *FENCE, jubilat*, and *The Hat*.

Who are we to be doing this? Well, first, a confession: we're readers, not poets. Don's creative writing career began, peaked, and ended with two poems in his junior high school's magazine; Diane's has yet to be launched; and Rob has been tempted to write interactive computer games, but not poems. We are publishers, originally from a very different neck of the publishing woods (legal publishing of all things), who discovered, about the time that Dana Gioia was writing his essay, that we shared both a mutual devotion to contemporary poetry and an excitement about the possibilities of the Internet. Don discovered a thin volume by W. S. Merwin in Diane's office, peeking out from behind a row of tomes like *Federal Rules of Evidence Manual* and *Liability of Corporate Officers and Directors*; Diane and Rob pitched the new technology ("bulletin boards" then, if you can remember them—no World Wide Web in those days) to a management group deputed to worry about such things, which included Don; an email exchange of favorite poems began; and before long we were contacting poets, editors, and publishers about the suddenly real possibility of bringing their work to the attention of an audience miles beyond their advertising budgets.

We're guessing that we came to poetry by routes not much different from yours: Diane found in the art a literary lifeline in the midst of an initial career in law practice and a second raising a family—each leaving scarce time for serious fiction but time enough for the poems that became more and more important to her. Before leaving for a stay in Italy, Don chanced on a notice in a magazine of an odd project by a poet with a Ouija board, so he packed James Merrill's *Divine Comedies* along with an edition of Dante from college days and came home eager for more. Rob matched Diane's and Don's fervor for poetry with his own vision of what the Internet could do for people and soon was borrowing books and imagining what poetry ought to look like in cyber-space.

Our first selection, Tom Vander Ven's "Sea Washes Sand Scours Sea," from *The Beloit Poetry Journal*, was published on April 7, 1997. A new poem (and sometimes an extra one or two) has appeared every day since, thanks early on to the editors and poets who saw the point of what we were proposing almost before they saw the Internet—Joseph Parisi at *Poetry*, Peter Davison and Wen Stephenson at *The Atlantic*, Marion Stocking at *The Beloit Poetry Journal*, R. T. Smith at *Shenandoah*, Jill Bialosky at W. W. Norton—and now thanks to the support and encouragement of hundreds of poets and publishers in the U.S. and abroad. We are so grateful for their belief in the value of Poetry Daily and for their encouragement and support. Our greatest pleasure has been getting to know these poets, publishers, and editors, experiencing the intensity of their labors, and bringing news of their work to others. We hope that Poetry Daily, both online and off, is a tribute to them.

But it is to our fiercely loyal readers that we dedicate this collection, selected from the first five years of Poetry Daily. As we had hoped, people from every walk of life, all over the world, not only visit us daily, but take the time to send us words of encouragement and, crucially, to make the financial contributions necessary to keep us in service to poetry every day, at no charge to anyone. Without both sorts of commitment we could not continue.

If you are a longtime online Poetry Daily reader, thank you, again and again, for your loyal support! If you are new to Poetry Daily, let us welcome you with this special collection. We hope you will enjoy this *off*line look at where we've been in our first five years *on*line. Keep looking in—there are more good things on the way!

january 1

V, x

Why is it modern poets are ignored
and only dead ones get adored?
That's how envy works, Regulus,
the dead make the safest rivals.
So we mourn Pompey's colonnade
and its nostalgic, leafy shade
just as our fathers praised the temple
Catulus restored not wisely nor too well.
Rome reads Ennius, though Virgil is to hand,
as Homer was a joke in his own land;
Menander's best plays were thought dull;
only Corinna knew her Ovid well.
So, little books, let's not rush to our fate.
Since death comes before glory, let's be late.

William Matthews
from *The Mortal City: 100 Epigrams of Martial*

january 2

An Attempt

for Osip Mandelstam

For us, all that's left
is a dried bee, tilted
onto one wing.

Not long ago, a bloom
fastened its tongue, while its belly
tried unsuccessfully
to tip it backwards.

We mustn't touch—
anything without water
is without give.

This bee is our scout—
one day, dust
will pronounce itself
in the armatures
of every flower.
But we'll not be closer.

Angela Ball
first published in *Ploughshares*, vol. 24, no. 4,
     Winter 1998–99

Forget How to Remember How to Forget

"I have a rotten memory" began
The American version of that long
French novel: and save for the telling word
Leaping in all its colors out of the
Grayish blank, or for the mad turn of phrase
That I, unyielding judge, committed to
My bedlam memory, I cannot come
Up with exactly what was said even
In a recent conversation. Books can
Remember, for they have written it all
Down—they are in themselves all written down—
And, as Phaedrus was famously told in
That lovely grove (and this was written down),
Writing is remembering's enemy.

Writing it down—thereby writing it up,
The "it" here being language or event—
Allows what was told to recall itself.
The flux of our experience will dry
Into mere flecks; once-great spots of time now
Are filmy moments of place, on the page,
In the full course—or somewhere on the banks—
Of all that streams behind me. And the dear
Name of oh, Whatshername, herself—oh, yes
Mnemosyne (lost for a minute in
An overstuffed, messy drawer, crammed with names)
Is all I have to call on for a guide
To wherever back up the relentless
River I might momently have to go.

And who, when hindsight frays, would want the most
Obvious compensation of foresight,
Prophecy creeping into the places
Recall was slowly vacating? Only
The young with so much to look forward to
And little to remember could call it
A reasonable deal, and better to
Go on climbing, as steps on steps arise
And it all keeps dissolving into that
Father of Waters that every fresh
Moment originates anew, the while
Some sort of sweet, silent judgment commutes
All that, accessible or not, streams out
Behind you into time already served.

John Hollander
from *Figurehead*

How the Demons Were Assimilated & Became Productive Citizens

The demons were more beautiful than the angels.
They had no qualms about plastic surgery.
They took to wearing black: didn't show dirt
In the city like Innocence, which anyway
Couldn't be worn between Labor Day and Easter.
They tired of grudging angels their gilded hair
& had theirs done. Their complexions were so pale
The blond looked natural, only more so.
They shrunk their wings into fashionable tattoos
So cashmere suits draped better from their shoulders.
Elocution lessons turned hisses to lisps.

The demons converted. They became Episcopalian,
Name-dropped high-ups in the Company of Heaven.
As for Evil, it became too much trouble:
The demons started to shirk the menial jobs
Which like good deeds, took one among the poor,
And bruised the manicure of rose-petal nails.
They preferred to stand by & watch Evil happen,
Or offended by odors & noise, even turned away.

They had become so beautiful, even the angels
(Who never looked in mirrors to comb their hair,
Afraid to be called vain, & never bought clothes
Since the old ones didn't wear out, just got shabby)
Left the lovely demons to languish, dropping all charges
On the spoiled creatures. They were that good.

A. E. Stallings
first published in *The Beloit Poetry Journal*, vol. 46, no. 6, Summer 1996
also from *Archaic Smile*

january 5

The Silence of the Stars

When Laurens van der Post one night
   In the Kalihari Desert told the Bushmen
      He couldn't hear the stars
Singing, they didn't believe him. They looked at him,
   Half-smiling. They examined his face
      To see whether he was joking
Or deceiving them. Then two of those small men
   Who plant nothing, who have almost
      Nothing to hunt, who live
On almost nothing and with no one
   But themselves, led him away
      From the crackling thorn-scrub fire
And stood with him under the night sky
   And listened. One of them whispered,
      Do you not hear them now?
And van der Post listened, not wanting
   To disbelieve, but had to answer,
      No. They walked him slowly
Like a sick man to the small dim
   Circle of firelight and told him
      They were terribly sorry,
And he felt even sorrier
   For himself and blamed his ancestors
      For their strange loss of hearing,
Which was his loss now. On some clear nights
   When nearby houses have turned off their visions,
      When the traffic dwindles, when through streets
Are between sirens and the jets overhead
   Are between crossings, when the wind
      Is hanging fire in the fir trees,
And the long-eared owl in the neighboring grove
   Between calls is regarding his own darkness,
      I look at the stars again as I first did

To school myself in the names of constellations
    And remember my first sense of their terrible distance,
        I can still hear what I thought
At the edge of silence were the inside jokes
    Of my heartbeat, my arterial traffic,
        The C above high C of my inner ear, myself
Tunelessly humming, but now I know what they are:
    My fair share of the music of the spheres
        And clusters of ripening stars,
Of the songs from the throats of the old gods
    Still tending even tone-deaf creatures
        Through their exiles in the desert.

David Wagoner
from *Traveling Light: Collected and New Poems*

january 6

The Nurse

My mother went to work each day
in a starched white dress, shoes
clamped to her feet like pale
mushrooms, two blue hearts pressed
into the sponge rubber soles.
When she came back home, her nylons
streaked with runs, a spatter
of blood across her bodice,
she sat at one end of the dinner table
and let us kids serve the spaghetti, sprinkle
the parmesan, cut the buttered loaf.
We poured black wine into the bell
of her glass as she unfastened
her burgundy hair, shook her head, and began.
And over the years we mastered it, how to listen
to stories of blocked intestines
while we twirled the pasta, of saws
teething cranium, drills boring holes in bone
as we crunched the crust of our sourdough,
carved the stems off our cauliflower.
We learned the importance of balance,
how an operation depends on
cooperation and a blend of skills,
the art of passing the salt
before it is asked for.

She taught us well, so that when Mary Ellen
ran the iron over her arm, no one wasted
a moment: My brother headed straight for the ice.
Our little sister uncapped the salve.
And I dialed the number under Ambulance,
my stomach turning to the smell
of singed skin, already planning the evening
meal, the raw fish thawing in its wrapper,
a perfect wedge of flesh.

Dorianne Laux
from *Awake*

january 7

Pine

i.
I thought wearing an evergreen dress
might be enough to express the longing
of the pine
though it or because it retains its scent
throughout the snowfall
and above the tree line. That's what I thought.

ii.
I needle my students
and a few write inflamed poems
to my ideological bent and my ankle bracelet.
I lay awake in the neighbor's light
through the curtain of flurries
we find in the real morning—
the one with real light.
And the only way to guide them
through their own compost
is to needle them harder—
to make them work not for me
but for the spruce
scraping at their windows. Still
X sends terrifying love letters
that send so much blood to the chest
the fingers are cold.

iii.
You say it's from *a crush*.

iv.
You say quit using these *he* and *hims*
when the specificity of *John*
is more engaging.
I needle: make me feel.

v.
Next time I make a C-note
from a poem
I will send you a red dress
I have tried on myself first.
The silk, light as the lotion
on the nape of your neck.

vi.
silk, rayon, chiffon,

vii.
You say it's the *he* in *heat*.

viii.
I see pine and I see
what I know is feeling.
I imagine stepping barefoot
under those trees
onto a bed of their
brown needles.
So prick my skin.

Kimiko Hahn
from *Mosquito & Ant*

january 8

Absence

There are men and women huddled in rooms tonight
discussing dark matter, the non-stuff, the anti-
things which fill the universe. Imagine writing
that grant. Their children are of relatively
specific dimension, their houses occupy
nearly calculable space. Seven have dogs.
One dreams of playing in the British Open
nude. Yes, exactly like your father.
Of special interest is the woman in an office
in Princeton in a swivel chair looking
through a window at the pond where Einstein's
said to have sat and thought about sailboats,
the little ones German children race on ponds.
She whispers Bolivia, a word she caught
on a map earlier and hasn't been able to shake.
She has never been there. She has never left
the east, finds Bar Harbor exotic, thinks
of lobsters as the first wave of an alien invasion.
Together with a colleague she is trying to total
the mass of everything, the mental equivalent
of 27 clowns cramming into a 60s vintage Volvo.
What she likes about the word Bolivia
beside the sexual things it does to the tongue
is her feeling that anything you do there
might cause people to dance. She would like
to dance now. If most of what exists
can't be seen or spread on toast
or wedged under a door in summer
when you want to fall asleep on the couch
to a wind that began somewhere near Topeka,
it's acceptable to dance on a desk in an office
paid for by the Rockefeller Foundation
in an attempt to resurrect that once
good name. And even as she pictures herself

clearing and scaling the desk,
she is striding to the board and brushing
away a series of calculations
and replacing them with another, more
elegant run, adding at the end the curlicue
of infinity which normalizes the equation,
which makes her noodling momentarily right
with God and explains how a pinhole
could have the density of a universe, how half
of Jupiter could lie balled in your shoe.
Bolivia, she says, spinning. Bolivia,
she repeats, grabbing Bill Morrison
by the collar. Bolivia, he answers,
embracing the odd particulars of revelation,
kissing her hand in a burlesque of manners,
knowing it's just made chalk beautiful,
aligned the glyphs of mass and spin
into a schematic of everything. Then briefly,
looking over his shoulder at the board,
she realizes in essence she's trapped
nothing, not the stars but the black leading
between the light, the same absence
she feels at night when looking up a force
like wind rises through her body, leaving
no trace except the need to be surrounded
by anything more comforting than space.

Bob Hicok
first published in *Boulevard*, vol. 12, nos. 1 and 2
also from *Plus Shipping*

What Do Women Want?

I want a red dress.
I want it flimsy and cheap,
I want it too tight, I want to wear it
until someone tears it off me.
I want it sleeveless and backless,
this dress, so no one has to guess
what's underneath. I want to walk down
the street past Thrifty's and the hardware store
with all those keys glittering in the window,
past Mr. and Mrs. Wong selling day-old
donuts in their cafe, past the Guerra brothers
slinging pigs from the truck and onto the dolly,
hoisting the slick snouts over their shoulders.
I want to walk like I'm the only
woman on earth and I can have my pick.
I want that red dress bad.
I want it to confirm
your worst fears about me,
to show you how little I care about you
or anything except what
I want. When I find it, I'll pull that garment
from its hanger like I'm choosing a body
to carry me into this world, through
the birth-cries and the love-cries too,
and I'll wear it like bones, like skin,
it'll be the goddamned
dress they'll bury me in.

Kim Addonizio
first published in *Another Chicago Magazine*, no. 32/33, Spring/Summer 1997
also from *Tell Me*

january 10

Fetch

Go, bring back the worthless stick.
"Of memory," I almost added.
But she wouldn't understand, naturally.
There is the word and the thing

adhering. So far so good.
Metaphor, drawer of drafting tools—
spill it on the study floor, animal says,
that we might at least see

how an expensive ruler tastes.
Yesterday I pissed and barked and ate
because that's what waking means.
Thus has God solved time

for me—here, here. What you call
memory is a long and sweet,
delicious crack of wood in my teeth
I bring back and bring back and bring back.

Jeffrey Skinner
first published in *The Iowa Review*, vol. 29, no. 1, Spring 1999
also from *Gender Studies*

How Came What Came Alas

Came the hammer, so to speak,
the what had been,

for some time, coming. Came
unlike the wrath I had so often

fancied. Came frog song
over pains of open soil.

Came bird song over brimstone.
Came collected. Came prepared.

No one called, with any voice,
me close to it.

No lightning loud to lord
over—the meek lights

of longing only. Came seeming, to me,
at first, unlovely as afterbirth—

came lovely as the body butting
all that is unlovely out.

Come wild, I prayed, come
fire-like upon my undergrowth,
come like the halbert here
upon my candid breast.

But such as would be fit
for such a coming came said,

came weary of the wilderness,
came kennelled in my head.

HeidiLynn Nilsson
first published in *Pleiades*, vol. 19, no. 2, Summer 1999

Nothing in That Drawer

Nothing in that drawer.
Nothing in that drawer.
Nothing in that drawer.
Nothing in that drawer.
Nothing in that drawer.
Nothing in that drawer.
Nothing in that drawer.
Nothing in that drawer.
Nothing in that drawer.
Nothing in that drawer.
Nothing in that drawer.
Nothing in that drawer.
Nothing in that drawer.
Nothing in that drawer.

Ron Padgett
from *New & Selected Poems*

january 13

A Dog's Grave

In thin sun that lifted its hands
from my shoulders,
leaving me cold, in a patch
of tall grass that took hold
of my legs so I stumbled,
next to a bent little tree
that tapped at my back
with its twigs, I fought hard
for a grave for my dog,
chopping through sod,
through a layer of ice,
through snow-soaked topsoil
that clung to the blade,
and then I unfolded the clay,
the warm yellow brown
of an old army blanket,
and dry as a place by the stove.

Ted Kooser
first published in *Witness*, special issue: "Animals in America," vol. XV, no. 2, 2001

Old Man Leaves Party

It was clear when I left the party
That though I was over eighty I still had
A beautiful body. The moon shone down as it will
On moments of deep introspection. The wind held its breath.
And look, somebody left a mirror leaning against a tree.
Making sure that I was alone, I took off my shirt.
The flowers of bear grass nodded their moonwashed heads.
I took off my pants and the magpies circled the redwoods.
Down in the valley the creaking river was flowing once more.
How strange that I should stand in the wilds alone with my body.
I know what you are thinking. I was like you once. But now
With so much before me, so many emerald trees, and
Weed-whitened fields, mountains and lakes, how could I not
Be only myself, this dream of flesh, from moment to moment?

Mark Strand
from *Blizzard of One*

january 15

What the Living Do

Johnny, the kitchen sink has been clogged for days, some utensil probably fell down there.
And the Drano won't work but smells dangerous, and the crusty dishes have piled up

waiting for the plumber I still haven't called. This is the everyday we spoke of.
It's winter again: the sky's a deep headstrong blue, and the sunlight pours through

the open living room windows because the heat's on too high in here, and I can't turn it off.
For weeks now, driving, or dropping a bag of groceries in the street, the bag breaking,

I've been thinking: This is what the living do. And yesterday, hurrying along those
wobbly bricks in the Cambridge sidewalk, spilling my coffee down my wrist and sleeve,

I thought it again, and again later, when buying a hairbrush: This is it.
Parking. Slamming the car door shut in the cold. What you called *that yearning*.

What you finally gave up. We want the spring to come and the winter to pass. We want
whoever to call or not call, a letter, a kiss—we want more and more and then more of it.

But there are moments, walking, when I catch a glimpse of myself in the window glass,
say, the window of the corner video store, and I'm gripped by a cherishing so deep

for my own blowing hair, chapped face, and unbuttoned coat that I'm speechless:
I am living, I remember you.

Marie Howe
from *What the Living Do*

january 16

from Unholy Sonnets

4

Amazing to believe that nothingness
Surrounds us with delight and lets us be,
And that the meekness of nonentity,
Despite the friction of the world of sense,
Despite the leveling of violence,
Is all that matters. All the energy
We force into the matchhead and the city
Explodes inside a loving emptiness.

Not Dante's rings, not the Zen zero's mouth,
Out of which comes and into which light goes,
This God recedes from every metaphor,
Turns the hardest data into untruth,
And fills all blanks with blankness. This love shows
Itself in absence, which the stars adore.

Mark Jarman
from *Questions for Ecclesiastes*

A '49 Merc

Someone dumped it here one night, locked
the wheel and watched it tumble into goldenrod and tansy,
ragweed grown over one door flung outward
in disgust. They did a good job, too: fenders split, windshield
veined with an intricate pattern of cracks
and fretwork. They felt, perhaps, a rare satisfaction
as the chassis crunched against rock and the rear window
buckled with its small view of the past. But the tires
are gone, and a shattered tail light shields a swarm
of hornets making home of the wreckage. How much
is enough? Years add up, placing one small burden on another
until the back yaws, shoulders slump. Whoever it was
stood here as the hood plunged over and some branches snapped,
a smell of gasoline suffusing the air, reminding us
of the exact moment of capitulation when the life
we planned can no longer be pinpointed on any map
and the way we had of getting there knocks and rattles to a halt
above a dark ravine and we go off relieved—
no, happy to be rid of the weight of all that effort and desire.

Kurt Brown
from *More Things in Heaven and Earth*

Nearly a Valediction

You happened to me. I was happened to
like an abandoned building by a bull-
dozer, like the van that missed my skull
happened a two-inch gash across my chin.
You went as deep down as I'd ever been.
You were inside me like my pulse. A new-
born flailing toward maternal heartbeat through
the shock of cold and glare: when you were gone,
swaddled in strange air, I was that alone
again, inventing life left after you.

I don't want to remember you as that
four-o'clock-in-the-morning eight months long
after you happened to me like a wrong
number at midnight that blew up the phone
bill to an astronomical unknown
quantity in foreign currency.
The dollar's dived since you happened to me.
You've grown into your skin since then; you've
    grown
into the space you measure with someone
you can love back without a caveat.

While I love somebody I learn to live
with through the downpulled winter days' routine
wakings and sleepings, half-and-half caffeine-
assisted mornings, laundry, stockpots, dust
balls in the hallway, lists instead of lust
sometimes, instead of longing, trust
that what comes next comes after what came
    first.
She'll never be a story I make up.
You were the one I didn't know where to stop.
If I had blamed you, now I could forgive

you, but what made my cold hand, back in prox-
imity to your hair, your mouth, your mind,
want where it no way ought to be, defined
by where it was, and was and was until
the whole globed swelling liquefied and spilled
through one cheek's nap, a syllable, a tear,
wasn't blame, whatever I wished it were.
You were the weather in my neighborhood.
You were the epic in the episode.
You were the year poised on the equinox.

Marilyn Hacker
from *Winter Numbers*

january 19

On a Portrait of Two Beauties

How old are these two, anyway?
Big and little sister, equally lovely.

In 100 years, smooth as two sheets of paper.
In 1,000, they still will glow like springtime.

Will the plum tree ever know the wind and moon?
Will reed and willow accept their dull fates?

Why not portray the other pleasures? Blame
the artist, gifted, but a bit dim about love.

Ho Xuan Huong
from *Spring Essence: The Poetry of Ho Xuan Huong*
translated by John Balaban

january 20

Landing under Water, I See Roots

—for Rita Dove

All the things we hide in water
hoping we won't see them go—
(forests fallen under water
press against the ones we know)—

and they might have gone on growing
and they might now breathe above
everything I speak of sowing
(everything I try to love).

Annie Finch
first published in *Partisan Review*, vol. LXVI, no. 2,
    Spring 1999
also from *Calendars*

january 21

Best

The Greeks said: never to be born is best;
next best, to die young in a noble cause.
"*Où sont les neiges d'antan?*" Villon asked.

"Where are yesteryear's snows?" is, I guess,
the phrase in English. Villon spoke in praise
of women not born when the Greeks said: "Best

not to exist at all." Yet the French poet pressed
on with his list: great beauties of the past.
"*Où sont les neiges d'antan?*" Villon asked.

In his great poem, only their names persist:
Joan, Beatrice, Blanche of the White Arms.
Were the Greeks right: not to live at all is best?

What would Blanche's lovers say to this
who are themselves just dust, all suffering
long gone as the snows after which Villon asked?

Beauty is like life itself: a dawn mist
the sun burns off. It gives no peace, no rest.
"*Où sont les neiges d'antan?*" we ask.
But the Greeks were wrong: to live and love is best.

Gregory Orr
first published in *Ploughshares*, vol. 23, no. 4, Winter 1997–98
edited by Howard Norman and Jane Shore
also from *The Caged Owl: New and Selected Poems*

january 22

Gravelly Run

I don't know somehow it seems sufficient
to see and hear whatever coming and going is,
losing the self to the victory
   of stones and trees,
of bending sandpit lakes, crescent
round groves of dwarf pine:

for it is not so much to know the self
as to know it as it is known
   by galaxy and cedar cone,
as if birth had never found it
and death could never end it:

the swamp's slow water comes
down Gravelly Run fanning the long
   stone-held algal
hair and narrowing roils between
the shoulders of the highway bridge:

holly grows on the banks in the woods there,
and the cedars' gothic-clustered
   spires could make
green religion in winter bones:

so I look and reflect, but the air's glass
jail seals each thing in its entity:

no use to make any philosophies here:
   I see no
god in the holly, hear no song from
the snowbroken weeds: Hegel is not the winter
yellow in the pines: the sunlight has never
heard of trees: surrendered self among
   unwelcoming forms: stranger,
hoist your burdens, get on down the road.

A. R. Ammons
from *Collected Poems: 1951–1971*

january 23

Why Fool Around?

How smart is smart? thinks Heart. Is smart
what's in the brain or the size of the container?
What do I know about what I do not know?
Such thoughts soon send Heart back to school.
Metaphysics, biophysics, economics, and history—
Heart takes them all. His back develops a crick
from lugging fifty books. He stays in the library
till it shuts down at night. The purpose of life,
says a prof, is to expand your horizons. Another says
it's to shrink existence to manageable proportions.
In astronomy, Heart studies spots through a telescope.
In biology, he sees the same spots with a microscope.
Heart absorbs so much that his brain aches. No
ski weekends for him, no joining the bridge club.
Ideas are nuts to be cracked open, Heart thinks.
History's the story of snatch and grab, says a prof.
The record of mankind, says another, is a striving
for the light. But Heart is beginning to catch on:
If knowledge is noise to which meaning is given,
then the words used to label sundry facts are like
horns honking before a collision: more forewarning
than explanation. Then what meaning, asks Heart,
can be given to meaning? Life's a pearl, says a prof.
It's a grizzly bear, says another. Heart's conclusion
is that to define the world decreases its dimensions
while to name a thing creates a sense of possession.
Heart admires their intention but why fool around?

He picks up a pebble and states: The world is like
this rock. He puts it in his pocket for safe keeping.
Having settled at last the nature of learning, Heart
goes fishing. He leans back against an oak. The sun
toasts his feet. Heart feels the pebble in his pocket.
Its touch is like the comfort of money in the bank.
There are big ones to be caught, big ones to be eaten.
In morning light, trout swim within the tree's shadow.
Smart or stupid they circle the hook: their education.

Stephen Dobyns
from *Pallbearers Envying the One Who Rides*

Riding Backwards on a Train

Someone always likes to ride backwards,
leaning his head against the window, reflection,
the clacking of the cars rocking him to sleep.
What does he see in the passing frames?
Stories. Stories like long tracts of land.
There goes an old house, a sycamore.
There goes an old house, a sycamore.
My mother was an old house, my father
a sycamore towering over her. In winter,
I teetered on a ladder, a weathered ledge,
and cleaned the gutters. When I dream
I am falling, I fall from that roof, born midair,
barely alive, then the ground, hard mercy,
a stranger's hand touching my shoulder.

James Hoch

first published in *The Kenyon Review,* New Series, vol. XXIV, no. 2, Spring 2002

january 2 5

Kepler Considers the Dimensions of a Sheep

The six directions which form a sheep
    are proof enough of Plan.
Plain to see why the head belongs on top:
    to view the view. And why
The ewe must brace her hooves
    against the earth. The belly
Rides beneath the back, to ease
    digestion on its downward tract.
As teats are neatly placed in reach
    of lambs, as baaah to bleat.
Front and back are circumspect
    in this respect:
To come and go requires it,
    while right and left are duplicates.
Probandum, one sheep, side by side,
Can progress, with alternating strides.

Linden Ontjes
first published in *Ploughshares*, vol. 27, no. 1, Spring
    2001
edited by Heather McHugh

january 2 6

Division

Inside the shed, he'd rigged
an oil drip into the barrel stove
so that the used sludge from his trucks
burned with split hickory while he
passed the winter piecing together furniture.
Just a sideline, he'd say, aiming
down a board to judge it in or out of true.
"It fills in the down months and tacks
some cash on the end of the year."

In those same white weeks at school
I learned division. First, you made a lean-to
for the big number to go under. The little
number waited outside. You could add on
as many zeros as you wanted.
The answer appeared on the roof.
December and January passed into February
and a whole bedroom suite came together.
On the roof, the smoke swirled into *O*s and *8*s.

Michael Chitwood
first published in *The Threepenny Review*, 88, vol. XXII,
    no. 4, Winter 2002

january 27

Numbers

I like the generosity of numbers.
The way, for example,
they are willing to count
anything or anyone:
two pickles, one door to the room,
eight dancers dressed as swans.

I like the domesticity of addition—
add two cups of milk and stir—
the sense of plenty: six plums
on the ground, three more
falling from the tree.

And multiplication's school
of fish times fish,
whose silver bodies breed
beneath the shadow
of a boat.

Even subtraction is never loss,
just addition somewhere else:
five sparrows take away two,
the two in someone else's
garden now.

There's an amplitude to long division,
as it opens Chinese take-out
box by paper box,
inside every folded cookie
a new fortune.

And I never fail to be surprised
by the gift of an odd remainder,
footloose at the end:
forty-seven divided by eleven equals four,
with three remaining.

Three boys beyond their mothers' call,
two Italians off to the sea,
one sock that isn't anywhere you look.

Mary Cornish
first published in *Poetry*, vol. CLXXVI, no. 3, June 2000

january 28

The Magic Mirror

I was standing in front of *The Magic Mirror*
   by Jackson Pollock in the Menil in late September.
     I was looking at a woman looking in the mirror—

abstracted, but with a feathered headdress.
   She was made of oil, granular filler, and glass
     fragments brushstroked across the canvas

in 1941, the year my parents turned fourteen
   and started "dating." The War was on,
     and black stormclouds loomed on the horizon.

I have imagined it all in slow motion—
   their two bodies coming together as one
     body exploding in rage into seeds and rain.

I was standing in front of *The Magic Mirror*.
   I was looking at a woman looking in the mirror.
     I was walking through the skin of the mirror

into the watery burial grounds of childhood.
   I felt the strokes—black, purple, yellow, red—
     raining down upon me, somehow freed

from the canvas—thick-skinned, light-filled—
   and suddenly I was summoning all the wounded
     animals inside me, totems of childhood,

and letting them go one by one—the mockingbird
  of grief, the nasty crow, the long-beaked
    hawk floating past a picture window flooded

with rain, heading for the Northeast Coast.
  Oh let the wind release me from the past
    wing by wing, bird by bird, ghost by ghost.

I was standing in front of *The Magic Mirror*.
  I was looking at a woman looking in the mirror.
    I was walking through the skin of the mirror

into the unexpected country of childhood.
  I watched my body dispersed and reunited
    somewhere else, transformed, transfigured.

Edward Hirsch
first published in *Five Points*, vol. III, no. 2, Winter 1999
also from *Lay Back the Darkness*

january 29

Oprah Out of Control

Headline in The Star

I have seen many horrible headlines
Of disasters on land and in air;
I have watched documentaries with breadlines
And pinched faces defining despair.
I have stood on the shores of the ocean
While the storm-surges darken and roll,
But I never heard such a commotion
As Oprah out of control.

I have seen Jenny Jones stand as witness
And Geraldo go down on his back,
Kathy Lee giving lessons on fitness
And Montel telling how to be black.
I have watched Jerry Springer take cover
When a guy finds his filly's a foal
Or a girl finds a *girl* is her lover:
But *Oprah* out of control?

Oh, I hope that the world will be saner
When the talk-shows at last reach an end,
When poor mom needs no guard to restrain her
And a friend kisses only a friend.
But I cling to my pillow—it's *so* soft—
And I shake to the depths of my soul,
And I shudder, in spite of my Zoloft,
At Oprah out of control.

R. S. Gwynn
first published in *Light Quarterly*, no. 32, Spring 2001

Purgatory Chasm

The earth has done this to itself. It heaved its rock
pectoral as an animal will, a brute mating. It must have
known that it would suffer endlessly thereafter

as the sea, reverberating, raised one steely claw, a second
and another: water's slow, erosive ritual.
That brand of love. The ghosts of razor grasses

watch from precipice and crevice, seething under
and above, swept hypnotized, as we are, by the shock
and aftershock of each anticipated wave. A minute.

A millennium. It's hazy, but we're here:
a study in repetition, breathing drowsy as the brume
we're watching struggle to disperse, particle

by particle, dulled by the hauled-out act, the redundant
sea and earth. Hapless would-be gas!
It's bound by laws of physics, laws of habit, laws

and love, love, love, the heat is overwhelming, but it isn't
our affair. We've traveled southwards
from the city, so ill-at-ease en route; you held

a radiant lemonade, and I, the satisfactory radio
wired in my head: disjunctive music's drowning out.
Slaking still and still devout, we make a pair

in judgment, cast it everywhere but in; we both
approved of, once, the vista, but now it's harrowed out
The Sea Mist Inn, peopled the cliff with a pack

of naturalists. Wave on wave, this rite continues. Earth will not
recoil from sea, sea digs the deeper groove
we cut through others to inspect. A little closer.

Close. The rusted rail and sign suggest all
take precaution, be responsible. Shift in sediment
or squall can force the careless over easy—

and often does, we pray: the granting of the asked-for.
And look, I've grasped your hand. Spurred
by passion as before, I pull us near enough to drop

into the chasm, doubled over. An answer, an idea.
We want this want but turn, demure.
We are not alone. All the world is here.

Timothy Donnelly
first published in *TriQuarterly*, no. 110/111, Fall 2001
also from *Twenty-Seven Props for a Production of Eine Lebenzeit*

january 31

Onomastics & the Falling Snow

The name and the spirit are inseparable.
    And most everything has a name except the falling snow,
By which I mean each flake, each one different,
    As one spirit is different from another, and close up,
Under a microscope, crystalline, like a thing made
    By a master watchmaker with a motor the size

Of a fingernail and an awl as fine as a hair.
    Sillier men than I have tried to name the flakes of snow
While standing hatless at a bus stop. From where comes
    This human urge to name each thing? Each man
And each woman, as though we're not all the same
    Thing repeated endlessly: the human race.

Did you know that among the ancient Hebrew tribes
    Children were given two names at birth,
One sacred, one profane? The child wasn't told
    The sacred one. So he walked around with two names,
One by which to be called in from the sheepfold
    And the other intricate, mysterious, useless, like the snow.

And in Norway, circa early twentieth century,
    There were so few hereditary names to pass down
Everyone must have thought everyone else a cousin. Maybe
    That's why they're so polite, so orderly. That's why,
If it's snowing in Oslo, there will always be
    A helpful soul standing beside you to offer space

The size of an umbrella while waiting for the bus.
    In America a name means nothing—a marker
To be called in, a convenience. You can look up an old, lost
    Acquaintance in a phone directory while passing through
A city, but until you call him up he's only the name
    Without the spirit. And his name won't tell us anything

About what he does with his days: Mr. Weaver at his loom,
    Mr. Lavender who makes soap; or how he looks:
Señor Roja for the color of his beard, or Mr. Gross,
    The fat man who stood in line waiting for
The greedy minions of the fanatic Empress Maria Theresa
    To take his money and bestow upon him a name

To be passed down to fat and skinny children alike.
    Or, if he were even poorer, and as a mean joke,
To be called the German equivalent of *Grease*, or *Monkey*
    Weed or *Do Not Borrow From* or *Gallows Rope*.
In Russia, in 1802, to raise an army, Czar Alexander
    Sent out a ukase ordering each Jew to take a last name—

Like writing a poem, mind-sprung
    And wholly inspired on first draft, then inscribing it
On the forehead of a neighbor, each one befitting:
    Isaac, *He Who Laughs*, or Mazal, *Lucky Man*,
Or Trubnic for *Chimney Sweep* or Soroka *The Magpie*,
    Meaning *The Gossip*. And babies in those days

Were sometimes given ugly names to turn aside
    The assiduous, bureaucratic Angel of Death;
Or, in illness, a child was renamed to befuddle
    The same angel coming down with his empty sack
To collect for God's heavens. But naming the snow,
    Each flake, each deliquescing cryptic coat of arms,

That would be a game for only the most inventive,
    Hopeless man. For after all, the snowflakes
Are the soon-to-be-dead, those who float awhile
    Then fall and, merging, pile up like corpses
On some northern battlefield, and there melt, flow
    Down as water to the river that has one name only.

It so happens it's snowing where I'm standing now
    At a bus stop in Oslo, between one moment and the next,
Feeling nostalgic, homesick, trying to remember the names
    Of everyone I've ever known. Hopeless, of course,
So to name is also duty, and is also good.
    So it worries me that my son, who is more like me

Than I care to think about, and who bears my last name,
    Could recite the names of each child
In his kindergarten class after only one week
    Of sitting with his hands folded on his desk.
He wasn't praying, he told me. He was waiting
    For the names to sink in so one morning he could say,

Suddenly, to each one, *Hi*, because it's good
    To be remembered by anyone, for the name and the spirit
Are inseparable. By the time we are old we have known
    So many people by name we could baptize each flake
Of falling snow while waiting for a bus.
    They grew away from me. They became snow,

Fuzzy at this distance, just beyond my reach,
    Waiting to be called upon again.

Steve Orlen

first published in *The Gettysburg Review*, vol. 11, no. 4, Winter 1998
also from *This Particular Eternity*

february 1

Lighting Up time

for Patrick Taylor

I

Rites of spring: roll out
your hibernating lawnmower,
dead grass wedged to blades;
line up the cans of paint,
sandpaper, brushes, rags.

II

The cottage garden
in the mauve light
of delphiniums.
Lilies with honeyed tongues.

Bird notes tossed
like blossoms.
A fern stretching
its wings.

III

Vulcanised rubber snails,
plump as a colony of seals,
make the viscous journey
to a meal of hosta leaves.

IV

Those daffodils,
You'd know it was
their first time:

so open, so eager to please,
so bright, so upright,
so unaware.

V

The raw nerve of yearning
triggered by hawthorn,
by the green of far-off hills
seen from your top-floor office
when sun pays out its light.

VI

That it might
always be spring,
a held note.

That we might
look forward
to long days

of growth:
haze lifting
like a screen,

waves peeling
off the Gulf Stream
one by one.

Dennis O'Driscoll
first published in *Verse*, vol. 13, nos. 2 and 3

february 2

Marriage

Marriage marriage is like you say everything everything in stereo stereo fall fall on the bed bed at dawn dawn because you work work all night. Night is an apartment. Meant to be marriage. Marriage is an apartment & meant people people come in in because when when you marry marry chances are there will be edibles edibles to eat at tables tables in the house. House will be the apartment which is night night. There there will be a bed bed & an extra bed bed a clean sheet sheet sheet or two two for guests guests one extra towel. Extra towel. How will you be welcomed? There will be drinks drinks galore galore brought by armies of guests guests casks casks of liquors liquors & brandies brandies elixirs sweet & bitter bitter bottle of Merlot Merlot Bustelo coffee. Will you have some when I offer. When you are married married there will be handsome gifts for the kitchen kitchen sometimes two of every thing. Everything is brand brand new new. Espresso coffee cups, a Finnish plate, a clock, a doormat, pieces of Art. And books of astonishing Medical Science with pictures. Even richer lexicons. When you are married married there will be more sheets sheets & towels towels arriving arriving & often often a pet pet or two two. You definitely need a telephone & a cell phone when you are married married. Two two two two lines lines lines lines. You need need separate separate electronicmail electronicmail accounts accounts. When you are married married you will have sets sets of things things, of more sheets & towels matching, you will have duplicates of things, you will have just one tablecloth. When you are married married you will be responsible when neighbors neighbors greet you. You will smile smile in unison unison or you might say he is fine, she is fine, o she is Just down with a cold, o he is consoling a weary traveler just now, arrived from across the Plains. She my husband is due home soon, he my wife is busy at the moment, my husband he is very very busy busy at the moment moment this very moment. Meant good-bye, good-bye. When you are married married sex sex will happen happen without delay delay. You will have a mailbox mailbox & a doorbell doorbell. Bell bell ring ring it rings rings again a double time. You do not have to answer. That's sure for when you are married people people understand understand you do not not have to answer answer a doorbell doorbell because sex sex may happen happen without delay delay. You will hear everything twice, through your ears & the ears of the other. Her or him as a case case may be be. He & he & she & she as a case case may be may be. When you are married married you can play play with names names & rename yourself if you like. You can add a name, have a double name with a hyphen if you like. You can open joint accounts when you are married. Marriage is no guarantee against depression. A shun is no guarantee against anything. Marriage is no guarantee against resolution. Revolution is a tricky word word. Here, you hear here? Marriage is sweeter sweeter than you think. Think.

—stereo

Anne Waldman
from *Marriage: A Sentence*

february 3

Self-Portrait, Double Exposed

Bellow-
ing skull heavy with brains
of pale prunes,
the eyeballs' continual dual eclipses,
cochlear snails coiled below
the skin, ellipses

of moles
trailing off mid-sentence
and the dense
shelf fungus of lungs. Crooked teeth. The nipples'
beribboned tambourines, miles
of intestines, ripples

of jagged
coastline where a gull glides
from the clouds
and over the fingers' ten shallow, brackish bays.
Pupas, polyps, checkered
crimsons, the steady buzz

of that
locust the heart. Liver
flies over
the stomach caw-cawing, over cells buttoned
    down
for evening: and hear the *thud*
thud as the pudenda

fall open
to the lines: "The world is
wholly his
who can see through its pretension."
But then what's left
to have? Stranded upon
the rocks as the rocks drift

off, both
too overwrought and too
naked, who
crouches here, hiding behind her shadow (turn a-
round, *look*—), dead in the path
of the navel's tornado?

Joanie Mackowski
first published in *The Paris Review*, no.158,
    Spring/Summer 2001
also from *The Zoo*

february 4

Farewell

At a certain point I lost track of you.

They make a desolation and call it peace.

When you left even the stones were buried:

The defenseless would have no weapons.

When the ibex rubs itself against the rocks, who collects its fallen fleece from the slopes?

O Weaver whose seams perfectly vanished, who weighs the hairs on the jeweler's balance?

They make a desolation and call it peace.

Who is the guardian tonight of the Gates of Paradise?

My memory is again in the way of your history.

Army convoys all night like desert caravans:

In the smoking oil of dimmed headlights, time dissolved—all winter—its crushed fennel.

We can't ask them: *Are you done with the world?*

In the lake the arms of temples and mosques are locked in each other's reflections.

Have you soaked saffron to pour on them when they are found like this centuries later in this country
  I have stitched to your shadow?

In this country we step out with doors in our arms.

Children run out with windows in their arms.

You drag it behind you in lit corridors.

If the switch is pulled you will be torn from everything.

At a certain point I lost track of you.

You needed me. You needed to perfect me:

In your absence you polished me into the Enemy.

Your history gets in the way of my memory.

I am everything you lost. You can't forgive me.

I am everything you lost. Your perfect enemy.

Your memory gets in the way of my memory:

I am being rowed through Paradise on a river of Hell: Exquisite ghost, it is night.

The paddle is a heart; it breaks the porcelain waves:

It is still night. The paddle is a lotus:

I am rowed—as it withers—toward the breeze which is soft as if it had pity on me.

If only somehow you could have been mine, what wouldn't have happened in this world?

I'm everything you lost. You won't forgive me.

My memory keeps getting in the way of your history.

There is nothing to forgive. You won't forgive me.

I hid my pain even from myself; I revealed my pain only to myself.

There is everything to forgive. You can't forgive me.

If only somehow you could have been mine,

what would not have been possible in the world?

(for Patricia O'Neill)

Agha Shahid Ali
from *The Country without a Post Office*

february 5

Candlelight

Crossing the porch in the hazy dusk
to worship the moon rising
like a yellow filling-station sign
on the black horizon,

you feel the faint grit
of ants beneath your shoes,
but keep on walking
because in this world

you have to decide what
you're willing to kill.
Saving your marriage might mean
dinner for two

by candlelight on steak
raised on pasture
chopped out of rain forest
whose absence might mean

an atmospheric thinness
fifty years from now
above the vulnerable head
of your bald grandson on vacation

as the cells of his scalp
sautéed by solar radiation
break down like suspects
under questioning.

Still you slice
the sirloin into pieces
and feed each other
on silver forks

under the approving gaze
of a waiter
whose purchased attention
and French name

are a kind of candlelight themselves,
while in the background
the fingertips of the pianist
float over the tusks

of the slaughtered elephant
without a care,
as if the elephant
had granted its permission.

Tony Hoagland
from *Donkey Gospel*

february 6

Love Poem with Toast

Some of what we do, we do
to make things happen,
the alarm to wake us up, the coffee to perc,
the car to start.

The rest of what we do, we do
trying to keep something from doing something,
the skin from aging, the hoe from rusting,
the truth from getting out.

With yes and no like the poles of a battery
powering our passage through the days,
we move, as we call it, forward,
wanting to be wanted,
wanting not to lose the rain forest,
wanting the water to boil,
wanting not to have cancer,
wanting to be home by dark,
wanting not to run out of gas,

as each of us wants the other
watching at the end,
as both want not to leave the other alone,
as wanting to love beyond this meat and bone,
we gaze across breakfast and pretend.

Miller Williams
from *Some Jazz a While: Collected Poems*

february 7

On guard

I want you for my bodyguard,
to curl round each other like two socks
matched and balled in a drawer.

I want you to warm my backside,
two S's snaked curve to curve
in the down burrow of the bed.

I want you to tuck in my illness,
coddle me with tea and chicken
soup whose steam sweetens the house.

I want you to watch my back
as the knives wink in the thin light
and the whips crack out from shelter.

Guard my body against dust and disuse,
warm me from the inside out,
lie over me, under me, beside me

in the bed as the night's creek
rushes over our shining bones
and we wake to the morning fresh

and wet, a birch leaf just uncurling.
Guard my body from disdain as age
widens me like a river delta.

Let us guard each other until death,
with teeth, brain and galloping heart,
each other's rose red warrior.

Marge Piercy
from *What Are Big Girls Made Of?*

Cold War

That first winter
he drove us across
the frozen surface
of Lake Champlain—
from Charlotte, Vermont
to Essex, New York and back,
in our VW bus,
the youngest at home
with our mother,
who knew nothing
until late that night
when my father, lighting
his pipe, said casually,
"I did it," and she,
unbelieving at first,
didn't speak, and then
in a voice that came
darkly, like the shadow
of a closing door:
"Are you some
kind of maniac?"

Weeks later
in the Mustang,
he maneuvered off the pier
and onto the rink
of lake, past stunned
hockey players,
accelerating
to the bruised
transparency of thinner
shield, then,
slamming his brakes,
spiraled us

into a vortex
degrees beyond our
understanding,
though the sheer
blind thrill of it
we mistook
for his happiness
wrenched free.

What failures
at violence, these
test drives, the earth's
ice sealed against
his folly,
his slow fall
not downward
but sprawling,
like fractures
in anchor ice,
or tributaries
bleeding in spring.
That February
might have been
fiction, but for the
pinging and shifting
of depths beneath us
the moment the Mustang
spun to its standstill,
a glazed world
turning through
milky oxygen,
and no sure direction
home.

The scooped
vinyl cushion
of back seat
made a dark lap
we squirmed in,
fearing and craving
these odd outings,
high on the cloudy
chemistry of love's failure—
or so we later learned.
Clues, though,
were everywhere,
shavings of crystallized
disappointment
beading on our mother's
tepid forehead
as she lined our mittens
along the radiator's
chipped ribs
and hung
our coats.

Sara London
first published in *The Hudson Review*, vol. LI, no. 4, Winter 1999

FEBRUARY 9

Song Beside a Sippy Cup

In the never truly ever
truly dark dark night, ever
blinds-zipped, slat-cut,
dark-parked light,
you (late) touch my toes
with your broad flat own
horny-nailed cold toes.
Clock-tock, wake-shock.

In the ever truly never
truly long long night, our
little snoring-snarling
wild-child mild-child
starling-darling wakes every
two, three (you-sleep) hours,
in the never truly ever
truly lawn brawn fawn dawn.

Jenny Factor

first published in *The Beloit Poetry Journal*, vol. 51, no. 4, Summer 2001

A Gentleman Compares His Virtue to a Piece of Jade

The enemy was always identified in art by a lion.

And in our Book of Victories
wherever you saw a parasol
on the battlefield you could
identify the king within its shadow.

We began with myths and later included actual events.

There were new professions. Cormorant Girls
who screamed on prawn farms to scare birds.
Stilt-walkers. Tightrope-walkers.

There was always the "untaught hold"
by which the master defeated
the pupil who challenged him.

Palanquins carried the weapons of a goddess.

Bamboo tubes cut in 17th-century Japan
we used as poem holders.

We tied bells onto falcons.

A silted water garden in Mihintale.
The letter *M*. The word "thereby."
There were wild cursive scripts.
There was the two-dimensional tradition.

Solitaries spent all their years
writing one good book. Federico Tesio
graced us with *Breeding the Race Horse*.

In our theatres human beings
wondrously became other human beings.

Bangles from Polonnaruwa.
A nine-chambered box from Gampola.
The archaeology of cattle bells.

We believed in the intimate life, an inner self.

A libertine was one who made love before nightfall
or without darkening the room.

Walking the Alhambra blindfolded
to be conscious of the sound of water—your hand
could feel it coursing down banisters.

We aligned our public holidays with the full moon.

3 a.m. in temples, the hour of washing the gods.

The formalization of the vernacular.

The Buddha's left foot shifted at the moment of death.

That great writer, dying, called out
for the fictional doctor in his novels.

That tightrope-walker from Kurunegala
the generator shut down by insurgents

stood there
swaying in the darkness above us.

Michael Ondaatje
from *Handwriting*

Misgivings

"Perhaps you'll tire of me," muses
my love, although she's like a great city
to me, or a park that finds new
ways to wear each flounce of light
and investiture of weather.
Soil doesn't tire of rain, I think,

but I know what she fears: plans warp,
planes explode, topsoil gets peeled away
by floods. And worse than what we can't
control is what we could; those drab,
scuttled marriages we shed so
gratefully may augur we're on our owns

for good reasons. "Hi, honey," chirps Dread
when I come through the door, "you're home."
Experience is a great teacher
of the value of experience,
its claustrophobic prudence,
its gloomy name-the-disasters-

in-advance charisma. Listen,
my wary one, it's far too late
to unlove each other. Instead let's cook
something elaborate and not
invite anyone to share it but eat it
all up very very slowly.

William Matthews
from *After All: Last Poems*

february 12

Tulips

Maybe our failed hopes rise like tulips
out of the cold ground,
and, when we look around,
there their satin bowls are, chocolates,

and swaying, velvety clarets, aglow
with memories of help we thought would
appear and beliefs we watered.
And we do have something to show,

goblet-like reminders of our stubborn
labors—or we don't, and refuse
odorless flowers and choose
to live without consolation.

Mark Halperin
first published in *River Styx*, issue 61, 2001

Sea Washes Sand Scours Sea

(for my daughter's wedding)

> *No hay camino. El camino se hace al andar.*
> —Antonio Machado

Walking the shore that day, each reaches down
for stones from time to time, the other talking,
her eye finding stones like purple berries,
his hand holding a cloud-light shell to her.

Seas they cannot yet see are ancient seas;
trees they will later pass are not yet trees.
Shore that he looks back to turns to haze,
and sand that she imagines turns to shore.

He says, "Sea washes sand scours sea."
"And sand drinks sea drowns sand," says she.
Voices of gulls call through them on the wind;
the dog circles out beyond their voices.

"All that proceeds recedes," he says at last.
"That you and I are here," she says, "is all."
The man watches the woman watches the man.
The woman loves the man loves the woman.

The day does not diminish other days;
they gain a newer language from the day.
Though wave by step their footprints wash away,
The day does not diminish other days.

Tom Vander Ven

first published in *The Beloit Poetry Journal*, vol. 47, no. 2, Winter 1996–1997

FEBRUARY 14

239

My lady, how comes it about—what all can see
from long experience—that rough mountain stone
carved to a living form, survives its own
creator, who'll end as ashes in an urn?
  Cause lesser than its effect. From which we learn
how nature is less than art, as well I know
whose many a lively statue proves it so,
which time and the tomb exempt, grant amnesty.
  Mine then, the power to give us, you and me,
a long survival in—choose it—stone or color,
faces just like our own, exact and true.
  Though we're dead a thousand years, still men can see
how beautiful you were; I, how much duller,
and yet how far from a fool in loving you.

Michelangelo
first published in *The Complete Poems of Michelangelo*
translated by John Frederick Nims

Modulation

When I am dead with you, fastened up, enameled,
dried on a hot stone and dropped in a well
to float with the other dead, not knowing them,
not knowing any name or step or skin,

when I am part of Law with you,
and have the terror of restless movement
worn away, so that I conform
in every particle to the rule of light,

when I am dead with you and stand
in bodiless perplexity inside the whim
of unimagined principle and cause, and feel
the fault that still I am myself,

still reasonable and cruel (and you
will be a heat of spinnings then), when we
are dead and witless to our dreams, collapsed
to less than ash, more thinly spread than space,

what will be the carrier, what atoms then
will boil, collect, and reappear unchanged,
remembering me in unfamiliar eyes,
and calling you in my forgotten voice?

Robert Clinton
from *Taking Eden*

february 16

Night Falling Fast

Was he gone for good? Or only an hour? Louise could never tell.
His hat was an after-
image fixed to the list of her eye. Was he tall and narrow,
did he wear white socks with black shoes, a fashion forgot-
ten so long ago but recently reborn as retro? Was he missing
to her? Had her heart's heart ever truly been his?

Or did she belong to whomever was wearing her arm
on his neck; her lip's sweetish lavender kiss
still hung in the air-
less room. Night falling fast in a shadowed locale
where a thin line could mean either fact or forensics:
the track of a fracture or the time it might take to wrap up a body.

The China dog tugged at its leash while in the radium light,
center and slightly, a zebra stood standing still.
The day had been ethereal until...
And where was the other when she needed a friend
to whom she could lend an ear
in return for a bed that was wider than one?

Her eyes remained anchored
on some furry distance; a furrow erased from her brow.
Let yourself go, she said to herself, and she did
know how after all. The night continued the day.
A murder of crows went by. What would she have?
The last beloved restored

to canvas and hanging, a knife through his heart?
Or a new who excelled where others had fizzled to Fail,
floundering fish on a shoal. Let go the leash
of the bad dogs that are dragging you this way and that.
And indeed, the hand could unclasp (Look at that!).
The leash fell at her feet.

Across the room, five fish in a tank made six meager moves,
the last through the castle that kept them
denizens of a splendid
language they spoke sotto voce.

Mary Jo Bang
from *Louise in Love*

Sonata

At ninety, the piano plays him.
He's like a man by the sea
the wind knows it must wear down,
sculpt to a profile,
then fill out again,
billowing his sleeves and trouser legs
into a younger musculature.
Over and again, the music grays
then reddens, the part
in its hair shifting left to center
until those few blades of sea grass
are all that's left to be
combed over the rocks,
and the thin fingers skitter,
leaving impressions in the keyboard
that waves wash level,
cleansing its audience of shell halves,
now glistening, now scoured dry.
And the house, the house just outside
this sonata's frame,
begs him to turn around
to pick his way back
along the stony runner,
his hands stopping his ears.
But, at ninety, the music plays the piano,
which plays the man, who finally, fearlessly,
plays himself, which is the landscape,
which is everything that ends.

Mark Cox
from *Thirty-Seven Years from the Stone*

February 18

Lightning Spreads Out across the Water

It was already too late
when the swimmers began
to wade through the heavy
water toward shore,
the cloud's black greatcoat
flinging across the sun,
forked bolts blitzing
the blind ground,
splits and cracks
going their own easiest way,
and with them, the woman
in the purple tank suit,
the boy with the water-wings,
one body then another.
And this is nothing about God
but how Stone Pond turned
at the height of the day
to flashpoint and fire
stalking across the water,
climbing the beach
among the screams
and the odor of burned skin
until twelve of them
curled lifeless on sand
or floated on the tipped
white caps of the surface,
and twenty-two more
walked into the rest
of their lives
knowing what waits
in the clouds to claim them
is random—

that nothing can stop it,
that afterwards the pond
smooths to a stillness
that gives back,
as though nothing could move it,
the vacant imponderable sky.

Patricia Fargnoli
from *Necessary Light*

My Gospel Is

I take my orders from the whiff
of the biscuit factory, the oily smell
of the bicycle repair shop.

I have caught myself in prayer,
nose lowered, longing
for the opposite side of the river,

for those white woods I've heard about
where one lets go at last the body's grip
and lifts, pale with knowledge, to hover

wingless in the windless air.
But I recover. A neighbor's cutting
lumber, loosing the pine plank's scent,

or a breeze is steeped in the stink
of marsh muck. My gospel is
the rolled-up rug discarded in a yard

and rained on, the fusty garden shed,
and the raised glass that stalls halfway
to the lips, the sweet milk gone bad.

Chris Forhan
first published in *New England Review*, vol. 21, no. 4, Fall 2000
also from *The Actual Stars*

Figure and Ground

In the summer I walked a trail, trying to accept things as they are.
Living among the small things.
For six weeks there was no rain; I took in the bright fields,
then the languid creek where two herons lifted over the water
as if their carriage were itself the air.
But it was God I was talking to now, not because the flowers
had a stricken beauty, but because for the first time
I commanded him, ordered him,
to notice me.

Christine Garren
from *Among the Monarchs*

Estuary

All winter we've been wheezing
gasping nights for breath.
Lace-edged, brackish, never freezing,
outside, the river crests.

Gasping nights for breath,
I sit upright, listen:
outside, the river crests;
inside, your breath glistens.

I sit upright and listen
for it: are you still or still breathing
inside? Your breath glistens
with the humidifier's misty heaving.

Are you? Still? You are still breathing!
We'll learn the names of birds
with the humidifier's misty heaving
background music to our words.

We learn to name the birds:
now you, at four, know grebes'
background music. Our new words:
coots' velvet necks, white beaks.

You, at four, know grebes,
grosbeaks, finches, buffleheads
and coots' velvet necks, white beaks.
We watch them mornings from the bed.

Grosbeaks, finches, buffleheads,
the busy estuary thrives.
We watch mornings from the bed.
The river nursery, *en masse*, rise.

Today, snow geese v'd north overhead.
Lace-edged, brackish, never freezing,
the river overflowed its bed
to end the winter of our wheezing.

Julie Fay
first published in *Shenandoah*, vol. 49, no. 4, Winter 1999

february 22

Charon

You who pull the oars, who meet the dead,
who leave them at the other bank, and glide
alone across the reedy marsh, please take
my boy's hand as he climbs into the dark hull.
Look. The sandals trip him, and you see,
he is afraid to step there barefoot.

Zonas, first century B.C.E.
from *Dances for Flute and Thunder*
translated by Brooks Haxton

february 23

Riddles

He opens her. She can't have him.
Day following night.
She can't have him but he opens her.
Clay and water.
He opens her because she can't have him.
Hive in a tree.
She can't have him until he opens her.
Peony and ant.
He opens her until she can't have him.
Wind in grass.
She can't have him while he opens her.
Cloud and rain.
He opens her, regretful she can't have him.
Phrase and mockingbird.
She can't have him regretful when he opens her.
Root and weak branch.

Kathleen Peirce
from *The Oval Hour*

February **24**

The Machinist, Teaching His Daughter to Play the Piano

The brown wrist and hand with its raw knuckles and blue nails
      packed with dirt and oil, pause in mid-air,
the fingers arched delicately,

and she mimics him, hand held just so, the wrist loose,
      then swooping down to the wrong chord.
She lifts her hand and tries again.

Drill collars rumble, hammering the nubbin-posts.
      The helper lifts one, turning it slowly,
then lugs it into the lathe's chuck.

The bit shears the dull iron into new metal, falling
      into the steady chant of lathe work,
and the machinist lights a cigarette, holding

in his upturned palms the polonaise he learned at ten,
      then later the easiest waltzes,
etudes, impossible counterpoint

like the voice of his daughter he overhears one night
      standing in the backyard. She is speaking
to herself but not herself, as in prayer,

the listener is some version of herself,
     and the names are pronounced carefully,
self-consciously: Chopin, Mozart,

Scarlatti,...these gestures of voice and hands
     suspended over the keyboard
that move like the lathe in its turning

toward music, the wind dragging the hoist chain, the ring
     of iron on iron in the holding rack.
His daughter speaks to him one night,

but not to him, rather someone created between them,
     a listener, there and not there,
a master of lathes, a student of music.

B. H. Fairchild
from *The Art of the Lathe*

february 25

Happiness

There's just no accounting for happiness,
or the way it turns up like a prodigal
who comes back to the dust at your feet
having squandered a fortune far away.

And how can you not forgive?
You make a feast in honor of what
was lost, and take from its place the finest
garment, which you saved for an occasion
you could not imagine, and you weep night and day
to know that you were not abandoned,
that happiness saved its most extreme form
for you alone.

No, happiness is the uncle you never
knew about, who flies a single-engine plane
onto the grassy landing strip, hitchhikes
into town, and inquires at every door
until he finds you asleep midafternoon
as you so often are during the unmerciful
hours of your despair.

It comes to the monk in his cell.
It comes to the woman sweeping the street
with a birch broom, to the child
whose mother has passed out from drink.
It comes to the lover, to the dog chewing
a sock, to the pusher, to the basket maker,
and to the clerk stacking cans of carrots
in the night.
          It even comes to the boulder
in the perpetual shade of pine barrens,
to rain falling on the open sea,
to the wineglass, weary of holding wine.

Jane Kenyon
from *Otherwise: New & Selected Poems*

february 26

Raptor in the Kitchen

Like an animal, I scavenge
after my child: half a peanut butter
sandwich, two tomatoes, skimmed from her
plate as if my blood could still

supply her flippery cavort.
No wonder a mother grows fat
with leavings, a bitch eating the afterbirth,
feral, destroying the fragrance

of nutritious young. Hawk
over chicks, eagle tearing the newly-
lambed, a raptor's shadow follows
me into the kitchen, onto the clown-faced

dish, desire to feed our own
the one command we share.

Joyce Peseroff
from *Mortal Education*

february 27

Vertigo

Mind led body
to the edge of the precipice.
They stared in desire
at the naked abyss.
If you love me, said mind,
take that step into silence.
If you love me, said body,
turn and exist.

Anne Stevenson
first published in *The Hudson Review*, vol. LII, no. 2,
    Summer 1999

february 28

Determinate Inflorescence: Ephemera

I am not making myself up for public consumption.
I enjoy consumption when it means an end to things.

Please deduce.
                          Each flower comes from the axil
of a small leaf which, however, is often so small
that it might escape notice and which sometimes
(as in the Mustard Family) disappears altogether.
(*Waving adieu, adieu, adieu.*) The summit, never
being stopped by a terminal flower may go on to grow
and often does so, producing lateral flowers
one after another, the whole summer long.

                                              Ok.

My raceme to your umbel. You terminal,
me currant, choke-cherry, barberry. You milk
weed, you flat cyme to my corymb, my kiss alas
like a moth on the right flower at the wrong time of day.

Liz Waldner
from *Self and Simulacra*

February 29

My Father's Hobby

My father's hobby was collecting sneezes. No stamps or coins for him. "The stuff of life," he said, "of life."

My mother and brothers shook their heads, his friends smirked, but he hurt no one, was an honest electrician, and everyone eventually shrugged it off as a harmless quirk. As his closest friend, Manny Borack, told my mom, "It could be worse."

Dad would mount the sneezes on glass slides he carried in his pockets everywhere he went. Some sneezes resembled flower petals, others seafoam, amoebas, insect wings, still others fanshaped fingerless foetal hands, splatters of raindrops, or empty cocoons.

Next he stained the specimens magenta, turquoise, egg-yolk yellow, and placed them in the glass cases that stood in all the rooms.

Late at night, when the family slept, he'd arrange handfuls of the slides on the light table in his study, and, switching off the lamp, he would peer down at them and smile.

One night, a small boy with bad dreams, I crept terrified through the darkened house to the study. He was bent over his collection, his face, surrounded by darkness, flowing in the table's light, as his lips murmured something again and again.

I slid my small hand into his and listened. He was rocking back and forth, bowing to the slides. "God bless you," he was saying, "God bless."

Morton Marcus
first published in *The Prose Poem: An International Journal*, vol. 5, 1996
also from *Moments without Names*

march 1

And in the Afternoons I Botanized

Where we sat, on the flagstone terrace behind the house,
Gin cooling in the spill of civilian twilight, ice cubes
Doing the dead man's float, with air rough to the touch,
The birch leaves blown yellow, in the lacerating shape of spades,
And thin boughs heaving a little with the season's sickness,
You said: We've come to calamity and the end of things.
Even the bees are weary, and the honey heavy, the petals depressed.
The wars you lose last longer than the wars you win.

And it was true. I could feel the same breeze, pallbearer of the birch,
October heading the dark cortège. Where others might trace
Lifelines in the palm, I read, on the back of my hand,
Liver spots like annotations on a last draft. No goldfinch
Flew to the feeder of wild seed; in the worked earth,
No chipmunk burrowed at the sweet root of the bulb.
And yet, in the mornings, fruit still hung fresh and firm,
Dew-dappled apples, frost smoke thick on the ground.

You said: If that crusty north-of-Boston poet had put us
In a poem, would we stand stiff as figures from a snow globe,
The trees bowed down around us, each branch bent
With the weight of meditation, the cling of imagery? Or would we
Lean on a worm fence, blood stropped in the heart,
Between us those moments where anger rubs on injury—
The tone medium wry, the pace pieced out in syllables
That stick in the throat, the ache of everything unsaid?

Well, better that than chintz and chimes, some teapot dame
Who'd make us talk on stilts, or in the weak repeats of
Rondeaus and rondels, French inventions that sound like
Girl groups from the Sixties. Would you rather lose yourself
In the cold echoes of Eliot, his vaulted voice dry as
Stone commencements at the graveside? Or find yourself
Edged out by the muscle of music in late Yeats?
We'll take our own line, broken, with a grain of sense and salt.

But no words slow down the dirt. And these drinks,
Essence of emptiness from the juniper berry, can't bring back
A duckweb spray of maple paddling in the slipstreams of spring,
Or the flowering crab, or panicles of japonica. You said:
At 47, I'm in my prime numbers, indivisible, entered
Only by myself and one other—odd and middling and absolute—
The mind still testing out every hedge against death,
The short con and the long shot, the bet called on the come.

It's no wonder we nail our days to the wall, and hang
Distractions of the calendar, slick colors over the Xed-out box:
Gaunt barge of Venice in the green canals; the loveknot puzzles of
Women in the pink; and from Monet, the blue and purple pulp of waterblooms.
So all our albums fail the past: pictures of picnics and the rose ribbons of
Girls dozy under the summer oak; your unparalleled apparel,
That dress the shade of bittersweet; and my brand-new panama,
Black band around the crown, hat like an elegy for the head.

You said: If we were characters cast in a play, could we choose
Some comedy written in the wit of Restoration, and call ourselves
Lord and Lady Vainhope, or the Fallshorts of a London season?
We'd stumble through contraptions of the plot, dull but not despised,
Wanting only to be better than we were, the axis of laughter
Set spinning by the jibes of gentlemen, the housemaid's joke.
A frump of mangled language, a squire's fat harrumph,
We'd ride out the raillery, redeemed as the footlights dimmed.

It might be worse. The Greeks would strap us both behind
A mask of agony, and raise, behind us both, tall columns
Glazed with gore, history dripping from the choral odes.
I'd rather see myself aggrieved in Italy, young and speaking
Blank verse in the twisted streets, a moonmad lover
Swooning over poison and a toy sword. These days,
They'd heap us unrehearsed in garbage cans, two bums
Practicing their rap before the bottom and the silence fell.

And what had the light left? A Chinese banner of a cloud
Burned across the sun, scarlet and gold of pennants at half-mast,
As the last glow lowered. Strung out among the spikes of dahlia,
A spider's tension stripped the air, a tripwire brushing
The dawdly fuss of a butterfly. You said: Sometimes I feel
Like a rabbit in the brightbeams, or a statue packed in sawdust,
Chained and crated and stowed away. How could I move,
Always made to bear up the dead weight of the self?

In this state of the ladybug and the buckeye whose shell
Battles back the winter like a scaled-down mace, where each
Politician and professor fights for his own empire of ideas,
Theories that colonize the brain, we've reached a common level:
Freaks under the tent, as damaged as Patty the Penguin Girl
Or the Dancing Pinheads, bad goods in the chromosomes, and pain
The price of admission, as the babies know, dangling brow-down inside the thighs,
Their first look at the world bloody and the wrong way up.

If we're all born, as Augustine said, between the feces and the urine,
We have a bone to pick with anatomy. And what was *his* problem—
Too much time spent cramped under the pelvic shelf? You can tell,
On every page, his pleasures in confession, nosing out the rank
And the dry rot, the mossy odors of the soul. I'd like to hear him
Alive and in Vienna, knees tucked up on the couch, as the dream doctor
Probed below the belt, fingers wrinkling in his beard: Vell, Herr Augustine,
Vunce more about your mother, and that voice calling from the vall.

Every rebel bred in appointed peace, every child squeezed from
Some squall in the loins, looks on love like a maggot,
That soft surgeon cleaning out the open festers where they hurt.
Who wouldn't sigh to live among the satisfied, in a mansion of
White linen, high polish, white paint, the windows unfolding on
A square of fountains from which the waters leaped in chandeliers?
All those who rise from rags to rages have had their infancy
Where the ends are mean and no gods ease the difficult middle.

You said: It comes clear now, that midsummer month of rain,
And the mushrooms over the lawn, large and limp, spread flat
Like severed ears listening for the next tremor, the resurrection of the flesh.
In the darkness, after the storms, everything sounded too loud, too close.
What could I do? There's only so much the rain can erase,
In natural baptism or new flood. That ooze draining through the night,
That rush and suck of water on the run—it frightened me,
As if heaven once more had breathed into the slippery limbs of mud.

By that stand of asters and the late mallow, where we sat
Like monks gone blind in the margin of manuscripts, and heard
Those arguments whose laws lead to the great Therefore, our hands
Stretched and met, both of us ghostly in the pale stains,
The mineral wastes of moonlight, deep dredge of shadows beneath our feet.
You said: Is there no way out of this helpless evidence?
And I put my shaken fingers to your lips, that wound
The words come from, worn down, drifting, like leaves in a sleepy wind.

Elton Glaser
first published in *Parnassus: Poetry in Review*, vol. 24, no. 1, 1999

march 2

The Year

When you did not come for dinner, I ate leftovers for days. When you missed dessert, I finished all the strawberries. When you did not notice me, I walked four miles uphill past you and into Florence and five miles the other way. When you did not like my dress, I wore it with gray silk shoes instead of gold ones. When you did not see my car had sunk into a snowdrift at the turn of your driveway, I took the shovel off your porch and dug myself out. When you stopped writing, I wrote. When you sent back my poems, I made them into earrings and wore them to work. When you refused to appear at the reunion, I went to the dentist who showed me X-rays of my teeth. When you did not tell me you would be in town, I met you on Main Street on the way to the library. While you had dinner with me, I walked past the window and looked in. You were not there.

Janet Bowdan
first published in *Denver Quarterly*, vol. 33, no. 4, Winter 1998

march 3

In Love with You

1

O what a physical effect it has on me
To dive forever into the light blue sea
Of your acquaintance! Ah, but dearest friends,
Like forms, are finished, as life has ends! Still,
It is beautiful, when October
Is over, and February is over,
To sit in the starch of my shirt, and to dream of your sweet
Ways! As if the world were a taxi, you enter it, then
Reply (to no one), "Let's go five or six blocks."
Isn't the blue stream that runs past you a translation from the Russian?
Aren't my eyes bigger than love?
Isn't this history, and aren't we a couple of ruins?
Is Carthage Pompeii? is the pillow the bed? is the sun
What glues our heads together? O midnight! O midnight!
Is love what we are,
Or has happiness come to me in a private car
That's so very small I'm amazed to see it there?

2

We walk through the park in the sun, and you say, "There's a spider
Of shadow touching the bench, when morning's begun." I love you.
I love you fame I love you raining sun I love you cigarettes I love you love
I love you daggers I love smiles daggers and symbolism.

3

Inside the symposium of your sweetest look's
Sunflower awning by the nurse-faced chrysanthemums childhood
Again represents a summer spent sticking knives into porcelain raspberries, when China's
Still a country! Oh, King Edward abdicated years later, that's
Exactly when. If you were seventy thousand years old, and I were a pill,
I know I could cure your headache, like playing baseball in drinking water, as baskets
Of towels sweetly touch the bathroom floor! O benches of nothing
Appear and reappear—electricity! I'd love to be how
You are, as if
The world were new, and the selves were blue
Which we don
When it's dawn,
Until evening puts on
The gray hooded selves and the light brown selves of...
Water! your tear-colored nail polish
Kisses me! and the lumberyard seems new
As a calm
On the sea, where, like pigeons,
I feel so mutated, sad, so breezed, so revivified, and still so unabdicated—
Not like an edge of land coming over the sea!

Kenneth Koch
from *On the Great Atlantic Rainway*

march 4

The Miraculous Mandarin

They knew how your good looks
would bring men
off the street,
how a cave is a good place
to invisibly linger—
no, not you,
you were to be out front,
the three brothers inside
waiting for wealthy victims,
waiting tense as spiders.
They promised you a cut.
And we must remember that all this
takes place in a poor country.
Well, you brought them in
all right, first a bankrupt cavalier
then a thin student, but
they weren't worth the air they
breathed—the brothers threw them out
their copper bits flung after them
and said move fast and quiet
if you know what's good for you,
and they did.

Then the mandarin came along,
a traveling collector with silk-lined
pockets and an oiled moustache.
He is called miraculous,
but how much of a miracle
was it, really, that he fell for you
on the spot—you *were* alluring—
that he rose to your dance,
his face a sad dog's,

and when the men pounced,
found gold, then tried
to smother him with his own silk sack,
his eyes, fixed to yours,
kept him alive, ready,
so that even when their knife
ripped open his guts,
he still breathed
and had to have you
though the murderers shrieked
"Die, die!" he could
not, lurching
like a haywire top,
a danse macabre that would not finish,
his eyes still on you, so
that was the miracle then:
that desire could keep the heart
beating against all odds...
but that's no revelation, is it,
nor that when
you gave yourself to him
right there in front of
the embarrassed schemers,
when you shimmied along his blood
and kissed his eyes shut
that only then could he die
for you, and did.

Deborah Tall
from *Summons*

Voir Dire

When he phoned the next morning from another state,
       saying that, after our dance,
    after my exit, in full view of all the guests,
        the waiters at long tables
of open bars, she lunged at him, tearing his tux,
      his dress shirt, scratching his chest,
drawing blood with her nails, demanding a response:
         "Why can't you love only me?"

    wasn't he describing me, our drama: our act,
        our scene? But last night I was
the other woman, catching his eye, pulling him
      close, soaked in his favorite scent,
poured into the tight dress, finally premiering
        a cameo role, complete
with the mysterious extra man, his arm snug
        as a stole across my back.

Still holding the telephone, I thought of my case,
        how I was called for jury
duty: the charge, Harassment and Assault. I couldn't
        answer him, but had to wait
for the coins to stop dropping, the sentence to stop,
        the blood to dry, the buttons
sewn back, and the tux left off at the dry cleaners,
        pretending our history

    was an invention and what justice lay in store
        would be served only by those
waiting for the sentence handed down in the end.

Elise Paschen
from *Infidelities*

march 6

Illumination

As if some monk bored
in the cold scriptorium
had let his quill

wander from the morning
Gospel, two tendrils
of wisteria

have scrolled
their green fervor
into the weave of a wicker

deck chair to whisper
with each spiral,
every sweet leaf

and dew sparkle,
Brother, come
with us, come home.

R. T. Smith
first published in *Poetry*, vol. CLXIX, no. 5, March 1997
also from *Messenger*

MARCH 7

The Wreck

But what lovers we were, what lovers,
even when it was all over—

the bull-black, deadweight wines we swung
towards each other rang and rang

like bells of blood, our own great hearts.
We slung the drunk boat out of port

and watched our sober unreal life
unmoor, a continent of grief;

the candlelight strange on our faces
like the tiny silent blazes

and coruscations of its wars.
We blew them out and took the stairs

into the night for the night's work,
stripped off in the timbered dark,

gently hooked each other on
like aqualungs, and thundered down

to mine our lovely secret wreck.
We surfaced later, breathless, back

to back, and made our way alone
up the mined beach of the dawn.

Don Paterson
from *The White Lie: New and Selected Poetry*

march 8

Irish Woman Washing

Before the mirror of a cement toilet in a trailer park at Doolin
She undresses to the waist, plugs the sink, fills it from alternate taps.

She splashes water under her arms, lathers soap between her palms.

I watch her back arc as she bends, her breasts fall, convex—
Two clouds watching from the sky.

The backs of her legs tense when a stream of cold water trickles down her belly.

She glances up, pulls a washcloth between her legs, rubs her crotch;
Finished, she checks her face for blemishes.

This is the way women have washed for centuries.

This is the way, in a Degas pastel—
Light catching on the curve of a back,
A rainbow lying in a pool at the feet
The toe dried carefully—the hair tied in a knot—
Combed from the roots.

All of us lined up—cow-eyed, sleepy, hungry at the sink—
Mild, fiery girls, not yet knowing that in a moment the world will change—

In the cold early morning air, half an hour, alone.

Laima Sruoginis
first published in *The Beloit Poetry Journal*, vol. 47, no. 3, Spring 1997

Domestic Work, 1937

All week she's cleaned
someone else's house,
stared down her own face
in the shine of copper-
bottomed pots, polished
wood, toilets she'd pull
the lid to—that look saying

Let's make a change, girl.

But Sunday mornings are hers—
church clothes starched
and hanging, a record spinning
on the console, the whole house
dancing. She raises the shades,
washes the rooms in light,
buckets of water, Octagon soap.

Cleanliness is next to godliness...

Windows and doors flung wide,
curtains two-stepping
forward and back, neck bones
bumping in the pot, a choir
of clothes clapping on the line.

Nearer my God to Thee...

She beats time on the rugs,
blows dust from the broom
like dandelion spores, each one
a wish for something better.

Natasha Trethewey
from *Domestic Work*

The Woman Who Allowed Light to Have Its Way with Her

She remembers
an absence of blue
billowing down,
playing loose with her,
the impetuous sailor
her mother warned her against
time after time. The light
did not invite her to dance,
nor shine upon her only.
In countless borrowed rooms
she swallowed
its gleaming intimations.
Later, in the dark, she lies
on the bed, recalling
the silvery edge of its breath,
like birch trees in spring.
She sparkles with shame.

Dannye Romine Powell
first published in *Ploughshares,* vol. 28, no. 1, Spring 2002
edited by Cornelius Eady

Woman with Chrysler

She smokes
slowly, like a bad
girl should. Imperial
plush and verve,
black over red,
with a smooth Detroit
rumble. Chrome
calls come
and get me.

I want
those headlights
half-hidden.
I want those taillights
that never
disappear. When she

looks at me in that American
way, I want to show her
how burning I can be,
how young.

Jeremy Countryman
first published in *LIT*, vol. 1, no. 1, Spring/Summer 1999

Femme Fatale

It's a crime story she's in:
betrayal and larceny, few clues.
Someone stole what she lived for,
made off like a thief in the night
or high noon. What shall she do?
Put a heel on each foot and set out,
making a snapping sound as she steps.
The man she loves smiles
from the drugstore's rack
of magazines, just in.
Looks like he's wrapped his movie,
dropped his wife on a Frisian Island
and is flying his girlfriend to St. Tropez.
The men who love her finger coins
in the stale linings of their front
pockets and whimper *What's your name?*
The job she wanted went
to the man who tells the truth
from one side of his mouth, lies
from the other: a bilingual.
The job she got lets her
answer the questioning phone all day.
Her disappointment has appetite,
gravity. Fall in, you'll be crunched
and munched, stretched
thin as Fettuccine. Watch out for her,
this woman, there is more than one.

That woman with you, for instance,
checking herself in the mirror
to see where she stands—
she's innocent so far, but someone
will disappoint her.
Even now you're beginning to.
Even now you're in danger.

Suzanne Lummis
from *In Danger*

Dearborn North Apartments

Chicago, Illinois

Rows of rectangles rise, set into brick.
And in every rectangle, there is a lamp.
Why should there be a lamp in every window?
Because in all this wide city, there is not
enough light. Because the young in the world
are crazy for light and the old are afraid
it will leave them. Because whoever you are,
if you come home late but it looks like noon,
you won't tense at the click as you walk in
which is probably after all only the heat
coming on, or the floorboards settling.
So when you fling your coat to its peg in
the hall, and kick off your heels, and unzip
your black velvet at that odd vee'd angle as if
someone were twisting your arm from behind,
then reach inside the closet for a hanger,
just to the dark left where the dresses live,
what happens next is a complete surprise.

Lola Haskins
first published in *The Southern Review*, vol. 37, no. 3, Summer 2001

march 14

Wrecked World

Your dishpan is quiet as a pond,
all the white ambition
shrunk to mild foam. You

have been away too long,
cups and plates tilt like glaciers.
Man: the toppler of worlds.

You wedge your hand
between what shifts
and slides, methodically

descend, layer by cool
layer, until your fingers crawl
along the smooth bottom,

amphibian.
This is where the knives lie,
mute battleships gone down

on their sides. How wonderful
to find them unaware
and then to pull one, nose

up, and up
until it hangs in the stunned air—
wrecker in a wrecked world.

Were you wrong to dredge it up?—
Is there not meat to cut, and pie?
Wrong to pour warm water

down the long length of its side,
to place it in the company of spoons,
who seem so soft, yet do not lie;

when you hold the knife
before one oblong eye—
concave or convex,

rightside up or upside down—
you see how the blade stretches
from your head to heart,

so much bigger than you thought.

Marilyn Annucci
first published in *Arts & Letters Journal of
Contemporary Culture*, issue 5, Spring 2001

In Alesia

In Alesia, our last town, our final stronghold,
we sent our women and our children out.
When Caesar sent them back, we, to feed our warriors,
we let them starve outside the walls of Alesia.
Our men fought well but not as well as Caesar's,
and in Alesia our handsome king conferred on us a choice:
You may kill me or deliver me to Caesar.
We could not kill him. Outside the breached walls of Alesia,
our broken stronghold, we delivered him to Caesar,
and we watched him throw himself down before Caesar
and we watched him throw out his arms, surrendering,
and we heard Caesar speak coldly to him, our handsome king,
and we saw him bound in chains. With scornful clemency
Caesar dismissed us. For a long time we heard nothing.
We plowed our charred fields, using each other as oxen.
Some of us found new gods, and some of those gods were Roman.
We paid our grain levies and, when he demanded them,
we sent our sons to Caesar and he made them soldiers.
In Alesia, we fathered new children and smiled sadly,
remembering our first children, first wives, our handsome king,
and then, in Alesia, we heard they'd kept him caged six years,
six years in a cage, our handsome king, our famous warrior,
six years before they dragged him through their capital,
some gray barbarian from some forgotten war, our handsome king,
our well-nigh savior, a relic of an old war six years settled.
We heard they tortured him and beheaded him, his head
jabbed on a pike and left till it fell off—
as we have ourselves, from time to time, honored the Romans.
We wish now we had killed him, our handsome king—
embraced him, kissed him, killed him, and buried him in Alesia.
If we were Romans, yes, we could have killed him,
and if he were Roman, he'd never have made us choose.

Andrew Hudgins
from *Babylon in a Jar*

march 16

The Sun on Your Shoulder

We lie together in the grass,
sleep awhile and wake,
look up at the cloverheads
and arrowy blades,
the pale, furred undersides
of leaves and clouds.

Strange to be a seed, and the whole
ascent still before us,
as in childhood
when everything is near
or very far,
and the crawling insect
a lesson in silence.

And maybe not again
that look clear as water,
the sun on your shoulder
when we rise,
shaked free of the grass,
tall in the first green morning.

John Haines
from *The Owl in the Mask of the Dreamer: Collected Poems*

Irish Poetry

for Michael Hartnett

We always knew there was no Orpheus in Ireland.
No music stored at the doors of hell.
No god to make it.
No wild beasts to weep and lie down to it.

But I remember an evening when the sky
was underworld-dark at four,
when ice had seized every part of the city
and we sat talking—
the air making a wreath for our cups of tea.

And you began to speak of our own gods.
Our heartbroken pantheon.

No Attic light for them and no Herodotus.
But thin rain and dogfish and the stopgap
of the sharp cliffs
they spent their winters on.

And the pitch-black Atlantic night:
how the sound
of a bird's wing in a lost language sounded.

You made the noise for me.
Made it again.
Until I could see the flight of it: suddenly

the silvery lithe rivers of the southwest
lay down in silence
and the savage acres no one could predict
were all at ease, soothed and quiet and
listening to you, as I was. As if to music, as if to
   peace.

Eavan Boland
from *Against Love Poetry*

march 18

Close Call

How suddenly she roused my ardor,
That woman with wide-open car door
Who, with a certain languid Sapphic
Grace into brisk rush-hour traffic
Stepped casually. I tromped the brake,
Her lips shaped softly, "My mistake."
Then for a moment as I glided
By, our glances coincided
And I drove off, whole rib cage filled
With joy at having not quite killed.

X. J. Kennedy

first published in *The Hudson Review*, vol. 54, no. 2, Summer 2001

also from *The Lords of Misrule: Poems 1992–2001*

Panty Raid

It is 1974 and out the institutional open windows
of the college dorm, nylon bikinis in floral prints
are plummeting like the cheap bodies of birds. And then

your mother's large white briefs like a mainsail, like
a flag of surrender, begin a slow dancing down current,
cinematic, lithe. All of the faces
are turning up, hushed, like those
holding a hoop to save a child burning. It is the opposite

of being lifted into the sky
the way I imagined my grandfather ascending
after the long pain of illness: this large pair of underpants
falling forever on the startled face
of an undergraduate boy.

For Paula Snow

Terri Ford
from *Why the Ships Are She*

march 2 0

Poem on the First Day of Spring

Everyone should write a spring poem.
        Louise Glück

Never, in the way of the Great Poets,
have I yearned to find myself in the domain of Nature,
rising, while first buds stud the trees,
to burst into a woman, open to the season.
Such anguish as it laid bare in them
I pity every famous ancient. Yes,
I despise their assumption: that we begin again in Spring.
Love, it is April, first light.
Listen, the birds, returned, pluck out ancient melodies.
Leave the shades drawn, let night stall in our bed.
Turn to me, naked, in no new way at all
but rolling our seasons into one, nameless.
How many years have we perfected this? Countless.
Losing track, each time is last, delicious, perilous.

Peter Cooley
from *Poetry*

Redwing Blackbirds

This morning they came like the dying
reclaiming their old lives, delirious
with joy right on the seam of Spring,
streaming in by the tattered thousands
like black leaves blowing back onto the trees.

But the homeless know what's expected by now,
and when the farmer fired into their body,
they rose all around me like trembling
black wounds gaping red at the shoulders,
a river of pain draining into the sky.

Tonight, as I look at the cold sky
and its flock of blue-white scars,
I can't yet turn from Orion's red star
whose trembling red light has travelled for years
to die now into any eyes that will hold it.

Fred Dings
from *After the Solstice*

Still Winter (Spring)

A warm, cheap snow, lightly wind-twirled,
rises (so it seems) from grates, puffs
out trees, fills the complicated furrows
of a woman's hat; it's all right to see
the worst reduced, as this snow is, to a
clumsy silliness no one could die from
or give up life distractedly sighing in,
but how close we are (still winter) to
what's merciless, as some whisper in the
happiest times: even this if walked into
steadily, boots soaking through, eyes
filling with white, could bring us down,
as something will, we who thought we
could endure anything, and almost did,
as everyone almost did, but didn't, as
spring, that staggers as it walks among
the cold stench of bodies and brisk
heartless blooms, the damp gaps
between the aging trees, reveals.

Charlie Smith
from *The Palms*

In the Clear Long After

Spring is cheap, but clean of sky. Long after she used to
meet him on the sly. He didn't say much, because to
speak you need a voice, need lead. Among the dead there were
such fresh ghosts, they were still breathing. Through their
mouths. Time, time, to adjust to an other. An ether
O so—No—too sweet. Intoxicated with permeability. 'Tis nox-
ious, to eat evanescence. However steadily, however slowly.
They stemmed into heady blows.
They missed
the stain. Of blue berries and argument. They missed
their lips. The yew and the thorns. They missed.
Their flaws.

O, to be stung by an errant bee. O, to sting.
O, to see you again. Covered in spring.

Olena Kalytiak Davis
first published in *Verse*, vol. 16, no. 3; vol. 17, no. 1

march 24

Spring

after Kenneth Koch

Let's not talk
At all this morning
I have too much to say
(Language is stubborn)
And the wind is singing
Against buildings and traffic
Let's hum softly into corners
And touch elbows
Under the table
Let's write a musical
(I mean our knees)

Let's get perfectly
Giddy and go into the city
(We'll see grimy salesmen
With neckties undone
And vacuum cleaners
Slung like lovers
Across their shoulders)
Oh to hear the sirens
Of early, windy Spring
Are you still listening
Let's not talk

You are distant and lovely
Like an imagined afternoon
And I see you this morning
As I have never seen
Fireflies in winter
Or handfuls of water
Or electricity

If I were in love
It would be with the low whir
Of memory
Rushing past and past
Like reels of a movie
Playing only for me

Let's not talk
Till everything's been said
(I could wait forever
This morning) though
If I mouth a word please
Remember in the Spring
You're so beautiful like
A fat checker taxi yellow
And white we may never
Learn our lines in time
To go on maybe never O mute
With this (love) let's not talk
For as long as day holds us
I am watching you
Shrug off sleep don't
Say a word I'm listening

Tracy K. Smith
first published in *Boulevard*, vol. 12, nos. 1 and 2

Last Shot

Before the game
Farnsworth had said
his heart felt on fire
and inside the heart
was trapped a small dark
horse kicking out
at the bolted door
of his body. Whether
he scored 33 or 34
no one seems to remember
but as for me there's
not enough beer and bean dip
in this county to save me
should the world erase
that clean pick and roll
in double-overtime and how
that orange globe of sun
rose from his fingers that night
to mount its peak three rims
above a landscape of smoke
and balded heads, swayed
and suspended itself
for what seemed a comet's lifetime,
until it finally left its arc
and descended as a ball on fire
travelling through a serene
and perfect net.
        It was the first
and only time some of us
cried out in joy so openly
and in public, and he pumped
his fists toward and through
the rafters so grandly
that with my own eyes I saw

the glow his body took
until it too ignited into flame
and out of his chest exploded
a herd of wild dark horses
galloping so fast
they left permanent shadows
on the blurred faces
of all those who applauded him.

Jon Veinberg
from *Oarless Boats, Vacant Lots*

march 26

The Figures

In memoriam:
Stephen Lacey, 1943–2000

Sunday morning. A summery
March 26th, and I'm pastor
again of The Little Church
Of Last Year's Fallen Leaves.
Mostly oak. Mostly white.
Some red. Some burr. Those
plastered together closest
to the dirt make up a black,
wet page. Text for a late
mass, perhaps. My raking,
a late call to prayer.
My parishioners, the usual
ones for the time of year:
the beetle, the hellgrammite,
the robin, the mole. My own
work's a kind of sweat
meditation. Join me. It's
the perfect weather for it,
and the clearing out will
go faster. By noon, we'll
lie back on a hill of grass,
the beer tasting crisper,
the crackers saltier than
we might ever have imagined.
And though I cannot now
know it, tomorrow, a young
friend will die of pulmonary
honeycomb fibrosis, as if
some strain of bees, finding
him choice enough to hive in,
drowned him in their sweetness.

Later, oh much, much later,
should you choose to read
in your Book of Hours,
look no further. You know
those figures in the old story,
aflame at the edge of the wood,
brightwinged and laughing.

Robert Dana
first published in *Prairie Schooner*, vol. 74, no. 4,
    Winter 2000

IX (Looking through the Window: Psalm 121)

from Scattered Psalms

> *I will lift my eyes to the mountains, where*
> *my help will come; my help from God, who*
> *makes heaven and earth.*
>
> Psalm 121:1–2

Was it Jonathan Edwards who'd repeat, continually,
One verse from the Song of Songs for an entire day?
I am the rose of sharon, the lily of the valley.

He believed that, in the repetition,
He could hear Christ's voice replace his own.
And while a god who'd use that kind of self-description

Would put me off—mine asks sarcastic questions
Like *Where were you when I laid earth's foundations?*—
I'm also given to wild expectations.

Here's my secret: help does come
When you invoke it with the hills or even hum
The melody for that one bit of psalm.

It's the sheer idea of lifting up your eyes,
The heady speculation that the mountains rise
Purely for the sake of lifting us,

As if the endless business of creation
Required even our participation.
But wouldn't we know it? It's a wild notion;

Besides, it's no mean trick to lift your eyes
And I've been making an untenable promise
In my impatience to repeat the phrase

That requires nothing of me: *help will come*—
It *is* an extraordinary claim—
I will lift my eyes to the mountains—pure momentum

Could make anything happen after that—
Unless it's part of a triumvirate:
Lifted eyes, my help, the mountains' height—

All approximations for the undiluted
And various emergences of God
A little like gas and liquid and solid

Versions of something wholly without substance.
But then—is it my failing?—there is a chance
That all I'll know of real deliverance

Is these blue-white mountains out my window
Still reeling from this morning's blast of snow.
They're uncannily beautiful without the Hebrew

So why don't I leave well enough alone?
Surely it's enough: a diamond-studded mountain.
Why insist on making it a stand-in

For what, if we could lift our eyes, we'd see.
(What help do I need? What is wrong with me?)
A lifted eye, a lily of the valley.

Jacqueline Osherow
from *Dead Men's Praise*

Even Love

Green light came down from the heaven of the jackals
and crisscrossed the room where the bed was slightly
disturbed, sheets damp, curtains swaying, curtains
on which strange birds were painted, their wings striped
and half-opened, birds of paradise with long tails
like umbrellas. The moon-colored bed that
the bodies floated on was tender as skin
itself. Even love, in some way, could be said
to be wasteful, which was what the jackals waited for,
fed on with their thorny fur and snarls. Tongues
hanging, covers already tearing where they lurked,
lamps overturned where they prowled for something spilled,
circling the bed, snapping at air and lace, foaming
over seed or blood on the pliant white soil.

Anne Marie Macari
first published in *Shenandoah*, vol. 51, no. 4, Winter 2001

MARCH 29

She Didn't Mean to Do It

Oh, she was sad, oh, she was sad.
She didn't mean to do it.

Certain thrills stay tucked in your limbs,
go no further than your fingers, move your legs through their paces,
but no more. Certain thrills knock you flat
on your sheets on your bed in your room and you fade
and they fade. You falter and they're gone, gone, gone.
Certain thrills puff off you like smoke rings,
some like bell rings growing out, out, turning
brass, steel, gold, till the whole world's filled
with the gonging of your thrills.

But oh, she was sad, she was just sad, sad,
and she didn't mean to do it.

Daisy Fried
from *She Didn't Mean to Do It*

BE-

A begat B begat C
and here we are at the depot,
surrounded by more baggage

than we could ever carry
alone, begirt, a little bedraggled,
but beguiled by what lies

before behind beyond us
and the power of a prefix
to make a noun a star:

bedecked, bedizened, bejeweled,
there must be something special
under all that finery, if only

a swirl of longing we've given
a name to, and a voice—why not,
we're all born ventriloquists,

so good we feel betrayed
when the world won't speak
for itself—but nothing escapes us,

no matter how far we fling it,
and we're never entirely taken in
by *trompe l'oeil* and *trompe l'oreille*,

we're proud of our double vision,
our ability to see and see through
the illusion—it's just that

sometimes we'd like to close one eye
and believe wholeheartedly in objects
that don't depend on us

for their definition, not a world
of absence but one in which
we'd have everything to lose.

Sharon Bryan
from *Flying Blind*

MARCH 31

The Book of Style

I often kept his suitors at bay.

Yet once a plan was made, I pulled
the florals out, extra nutmeg, and
a few flasks, hidden discreetly, properly,
within the room's deep crevices
in anticipation of our smoking dramas.

He called himself an artist manqué
when he dressed in his theatre-maroon.
(The preface of this book reads,
"I impresarioed his evenings."
The pages show their gold on one side,
and the margins are narrow like these hours.)
He never really wanted—nor would ever
break a vein over—my, this, sex.
He said, "it would seem taboo,
like cousins together."

A particular icy night, unexpectedly,
a visitor came over wielding a knife.
I was called to placate him, deflect
his quaint violence. So I went to our faunish
    guest

and kissed and kissed his tense arms,
staining them with candle burns,
only to save us. (It's as though I were
the rush of violins, a tempered accompaniment
to their romantic collage.)

I brought the tray
with the hand-blown pipe and delicate
syringes with their silver arrows pointing away,
then robed them both in matching silks.

(On the way to impoverishment,
I learn my late night lessons
from these young swans that punish my dreams.)

Later that night, I knew this visit was outdated,
his welcome, outstayed; so I signaled
to our guest in the dark to show him out.
I pulled him by his coat's lapels
to the door, and he said to me,
"You're saner than usual,
but still exercising your mystical rights,"
then pushed himself against the posturing wind.

Back in our haven the ice trees began
to strike their light through the breaks
and tears in the curtains.
And I slowly woke him up

by calling out names: this boy's,
our latest visitor, and old lovers'
like the one who abandoned him
in Amsterdam. I cursed them,
then he'd join me, describing
some elaborate blackmail, imagining them
covered in stab wounds.
It became our carnival where
we illustrated the turbulence of cut jewels.

I think he cherished
my body for a moment,
draping the boy's robe over me,
and I almost asked him,
"Couldn't we summon from all
this foreplay another heady scent?"

The luster from the glass and silver
arched over the chairs and pillows
like dense vines, and we found
our old elegance of the inarticulate again.

It's winter, always, when I'm reminded
of him, and, you know, there was
a *petit bateau érotique* for us once
and danger. And the tragic, the maudlin,

hushed talk—it still goes on about us.

Molly Bendall
from *Dark Summer*

APRIL 1

Diagnosis

for David Lehman

I woke up this morning feeling
incredibly Gorky. So I made an appointment
to see my Doctorow. He said my Hemingways
looked a little swollen and sent me to
get an M. R. James and a complete Shakespeare.
By that time, I began to feel a slight Trilling
in my Dickinsons and some minor Kipling
in my left Auden. The entire experience
was extremely Dickey.

I was referred to an H.D., who asked
about my cummings. She detected traces
of Plath in my Sextons and suggested
I might also have some Updike
trapped in my Yeatsian system.
She recommended that to keep Orwell
and prevent inflammation to my Balzac,
I elevate my Flaubert once a day.

Terence Winch
from *The Drift of Things*

APRIL 2

Bewilderment Is Love

Your whole life you've hailed police cars
when all you want's a cab.

Once you put a dollar in a stranger's coffee,
you thought it was an empty cup.

Your baby's cry means *change me*,
you think it wants to be a different baby.

Sweetheart, one thing is another,
you're confused because you care;

why not hire a stand-in
to handle your affairs?

Lesley Dauer
first published in *Grand Street*

APRIL 3

Song

Her nose is like a satellite,
her face a map of France,
her eyebrows like the Pyrenees
crossed by an ambulance.

Her shoulders are like mussel shells,
her breasts nouvelle cuisine,
but underneath her dress she moves
her ass like a stretch limousine.

Her heart is like a cordless phone,
her mouth a microwave,
her voice is like a coat of paint
or a sign by Burma Shave.

Her feet are like the income tax,
her legs a fire escape,
her eyes are like a videogame,
her breath like videotape.

True love is like a physics test
or a novel by Nabokov.
My love is like ward politics
Or drinks by Molotov.

William Logan
first published in *The Gettysburg Review*, vol. 11, no. 1,
    Spring 1998
also from *Night Battle*

Aprіl 4

Before a Departure in Spring

Once more it is April with the first light sifting
    through the young leaves heavy with dew making the colors
remember who they are the new pink of the cinnamon tree
    the gilded lichens of the bamboo the shadowed bronze
of the kamani and the blue day opening
    as the sunlight descends through it all like the return
of a spirit touching without touch and unable
    to believe it is here and here again and awake
reaching out in silence into the cool breath
    of the garden just risen from darkness and days of rain
it is only a moment the birds fly through it calling
    to each other and are gone with their few notes and the flash
of their flight that had vanished before we ever knew it
    we watch without touching any of it and we
can tell ourselves only that this is April this is the morning
    this never happened before and we both remember it

W. S. Merwin
from *The River Sound*

Five Panels

The way a word, feathering air, may outlast a building,
the way desire builds and builds toward nothing.

The scent each April of this and so many other past
beginnings, coming up again, reminding air, lily, iris.

The armfuls of you are never enough. Forsythia's sulfur
shower blooms. A sleep of bees, then their gold spasm.

All day rain borne down upon the green land till sunlight
opened, climbing the white shoulders of a cumulus.

Sheep graze among flowers and the grass of their pure hunger.
The oceans whose salt you crave, the city of stars.

Mark Irwin
Denver Quarterly, vol. 34, no. 2, Summer 1999

APrIL 6

Silver

On the butcher block table
is the silver that has been housed
in a molded cardboard box in my mother's basement
and handed down to me as my inheritance.
It was great grandmother's silver;
she died in Russia before I was born.
From great grandmother's table
this silver came to rest in another
drawer in the cherry bureau
of her daughter's house in Cleveland.

It came to me as I began my work.
This silver had been set, and washed,
and laid down again, night after night,
with bowls of borscht, roasted potatoes,
brisket so tender it could be cut with a fork,
in the evening candlelight after the Sabbath.
It was this butter knife
my father held in his hand, and raised
against his father in anger.
This fork he eagerly
brought to his lips
as he listened to the hushed talk
of babies lost and relatives killed in the war.

It took all day to polish the servings for twelve,
the salt and pepper shakers, sugar bowl, and creamer
all wearing the monogrammed inscription
of the family initial.
Afterwards I was tired.
I looked at my days work spread out on the butcher block,
sparkling against the last stain of sun
the way one might come upon
a dark family secret
rubbed out after a month,
a year, a decade of tarnish.

Jill Bialosky
from *The End of Desire*

APRIL 7

Virtue

All the houses are white;
all the yards have yellow flowers
attended by bees.
If you must be born female
try coming as an insect—
they have the edge. Bees
spoil their little brothers just
so long and then they're through.
The queen has a hundred lovers,
her daughters, none. A nation of sisters
lives forever: wasps and ants.
Here in New England
you'll come across old family plots
—farmers with two or three wives
set down in a row; prayers and faint praise
for the good woman, wife, mother:
modest and weary, homely as a shoe.
How she stirred and kneaded,
baked, sewed, scrubbed, and bore down.

I let the ants come in my kitchen
and carry off bread crumbs.
Girl soldiers, all discipline and grit.
Flies buzz the heads of stupefied cows,
up to their knees in yarrow,
hissing: "wake up, wake up!"
Their teats swell, heavy with milk,
long after they're done
being anyone's mother.
In the corner of the garage
a spider devours her mate,
wraps up what she can't finish
and hangs it to dry. Mosquitoes
murmur for blood in the high grasses.

A car door slams down the street.
Milk and honey, butter and jam,
what virtue in living as a slave?
In the kitchen I unpack groceries:
sweet peas, cider, wild honey, pears
burst from the flowering branch.

Cynthia Huntington
first published in *The Massachusetts Review*, vol. XL,
    no. 2, Summer 1999
also from *The Radiant*

The Try-Outs

"*Rat!* Torturing my *BRAIN!*" is the aria
my mother sang, trying out to be a singer
in a downtown theater. All month, she had practiced,
"*Rat!*" leaping out in sharp coloratura
from that mouth that drew back from kissing my father,
her mouth I kissed as if it were sacred,
"*Rat!*" suddenly in the pantry, then the pause, then
torturing and *my* run together in a
slurred mutter, then that radical, stridulating
high, off-key note, "*BRAIN!*"
—this was how a woman tried
to enter the world, *Rat torturing my*
brain vacuuming, *rat torturing my*
brain doing the dishes, atonal
shriek like choir gone wrong, or as if
the housework, itself, screamed, matter
and dirt-on-matter squealing, the dust-rings of
Saturn grating on each other. Backstage,
the folds of a massive curtain, and the mothers were
going behind its lank volutes,
one by one, and trying out,
Rat torturing my brain, I could tell
my mother by her pitch, about an eighth of an
inch below the note, and by
the way my skin tightened, and rose, and I
cried, when she sang. I would stop making
the paper Easter basket, and shudder
till another mother sang. At least I thought they were all mothers,
those grown-up women, although I was the only
child, there, cutting strips of
construction paper in the bad light
down at the base of the blackout aurora,
cloak of a potentate, where you wait
to be born, where your mother prays to be famous.

I never wondered just how the rat
tortured her brain, I cut out bunnies and
chickens and stood them up inside a basket
by bending them hard at the ankles, and taping
their feet to the floor. My jaws moved
with the scissors, chewing—it was a sort
of eating, that making, a having by pouring
forth, hearing from the dark the soprano
off-key cries of my kind.

Sharon Olds
from *Blood, Tin, Straw*

Rusted Legacy

Imagine a city where nothing's
forgiven   your deed adheres
to you like a scar, a tattoo   but almost everything's
forgotten   deer flattened leaping a highway for food
the precise reason for the shaving of the confused girl's head
the small boys' punishing of the frogs
—a city memory-starved but intent on retributions
Imagine the architecture   the governance
the men and the women in power
—tell me if it is not true you still
            live in that city.

Imagine a city partitioned   divorced from its hills
where temples and telescopes used to probe the stormy codices
a city brailling through fog
thicket and twisted wire
into dark's velvet dialectic
sewers which are also rivers
art's unchartered aquifers   the springhead
sprung open in civic gardens left unlocked at night
I finger the glass beads I strung and wore
under the pines while the arrests were going on
(transfixed from neck to groin I wanted to save what I could)
They brought trays with little glasses of cold water
into the dark park   a final village gesture
before the villages were gutted.
They were trying to save what they could
—tell me if this is not the same city.

I have forced myself to come back like a daughter
required to put her mother's house in order
whose hands need terrible gloves to handle
the medicinals   the disease packed in those linens
Accomplished criminal I've been but
can I accomplish justice here? Tear the old wedding sheet
into cleaning rags? Faithless daughter
like stone   but with water pleating across
Let water be water let stone be stone
Tell me is this the same city.

This *I*—must she, must she lie scabbed with rust
crammed with memory in a place
of little anecdotes   no one left
to go around gathering the full dissident story?
Rusting her hands and shoulders stone her lips
yet leaching down from her eyesockets tears
—for one self only? each encysts a city.

Adrienne Rich
from *Midnight Salvage: Poems 1995–1998*

At the Center

Six feet by three feet patch
swells upward, slightly

greener toward the chest.

Plastic carnations, polka dots.

Behind, tall wheat,
some pines, a ragged fence.

And the occasional clink clunk
of the cowbells we hung here

once, when we came out
with Phoebe and Tobin, two blonde babies
tumbling, one still at the breast.

But now you are nowhere in evidence, down there
dressed in the green sweater I knitted for you
when we first met.

On the horizon, 350 degrees of raw mountains;
the passing brush of wind—
sunshine's glint.

At the center, a handful of whiskery
wild roses in a pot

and a clump of sunflowers that burns
like a yellow warning light, stuck, swinging
in the middle of a deserted intersection

surrounded by old ranch houses, faint flecks of snow
still visible on the mountains.

Patricia Goedicke
first published in *The Hudson Review,* vol. 55, no. 1,
     Spring 2002

APrIL 11

Covered with Dew

Covered with dew,
country of tender leaves,
how many more millennium
before you grow weary of giving birth?
Cradle of misfortune,
so lovely that no one
has time to forego
your green graveyard,
your dust rich with salt
deposited by tears that
borne by river beds
replenish them with fish;
even your weeping is fertile,
inexhaustible mother.
Heedlessly, you raise up
lambs into sheep for slaughter,
bring forth live herbs from the dead
and out of suffering, love.
Peace and repose to you,
reckless provider;
forgotten under a bloodied sky
and grayed with cold—good night.

Ana Blandian
first published in *Great River Review*, no. 33, Fall/Winter 2000–2001
translated from Romanian by Kathleen Snodgrass, with Dona Rosu and Luciana Costea

This Fog

Well, now I'm lost in fog. Not metaphorically.
Not in the middle of life's journey. But mid-way
Between green can "8" and Hadley Harbor,
Which should be beyond that atheistic whiteness
That might as well be the edge of the earth. I cling
To the one gray-black rocky finger of land
Included in the mortal circle I can see.
Depth should be four feet or better to the west of that
So I'll drop anchor as soon as I get there,
Wait for death in one spot, not sailing and motoring
Against a current fast enough to make green can "8"
Look like the smokestack of a drowned steamer
Going full speed ahead even as it's sinking.
Oh God, I think, though I do not think I believe
In petitionary prayer. The sea is bigger than I am,
And I always do something to reawaken a sense of contingency.
Who else to talk to? My voice to the living
Would sound pathetic and posthumous as the cockpit voice recorder
Recovered from crashes, or the too-human postures
Of the charcoal-colored Mt. Vesuvius victims
Reaching for help, still, after two thousand years.
So, by the compass, I'm going to have to save myself,
Believe in my belief that's Timmy Point,
No parent, or instructor, to nod a calm confirmation.
Lower an anchor, and hope the one rock I can see,
Shaped like an anvil, isn't taken from me too
By this fog. This fog which, if I live, will soon be metaphor.

Alan Feldman
first published in *The Virginia Quarterly Review*, vol. 75, no. 2, Spring 1999

APRIL 13

You Are Right

In your super-logical
analytical,
bumbling way,
with halting speech
and much digression,
you explain that male
mathematicians are rarely
verbal...

> "oh by the way,
> did I mention that this theory
> is largely unproven, but
> nevertheless, quite probable?"

because of a prenatal
super-dose of testosterone
to the left side of the brain
which suppresses the right
side of the brain
where you are currently
trying to express
your lack of verbal agility

while at the same time
peeling an orange,
stroking your mustache,
pulling your ear,
and making little
finger-steeples.

And I am about to conclude
that you are right.

Cathryn Essinger
from *A Desk in the Elephant House*

Luna Moth

No eye that sees could fail to remark you:
like any leaf the rain leaves fixed to and
flat against the barn's gray shingle. But

what leaf, this time of year, is so pale,
the pale of leaves when they've lost just
enough green to become the green that *means*

loss and more loss, approaching? Give up
the flesh enough times, and whatever is lost
gets forgotten: that was the thought that I

woke to, those words in my head. I rose,
I did not dress, I left no particular body
sleeping and, stepping into the hour, I saw

you, strange sign, at once transparent and
impossible to entirely see through, and how
still: the still of being unmoved, and then

the still of no longer being able to be
moved. If I think of a heart, his, as I've
found it...If I think of, increasingly, my

own...If I look at you now, as from above,
and see the diva when she is caught in mid-
triumph, arms half-raised, the body as if

set at last free of the green sheath that has—
how many nights?—held her, it is not
without remembering another I once saw:

like you, except that something, a bird, some
wild and necessary hunger, had gotten to it;
and like the diva, but now broken, splayed

and torn, the green torn piecemeal from her.
I remember the hands, and—how small they
seemed, bringing the small ripped thing to me.

Carl Phillips
from *From the Devotions*

APRIL 15

The Accountant

This being Cambridge, he too
(a minor in Classics from
Brandeis U.) has read Herodotus,
but now it's no longer the cycles
of history that move him,
but the more grounded questions
of whether to file *married,
filing separately*, or *married,
filing jointly*, whether to declare
one's home *temporarily converted
to rental property*, or *domiciled
abroad*, to partially depreciate
one's decline, or await the single large loss
of sale in a falling market. And then
a friend tells me studies have shown
accountants to be the happiest professionals,
forever working toward some tangible outcome
in a world already codified, and I think again
of my own scribe, Don, reading the *Oresteia*
for no particular purpose beyond pleasure,
as he follows the unambiguous oracle
of his ordinary occupation, delighted
merely to ponder the possibility
that things may yet add up to add up.

Michael Blumenthal
from *Dusty Angel*

APRIL 16

Time to Hear Ourselves Think

We've missed that for years, not so much
The thinking itself—that goes on regardless—
But the hearing of it, small waterwheels
Turning in millponds, the press and hiss

Of steam irons in storefront laundry shops,
Gears changing, the tick in the clock
Hopping upstairs. It's as if,
In muffled slow motion, through shock and aftershock,

We kept feeling with our hands—all thought
Outside ourselves, all concepts
Those railroad stations we were always leaving,
Elevators, the courthouse steps

Hurrying toward collapse. But now that we have
Stolen this time, I'm beginning
To hear numbers—I swear it—
Little formations of numbers gathering

Strength as their flanks swing east, and pigeons
Cooing in bank alcoves, and my own
Pencil tapping, ears popping, the spitting sound
Made when tires roll over tiny stones

And it's almost frightening to think
Of what was going on, how much lies there
Scattered, or wounded, or dead
In ourselves that we could not hear.

Dick Allen
first published in *Poetry*, August 1996
also from *Ode to the Cold War: Poems New and Selected*

The Bather

Where the path to the lake twists out of sight,
A puff of dust, the kind bare feet make running,
Is what I saw in the dying light,
Night swooping down everywhere else.

A low branch heavy with leaves
Swaying momentarily where the shade
Lay thickest, some late bather
Disrobing right there for a quick dip—

(Or my solitude playing a trick on me?)
Pinned hair coming undone, soon to float
As she turns on her back, letting
The dozy current take her as it wishes

Beyond the last drooping branch
To where the sky opens
Black as the water under her white arms,
In the deepening night, deepening hush,

The treetops like charred paper edges,
Even the insects oddly reclusive
While I strained to hear a splash,
Or glimpse her running back to her clothes...

And when I did not; I just sat there.
The rare rush of wind in the leaves
Still fooling me now and then,
Until the chill made me go in.

Charles Simic
first published in *AGNI*, no. 53

Each Moment a White Bull Steps Shining into the World

If the gods bring to you
a strange and frightening creature,
accept the gift
as if it were one you had chosen.

Say the accustomed prayers,
oil the hooves well,
caress the small ears with praise.

Have the new halter of woven silver
embedded with jewels.
Spare no expense, pay what is asked,
when a gift arrives from the sea.

Treat it as you yourself
would be treated,
brought speechless and naked
into the court of a king.

And when the request finally comes,
do not hesitate even an instant—

Stroke the white throat,
the heavy, trembling dewlaps
you'd come to believe were yours,
and plunge.

Not once
did you enter the pasture
without pause,
without yourself trembling.
That you came to love it, that was the gift.

Let the envious gods take back what they can.

Jane Hirshfield
first published in *Five Points*, vol. II, no. 1, Fall 1997
also from *The Lives of the Heart*

Flight

The river slops under the bridge,
rubs the muddy turn of the bank
and glistens in sunlight,
straightaway and brilliant as a landing strip.

Call it a kind of redemption,
the way the simple light purifies,
though any dipped cup comes back so murky
no one could gag it down—
a failure of vision, let's say,
too much common sense—
the rim just touching the lips.

A quick gulp would reveal
what the heron knows.
At such a thought,
the stomach jumps like a fish;
but already the sun has shifted,
and whatever winged thing lingered there
has flown.

Neal Bowers
first published in *Poetry*, vol. CLXXII, no. 2, May 1998
also from *Out of the South*

The Hayfork

I could get up from this kitchen table, I think,
and go see for myself whether, even now,
in the worn planks of the old barn floor,
there might still be two holes I saw made there
forty years ago, in a single second along
the ponderous time-line of farming. Well,

I might get over there one of these days.
Meanwhile, what can I see from here? We entered
the barn's second story through a big sliding door
at the top of an earthen ramp. There was a haymow
on either side of a wagon-wide aisle-way.
A rail under the ridgepole ran gable to gable.

High in a dark far end, when I was a boy,
the old hayfork still hung there, barely visible
in cobwebs and thin strips of sunlight
that burst between weathering boards. Shaped
like a three-foot inverted U, a giant staple,
it rusted toward absolute darkness against which

stark blobs left by last season's mud-wasps
stood out like white spots on a heifer.
Who knew how long it had been there? Loose hay
was giving way to bales before I was born,
though here and there I've seen it made, the teams
of work-horses pulling the loader and wagon,

a man with a pitchfork working everyday magic
on top of the rack, the slow ride to the barn,
drawing the load up under the rail and the trip-stop.
A man dragged the fork down, hauling against
the tow-rope's weight the forty pounds of steel
with two barbed ends that grabbed the wads of hay.

Then the team, unhitched from the wagon, pulled
on the tow-rope, moving away from the barn,
lifting the hay toward the roof. A click
as the trolley-hook caught, then the hay
rode back along the rail into the mow
where men forked it away for the winter.

So to a day when I was twelve or thirteen,
when the baled hay we were making was plentiful,
stacked in the mow almost up to the roof,
and we were standing around in the aisle-way
after the wagon backed out, catching breath,
getting ready to go back to the field. One man

up in the mow took a notion and snatched
at the tag-end of rope still fastened to the hayfork,
so it whirred down the track to a place just above
the middle of the aisle-way, hit the trip, and dropped,
all faster, it seemed, than the noise of the track
could make us look up, and plunged its two points

into the floor just beside the left foot of Joe Trammel,
who stood there, leaning away from it, looking down
and then up, and around at all of us, a barnful
of men struck reverently silent in the presence
of whatever it was, the good luck that kept Joe
from injury, the bad luck that gave him his worst scare

in years, the innocent thoughtlessness that led
to that yank on the rope, the way things can go
for years without happening, biding their time
in a dust-whirling, cobwebby barn I can see
and smell and hear right now, staring down
at the grain in the wood of this kitchen table.

Henry Taylor
first published in *Shenandoah*, vol. 48, no. 2, Summer 1998

Infidelities

Wet air, rain oncoming,
And carrying with it brine
And creosote, harbor and breakwater,
Scent of spray and shipwreck,
Not inland rain. This is air
Hollowed to bear the traces
Of other geographies across the landscape.
With such randomness this scent
Arrives, almost like the discovery
Of an infidelity, unknown until
It surrounds us, the wind blowing
The backs of leaves, silvering
Like fresh spawn when something
Rises suddenly from below them.

The scent of wet air is brief,
Turning dark and thin,
Betraying itself, until it becomes
Memory, unhealed, repeating
Like forsythias, each late April
Blooming across the hillside,
Before sicklewort, larkspur, or yarrow
Begin to cure the air, draw
The wounds dry. Time heals, some
Console. Shafts of hollyhocks
Bloom by deep summer: infusions
Could be made to calm memory
Or dye anger, but past the trees
Lie ruined harbors the air still pulls from.

The world resumes. For one, infidelity
Reveals desire never rests with only one,
And for another, infidelity is
Deportation, a rusted ship waits:
Again, we are meant to learn to suffer
At another's pleasure, and to enter the world again
As it is, itself betrayed already by those before us.
The hillsides begin their own work of the summer:
Myrtle's blue covers the ground, the scent of allium
    drifting...

For the one who is faithless, there is nothing
To add, the world resumes with its
Consequences already discounted.
And for the others, their words have been
Pulled from their dark hold, and cast down.

James McCorkle
first published in *New England Review*, vol. 20, no. 2,
    Spring 1999

APRIL 22

Anniversary

When the world was created wasn't it like this?

A little flame illuminating a rough sea, a question

of attraction, something fermented, something sweet?

And then a bird or two were added, the crow of course to

joke about humanity, and then another kind so beautiful

we had to hear them first, before our eyes could be imagined.

And it was, we were then—and there was no separation.

The cries of a planet formed our becoming.

We peered through the smoke as our shoulders, lips,

emerged from new terrain.

The question mark of creation attracts more questions

until the mind is a spiral of gods strung out way over

our heads, traveling toward the invention of sky.

Move over and let us sleep until the dust settles,

until we can figure this thing out.

What was created next is open to speculation or awe.

The shy fish who had known only water

walked out of the ocean onto dry land,

just like that, to another life.

Frog imagined meals of flying things and creatures in flight imagined hills

of daubed dirt and grass in which to settle and make others

to follow in their knowledge which they were building

as sure as houses on the tangled web.

And in that manner we became—elegance of fire, the waving grass.

And it's been years.

Joy Harjo
from *A Map to the Next World*

Madrigal

How the tenor warbles in April!
He thrushes, he nightingales, O he's a lark.
He cuts the cinquefoil air into snippets
With his love's scissors in the shape of a stork.

Hear the alto's glissando, October.
She drapes blue air on her love's shoulders,
On his velvet jerkin the color of crows.
Her cape of felt & old pearls enfolds her.

How the baritone roots out in May!
His depths reach even the silence inside
The worms moving level, the worms moving up,
The pike plunging under the noisy tide.

Hear the soprano's vibrato, November,
Water surface trembles, cold in the troughs.
She transforms blowing hedges into fences,
She transforms scarlet leaves into moths.

Mary Leader
from *The Penultimate Suitor*

Triage

It is a kind of triage, a setting
of priorities, this loving the bud
and hating the wilted flower: the red
of geraniums, another siren, another
little death resting in a bush, where
the air is different, the light
is different, the very molecules

we are, are different. All the stars
are out tonight, and I am spilling
salt, watching its crystals fall
into the patterns of stars, into
beautiful sadnesses. Vega, Sirius,
Alpha Centauri: I am wishing
on them until I run out of names.

It is the month of buds
and the vines begin their strangulations.
This life is a falling-away,
a discarding, though we collect
many things—our supplies of helium
and laughter are not in danger.
Still the end of winter turns

into itself: we must stay
in our own bodies, and though
we may leave cells on the pages
or on doorknobs we turn,
the stars keep turning out to be
only the idea of stars
before their light can reach us.

Margot Schilpp
from *The World's Last Night*

APRIL 25

Hybrid Magnolias in Late April

You bent to whisper to a small granddaughter,
Exposing the bald priestly back of your head,
Lifting her then and handing her to me:
    See you in April.

Never the same, these northern magnolias,
As the great starred candelabra ghosting,
Even before I left them, the deep-shaded
    Lawns of my boyhood.

And yet these too break wholly into blossom,
What somebody called the early petal-fall:
I walk out one day and the limbs are bare;
    Then they are burdened

With the flared tulip shapes of opening blooms.
Two rainy indoor days in a row, then out,
The sun is out, and a fallen constellation
    Litters the grasses.

What would you be up to this April morning?
Muttering to yourself, looking high and low
For the good stick fashioned out of laurel?
    I have it with me.

Patience. Lean back and light another Lucky.
Whatever will kill you dozes in your rib cage.
Read a few more pages in the *Little
    Flowers of St. Francis*,

Then throw a window open on the fragrance
Of even this, the northernmost magnolia.
By now the child you lifted in your arms has
    Slipped from their circle

To cherish and polish your crooked old stick
Into a poem of her own so tender and deft
I can hold its wrong end and reach you the worn
    Thumb of its handle.

Gibbons Ruark
from *Passing through Customs: New and Selected
    Poems*

Rehab

Two springs, I filled our rooms with chirping fleets
of fledglings quiet women of the zoo's
Bird Rehab Center fetched from fallen nests.
My tasks were just to feed them, keep them warm
and shoo away the cats that gathered on
the balcony above our lush courtyard.
Mockers, jays, tough proletarian birds
grew fast and pulsed away; though even as
I brought more tiny eaters home in boxes,
the grown ones gathered every morning, into
summer, on the railing of the balcony
at 6:15 a.m., and squawked until
I stumbled out and dropped a pinch of moist
cat food down each screamer's gullet, to bid
it pop upon the air and disappear.
Then I padded in and fed the babies.

Those were good years in a marriage most would judge
a good one, all and all. We worked hard and laughed
a lot, pursuing separate interests, and came
together every night with no agenda
but the comfort of our coupling, and sleep.

When weak ones shriveled, I grew despondent,
isolating them until they died or
rallied, and when they quit their begging, and when
their hideous small faces—the bulging
monster eyes lidded with veins—dangled back
upon their too-delicate necks, I cupped
them in one hand and stroked them with a finger
until the last perceptible breaths had ceased.

Richard Katrovas

first published in *The Virginia Quarterly Review*, vol. 77, no. 2, Spring 2001

APRIL 27

Out of Hiding

Someone said my name in the garden,

while I grew smaller
in the spreading shadow of the peonies,

grew larger by my absence to another,
grew older among the ants, ancient

under the opening heads of the flowers,
new to myself, and stranger.

When I heard my name again, it sounded far,
like the name of the child next door,
or a favorite cousin visiting for the summer,

while the quiet seemed my true name,
a near and inaudible singing
born of hidden ground.

Quiet to quiet, I called back.
And the birds declared my whereabouts all morning.

Li-Young Lee
from *Book of My Nights*

APRIL 28

Marriage Patois

After a thousand days,
our language is fixed
as the Madagascar-shaped mole
on your neck,
and the pink levees
of your eyelids.
Like avid expatriates,
we're perfecting the accent
of our new country,
trading in the rug
of our old tongue.

I say fire the translators,
no more dictionaries.
We're natives now
because last night
I dreamt I stood
in our garden
and spoke my name for you.
With each sound,
one of my teeth fell out,
and from each glyph they made
in the dark loam,
a wild orchid grew.

Megan Sexton
first published in *Prairie Schooner*, vol. 74, no. 4,
    Winter 2000

APRIL 29

Star Apocrypha

Where stars are concerned, I am as enthusiastic
    as the next one—those planets just forming

across the cosmic lot, the cold blue quasars finally
    arriving after fifteen billion years,

one apparently as hopeful as the next. I think we all
    came to live in this world so why

should the sea in its white glitter, fasting for the sun,
    or the stutter in a line of clouds have us

thinking of death, the continuing resolution of the dark
    that reads entirely across the sky? For exuberance

we have the shoal of stars, the command performance
    and grand galactic archipelagoes, the sea foam

and abacus of stars. Yet all the time, finite by definition—
    they have done the math. On a smaller scale,

I can no longer enjoy even a small espresso without
    considering the atomic consequences—

arrhythmia, free radicals, and pancreatic dissolution, but
    there are other examples—St. Catherine of Siena

living for years on nothing but the host of air, levitating
      as purely as the stubborn light she was becoming.

Why then be on earth? Yet even I fly through the blue night
      sometimes, in my astral body, light as the bread

she would not eat, and for a while there, above the palm trees
      and cypresses, all things seem possible to a man,

who, though he knows his weight on earth, can, among his friends,
      lift off the sidewalk, rise to the occasion of wind,

of his improbable dreaming soul, as it floats away, effortless
      in its modesty, in his star-white shirt—and godwit

or sanderling, be as congenial, as satisfied to receive the sun
      off the spume of waves, the gilded aura of thought

lifting from the star pine's boughs, the small contributions
      to the infinite panoply, the boundless savor of light....

The dove who arrives on my balcony, and paces the railing
      in her flame-colored feet, is not a poetic truth,

but an earthly one who stands for her grey apprehensive self,
      dark unmetaphorical eye eyeing me

before she flutters off into the half-mystical eucalyptus
      that this morning is separating wind from wind

to no avail, and which, along with the doves, seems to
    repeat the long Aramaic vowels of the Essenes

swirled through canyons of the Dead Sea, almost as old as sand.
    I decipher nothing and, unlike them, I give up little,

and for lasting imperfection turn to the waves, as close to
    the scroll of stars, as beyond time, as we're going to get.

Today, what more shall we believe about ourselves? Half the time
    the stars go missing. Eye of the dove, dark as the unlocked

heart of space, there must be something else....Starry needles
    just sew and unsew the dark so that the days return—

how long has the sky been waiting for all of this to arrive?
    All we are is respiration—no distance and little wind,

a verse which could quit any time—*et cum spiritu tuo*—
    the last breath gone out with the wild idea of us.

Christopher Buckley
from *Star Apocrypha*

North Point North

I

In these I find my calling:
In the shower, in the mirror, in unconscious
Hours spent staring at a screen
At artifacts complete unto themselves.
I think of them as self-sufficient worlds
Where I can sojourn for a while,
Then wake to find the clouds dispersing
And the sidewalks steaming with the
Rain that must have fallen while I stayed inside.
The sun is shining, and the quiet
Doubts are answered with more doubts,
For as the years begin to mirror one another
And the diary in the brain implodes,
What filters through the theories on the page
Is a kind of settledness, an equilibrium
Between the life I have and what time seemed to hold—
These rooms, these poems, these ordinary streets
That spring to life each summer in an intricate construction
Blending failed hopes and present happiness—
Which from the outside seems like self-deception.

There is no end to these reflections,
To their measured music with its dying fall
Wherein the heart and what it seeks are reconciled.
I live them, and as though in gratitude
They shape my days, from morning with its sweetest smile
Until the hour when sleep blows out the candle.
Between, the present falls away,
And for a while the old romance resumes.
Familiar but unrecognized, an undiscovered place
Concealed within the confines of this room,
That seems at once a form of feeling and a state of grace

Prepared for me, written in my name
Against the time when time has finally merged
These commonplace surroundings with what lies behind the veil—
Leaving behind at least a version of the truth
Composed of what I felt and what I saw outside my window
On a summer morning; melding sound and sense,
A music and a mood, together in a hesitant embrace
That makes them equal at the end.

II

There may be nothing for a poem to change
But an atmosphere: conventional or strange,
Its meaning is enclosed by the perception
—Better, by the misperception—
Of what time held and what the future knew;
Which is to say this very moment.
And yet the promise of a distant
Purpose is what makes each moment new.

There may be nothing for the soul to say
In its defense, except to describe the way
It came to find itself at the impasse
Morning reveals in the glass—
The road that led away from home to here,
That began in wonderment and hope,
But that ended in the long slope
Down to loneliness and the fear of fear.

The casuistry is all in the event,
Contingent on what someone might have meant
Or might still mean. What feels most frightening
Is the thought that when the lightning
Has subsided, and the clearing sky
Appears at last above the stage
To mark the only end of age,
That God, that distant and unseeing eye,

Would see that none of this had ever been:
That none of it, apparent or unseen,
Was ever real, and all the private words,
Which seemed to fill the air like birds
Exploding from the brush, were merely sounds
Without significance or sense,
Inert and dead beneath the dense
Expanse of the earth in its impassive rounds.

There may be no rejoinder to that thought.
There may be nothing that one could have sought
That might have lent the search significance,
Or even a kind of coherence.
Perhaps. Yet closer to me than the grandeur
Of the vast and the uncreated
Is the calm of this belated
Moment in its transitory splendor.

III

Someone asked about the aura of regret
And disappointment that surrounds these poems,
About the private facts those feelings might conceal,
And what their source was in my life.

I said that none of it was personal,
That as lives go my own life was a settled one,
Comprising both successes and misfortunes, the successes
Not especially striking, the misfortunes small.

And yet the question is a real one,
And not for me alone, though certainly for me.
For even if, as Wittgenstein once claimed,
That while the facts may stay the same

And what is true of one is true of both,
The happy and unhappy man inhabit different worlds,
One still would want to know which world this is,
And how that other one could seem so close.

So much of how life feels lies in the phrasing,
In the way a thought starts, then turns back upon itself
Until its question hangs unanswered in the breeze.
Perhaps the sadness is a way of seeming free,

Of denying what can change or disappear,
Of tearing free from circumstance,
As though the soul could only speak out from the
Safety of some private chamber in the air.

Let me try once more. I think the saddest moments
Are the ones that also seem most beautiful,
For the nature of a moment is to fade,
Leaving everything unaltered, and the landscape

Where the light fell as it was before.
And time makes poetry from what it takes away,
And the measure of experience
Is not that it be real, but that it last,

And what one knows is simply what one knew,
And what I want is simply what I had.
These are the premises that structure what I feel,
The axioms that govern my imagination,

And beneath them lies the fear—
Not the fear of the unknown, but the fear of growing old
Unchanged, of looking in the mirror
At a future that repeats itself ad infinitum.

It could be otherwise so easily.
The transience that lectures so insistently of loss
Could speak as clearly of an openness renewed,
A life made sweeter by its changing;

And the shadows of the past
Could seem a shade where one could linger for a while
Before returning to the world, and moving on.
The way would be the same in either case,

Extending for an unknown span of years
Experienced from two perspectives, a familiar course
Accessible to all, yet narrowing,
As the journey nears its end, to one.

The difference isn't in the details
Or the destination, but in how things feel along the road:
The secret of the quest lies all around me,
While what lurks below the surface is another story,

One of no more consequence or import than the last.
What matters isn't what one chances to believe,
But the force of one's attachments,
And instead of looking for an answer in a dream

Set aside the question, let the songs continue
Going through the motions of the days
And waking every morning to this single world,
Whether in regret, or in celebration.

IV

Each day begins as yesterday began:
A cat in silhouette in the dim light
of what the morning holds—
Breakfast and *The New York Times*, a man
Taking a shower, a poem taking flight
As a state of mind unfolds
So unpredictably.
Through the hot summer air
I walk to a building where
I give a lecture on philosophy

In the strict sense; then go home to the cat.
A narrow life; or put another way,
A life whose facts can all
Be written on a page, the narrow format
Of this tiny novel of a day,
Ulysses written small,
A diary so deep
its rhythms seem unreal:
A solitary meal.
Some records or a movie. And then sleep.

V

At the ending of the remake of *The Thing*
Kurt Russell and one other guy
Are all that's left of what had been the crew
Of an Antarctic outpost. Some horrifying presence
—Some protean *thing*—establishes itself
Inside the person of an ordinary man
And then, without a warning, erupts in devastation.
The two survivors eye each other slowly,
Neither knowing whether one of them
Still holds the horror. "What do we do now?"
The second asks, and Russell says,
"Let's see what happens," and the movie ends.

"Horror" is too strong, but substitute the fear
I spoke about before, and the scene is apt.
I don't know, as no one really knows,
What might lie waiting in the years to come,
But sometimes when the question touches me I feel afraid—
Not of age, but an age that seems a prolongation of this afternoon,
That looks ahead, and looks instead into itself.
This is the fear that draws me back inside:
That this is all there is, that what I hold so easily
Will vanish soon, and nothing like it will be given me again.
The days will linger and the nights rehearse themselves
Until the secret of my life has finally emerged—
Not in devastation, but in a long decline
That leads at least as surely to a single end.

And then I turn away and see the sky
That soars above the streets of North Point North,
Reducing everyone to anonymity, an anonymity
In which I find a kind of possibility, a kind of freedom
As the world—the only world—rolls on its way,
Oblivious to anything I might say, or that might happen in a poem.
A poem can seize and hold a moment fast, yet it can
Limit what there is to feel, and stake a distance from the world.
The neighborhood around me wakes each day to lives
No different than my own, lives harboring the same ambitions
And regrets, but living on the humbler stuff of happiness.
The disappointments come and go; what stays
Is part of an abiding presence, human and serene.
The houses wait unquestioning in the light
of the approaching summer evening, while a vast
Contentment answers from the air.
I think I know where this is going to end,
But still my pleasure is to wait—
Not wait, perhaps, for anything within,
But for what lies outside. Let's see what happens.

John Koethe

first published in *The American Poetry Review*, vol. 29, no. 6, November/December 2000
also from *North Point North: New and Selected Poems*

The Cowboy and the Farmer Should Be Friends

a former
leading man
in that mirror
now beloved
for his character
roles

crack down
the center
half cowboy
half nester

tear down
them fences
luke
shoot them sheep

ride hell
for leather
billy
get help

Robert Hershon
from *The German Lunatic*

Like

When that fallen leaf of a girl,
       my milkmaid,
           banana-pan-cake,
              Listerine, little tickle,
          honey muffin, desperado,
      Mystic, Connecticut,
difficult situation,
       forever amber waves of loving debate,
         her eyes like dying doves,
           like my own desire,
         her milky/dewy/cloudy neck
      a chrysanthemum of hopefulness,
her hair burning like a hay fire,
       like a gas jet,
         like a matchstick,
           the czarina's hot jewels,
        an act of forgiveness,
     a misunderstanding,
burning, I tell you, just like fire,
       her breasts like the snowcones of my youth,
         like macaroons, a fine flan,
           strawberry PopTarts
       (with powdered sugar and water icing),
     yet, truth be told, really more
like the mammary glands of cute, young monkeys,
     her belly a valley of despair
       for travelers from third world
         (that is, developing) countries,
      her thighs a memory...of something,
    her feet like Peppermint candy,
like a clam's treasure offered up nightly
     at the sandy fish shacks
       along Little Compton, RI
         (the best-kept secret of our ocean state,

the smallest one in the union
and yet not any less
beautiful for all that),
finally spoke to me, her lips
like diamonds, like sapphires,
like the best canned spaghetti,
I listened like a chimpanzee,
like a defrocked priest,
like the last dying fish
in an unclean fishbowl
atop a dead woman's antique bureau,
to her words as if
I had a red ribbon tied around my neck
a coughdrop lodged in my larynx,
hairball in my idiotic kitty-licking throat,
like I was the cat falling
sixty floors from a luxury building
and who knows goddamned well
that it's not going to land
on its famous feet this time, jack,
no matter how many ambulances are waiting,
their cherries circling like helicopter blades,
their white doors as open as Thanksgiving,
spewing forth neatly groomed ambulance men,
with their asphalt-black hair slicked back
like a duck's happy ass in a bucolic setting
of wild bunnies
and fearless, full-grown fawns,
where like-minded lovers
can hold each other's hands
like lovers holding each other's hands
on a bright winter morning

when the new snow
    has made everyone as happy
        as the first day of spring
            when it feels like—
    "I don't love you,"
   she said, just like that,
and, brother, let me tell you,
    that I felt like,
      I felt like,
        I felt

Cathleen Calbert

first published in *Poetry Northwest*, vol. XLI, no. 1, Spring 2000

The Wave

As when far off in the middle of the ocean
A breast-shaped curve of wave begins to whiten
And rise above the surface, then rolling on
Gathers and gathers until it reaches land
Huge as a mountain and crashes among the rocks
With a prodigious roar, and what was deep
Comes churning up from the bottom in mighty swirls
Of sunken sand and living things and water—
So in the springtime every race of people
And all the creatures on earth or in the water,
Wild animals and flocks and all the birds
In all their painted colors, all rush to charge
Into the fire that burns them: love moves them all.

Virgil

first published in *The Threepenny Review*, 85, vol. XXII, no. 1, Spring 2001
translated by Robert Pinsky

For the Other World

For those who ran in the streets,
there were no faces to welcome them back.
José escaped and loved the war.

For those who swam with the bitterness
of a scorched love,
there was a rusted car to work on.

For those who merely passed
and reclined in prayer,
there was the smooth length of the tower.

For those who dedicated tongues
to the living and the dying,
there were doorways painted in bright colors.

For those who left their children
tied to the water heater,
there was a shout and a name.

For those whose world
was real and beautiful,
there was a cigarette and a saint.

For those who asked José
to stay and feed his children,
there were flowers at the funeral.

For those who carried a shovel
tattooed on their backs,
there was a wet towel and a bottle.

For those who swept the street
of superstition and lies,
there was a turquoise house to come home to.

For those who came home late
and put up their swollen feet,
there was love and the smell of dirty socks.

For those who feared the devil
and spit on his painted arms,
there was a lesson in rosaries.

For those who had to leave
before the sun faded,
there was asphalt and a bus and José.

For those who stared at the wet plaster
and claimed the face of Christ appeared,
there was confinement and stale bread.

For those who talked with each other
and said it was time to go,
there was lead in the paint and on the tongue.

For those who left children behind,
there was another world made
of sulphur and sparrow nests.

For those who accused their ancestors
of eating salt, there were these hands,
folded fingers tracing what was left after the
  sweat.

Ray González
first published in *Crab Orchard Review*, vol. 4, no. 1,
  Fall/Winter 1998

The Passionate World

is round. For days we sail, for months,
and still the way is new; strange stars.
Drawn to you, taut over time,
ropes connect this floating floor
to the wind, fraying into sound.

To arrive is to sleep
where we stop moving.
Past the shoal of clothes
to that shore, heaped with debris
of words. A hem of salt,
white lace, on sea-heavy legs.

Love longs for land. All night
we dream the jungle's sleepy electricity;
gnashing chords of insects swim in our ears
and we go under, into green. All night
love draws its heavy drape of scent against the sea
and we wake with the allure of earth in our lungs,
hungry for bread and oranges.
Salamanders dart from your step's shadow,
    disappear
among wild coffee, fleshy cacti, thorny succulents
    and
flowers like bowls to save the rain.
We are sailors who wake when the moon intrudes
the smoky tavern of dreams, wake to find a name
    on an arm
or our bodies bruised by sun or the pressure of a
    hand,
wake with the map of night on our skin,
traced like moss-stained stone.

Lost, past the last familiar outpost,
flat on deck, milky light cool on our damp hair,
we look up past the ship's angles to stars austere
as a woodcut, and pray we never reach
the lights of that invisible city, where,

landlocked, they have given up on our return.
But some nights, woken by wind,
looking up at different stars,
they are reminded of us, the faint taste of
salt on their lips.

Anne Michaels
from *Poems—The Weight of Oranges, Miner's Pond,
    Skin Divers*

MAY 6

A Sketch from the Campaign in the North

Just before dawn the women are washing
skirts and blouses, slacks from Hong Kong,
scrubbing their cotton on pockmarked boulders,
cleaning their limbs with mud and lemons
along the turbid river.
At the edge of the jungle, in surplus tents,
the men are talking without weakness or strength
of the recent change in the government.
On the other bank the soldiers are waiting
for the sun to rise from the hills behind them,
not smoking, not talking, in place and unmoving
as the leaves above them waver.
The day unfolds as if kept in a folder
on a desk in the capital.
The sun rises and blinds the river
the soldiers line up and fire from its cover
the air is gravid with sulfur
the river takes blood without changing color
a siren signals the end of the hour
and later in the capital
word is leaked to the foreign papers—
not even their souls climbed free to safety.
There are no handholds up that wall of light.

Vijay Seshadri
from *Wild Kingdom*

Crossroads

Crossed over the river and the river went dry
Crossed over the river, the river went dry
Saw myself drowning and I couldn't see why

Come up for air and the day said noon
Come up for air, said the air read noon
Day said, Son, you better mind something soon

Sink back down, felt my spirits leave high
Sink back down, I felt my spirits lift high
Didn't know if I was gonna die

A man give his hand and he pulled me to the shore
Man give his hand, pulled me over to the shore
Told me if I come I wouldn't drown no more

Me and the man walked and talked all day and night
Me and the man, we walked, we talked all day and night
We startled wrestling till the very lip of light

I put my mind on evil sitting in my soul
Put my mind on evil just a-sitting on my soul
Struggling with the devil make a soul old

I looked at my face and my life look small
Looked hard at my face and this life it look so small
All of a sudden didn't bother me at all

Returned to the river and I stood at the shore
Went back to the river and I stood right at the shore
Decided to myself needn't fight no more

Forrest Hamer
first published in *TriQuarterly*, no. 103, Fall 1998
also from *Middle Ear*

Pittsburgh, 1948, The Music Teacher

I don't know where my mother got him—
whose caricature he was—or how
he found me, to travel by streetcars
on Saturday mornings to the Negro
home, our two rooms and bath on Hornsby's
second floor. His name was Professor
Something-or-Other Slavic, portly,
florid man, bald pate surrounded
by stringy, gray hair. Everything
about him was threadbare: wing collar,
string tie, French cuffs, cutaway coat.
His sausage fingers were grimy, his nails
dirty. I think, now, he was one of the War's
Displaced Persons, who accepted with grace
coming to give violin lessons
to a 15-year-old alien boy
(displaced here myself from a continent,
from a country I couldn't name,
and a defector from Alabama).
I was the debt he had to pay
on the short end of a Refugee's desperate
wager, or prayer, to redeem the body
before the soul. I don't know why
my mother didn't give him
his paltry three dollars. I had to do it.

One morning he stood
at my side waving his bow
in time to my playing, swayed
once and crumpled to the kitchen
floor that she had made
spotless for him, taking
the music stand down.
I stood terrified until she
ran in and we helped him to his feet.
He finished my lesson in dignified shame,
and I knew, from pure intuition,
he had not eluded the hounds of hunger.

Outside of death camps I'd seen liberated
in newsreels and *Life*, it was the first time, I think,
I'd felt sorry for anyone white.

Gerald Barrax
first published in *Prairie Schooner*, vol. 71, no. 3, Fall
     1997

The Right Meaning

"Mother, you know there is a place somewhere called Paris. It's a huge place and a long way off and it really is huge."

My mother turns up my coat collar, not because it's starting to snow, but in order that it may start.

My father's wife is in love with me, walking up, always keeping her back to my birth, and her face toward my death. Because I am hers twice: by my good-bye and my coming home. When I return home, I close her. That is why her eyes gave me so much, pronounced innocent of me, caught in the act of me, everything occurs through finished arrangements, through covenants carried out.

Has my mother confessed me, has she been named publicly? Why doesn't she give so much to my older brother? To Victor, for example, the oldest, who is so old now that people say, "He looks like his father's youngest brother!" It must be because I have traveled so much! It must be because I have lived more!

My mother gives me illuminated permissions to explore my coming-home tales. Face to face with my returning-home life, remembering that I journeyed for two whole hearts through her womb, she blushes and goes deathly pale when I say in the discourse of the soul: "That night I was happy!" But she grows more sad, she grows more sad.

"How old you're getting son!"

And she walks firmly through the color yellow to cry, because I seem to her to be getting old, on the blade of the sword, in the delta of my face. Weeps with me, grows sad with me. Why should my youth be necessary, if I will always be her son? Why do mothers feel pain when their sons get old, if their age will never equal anyway the age of the mothers? And why, if the sons, the more they get on, merely come nearer to the age of the fathers? My mother cries because I am old in my time and because I will never get old enough to be old in hers!

My good-byes left from a point in her being more toward the outside than the point in her being to which I come back. I am, because I am so overdue in coming back, more the man to my mother than the son to my mother. The purity that lights us both now with three flames lies precisely in that. I say then until I finally fall silent:

"Mother, you know there is a place somewhere called Paris. It's a huge place and a long way off and it really is huge."

The wife of my father, hearing my voice, goes on eating her lunch, and her eyes that will die descend gently along my arms.

César Vallejo
from *Neruda & Vallejo: Selected Poems*
translated from Spanish by Robert Bly

MAY 10

#2

Driving a cardboard automobile without a license
                    at the turn of the century
            my father ran into my mother
                                on a fun-ride at Coney Island
            having spied each other eating
                        in a French boardinghouse nearby
And having decided right there and then
                    that she was right for him entirely
            he followed her into
                        the playland of that evening
            where the headlong meeting
                            of their ephemeral flesh on wheels
            hurtled them forever together

And I now in the back seat
                    of their eternity
                            reaching out to embrace them

Lawrence Ferlinghetti
from *A Far Rockaway of the Heart*

Prayer to the Muse of Ordinary Life

I seek it in the steamy odor
of the iron pressing cotton shirts
in the heat of a summer afternoon,
in my daughter's ear, the warm pink
cone, curling inward. I seek it
in the dusty circles of the ceiling fan,
the kitchen counter with its painted shells
from Hilton Head, the creaking boards
in the bedroom floor, the coconut
cookies in the blue glass jar.
The hard brown knob of nutmeg nestled
in the silver grater and the lemon
yogurt that awaits. I seek it not
in books but in my life inscribed
in two brief words—*mother*, *wife*
—the life I live as mistress of an unkempt
manse, volunteer at firstborn's
school, alternate Wednesdays'
aide at youngest's nursery, billpayer,
laundress, cook, shrewd purchaser of mid-
priced minivan. I seek it
in the strophes of a life
like this, wondering what
it could be like, its narratives
drawn from the nursery and playpen,
its images besmirched with vomitus
and shit. The prayer I pray is thus:

If you are here,
where are you?
If you exist,
what are you?
I beg you
to reveal yourself.
I will not judge,
I am not fancy.
My days are filled
with wiping noses
and bathing bottoms,
with boiling pots
of cheese-filled pasta
for toothless mouths
while reading Rilke,
weeping.

My life is broken
into broken pieces.
The fabric is rent.
Daily, I roll
the stone away
but all is dark
inside, unchanged.
The miracle has not
happened yet.

If you are anywhere
nearby, show me
anything at all
to prove you do exist:
a poem in small, soiled
nightie, a lyric
in the sandbox voices
raised in woe.

Release a stanza
from the sink's hot suds
where dirty dishes glow.
Seal a message inside:
encourage me
to hold on.
Inform me
in detail
exactly how to do it.

Kate Daniels
from *Four Testimonies*

An Interval of Five Tones Being the Dominant

Five is the sum of this world figured by the senses,
and the tally of the planets to the naked eye,
four directions with one person wandering at the pivot.
Five is the head and hands and feet, the five wounds,
and the five loaves for the hunger of five thousand.

Torah has five books with twice five laws
inside an ark of shittimwood, the twice five curtains
of the tent, the scarlet, blue, and purple linen, stitched
with cherubim, the wooden pillars overlaid with gold
with hooks of gold and sockets made of brass.

After Empedocles, four elements made up the world,
tinged, Aristotle thought, with aether, called
in alchemy quintessence, which is five. The Five Wits,
once upon a time, were common sense (or mother wit),
imagination, fancy, estimation, and remembrance.

In the House of Number, one is union. Two division.
Three joins one more to the halves of being.
Four, two twos, divides division; four seeks judgment.
Five holds two and three in consort. In the pentad
mystery trembles under the star of calculation.

Five enumerates the hand. The fist unclenches and flames
wobble from the upheld palm which is the sign of peace.
Five times a day, Muhammad cries out from his balconies.
Farewell and peace. Beside the corn, the passion flower
climbs the fence and wavers over a green bay full of starfish.

Brooks Haxton
from *The Sun at Night*

Stories

Nights she counted coins from my father's vending machines,
stacked nickels dimes pennies into houses, neighborhoods,
with streets & backyards & little boys under kitchen tables
watching their mother's feet tapping, her nails on waxy wood
splaacckkcctt splaacckkcctt until her eyes got sleepy & she
picked me up & carried me to the tub, water jumping
raauuummppphh & slid me down the steaming, her breasts
wet & soapy as she scrubbed me a plump pink chicken,
humming lala aaa uuiieeoo laaa & lifted me high & kissed me,
singing, My darling little man! & carried me to my room
to dry me in a big soft towel while I pretended not to like it,
twisting as she rubbed harder, Ticklish, eh! she laughed, ticklish
little rabbit, her fingers crinkly with talcum, jumping on my stomach
until I howled—Oh, I could eat you up *arruummpphh!* munching
my fingers toes, my heart *kaalluummpping* as she told stories
about being a girl when every yard had gardens like countries
in Europe with cherry & black plum & apple & pear trees
& her hair so long her mother braided it in pink ribbons & all
the women wore kerchiefs & bright peasant dresses waving
like flags up one street & down another smiling good morning
telling every brilliant thing their children did with one hand tied
behind their backs & all the old widows deep in windows, window
widows she called them, always complaining but everyone spoke
five languages at once & every house was white with red shutters

& she & her sisters walked around flirting with boys in derbies
& every spring Saturday she helped her mother do wash in the backyard
& the splashing soaked the air & the grass glistened & everywhere in branches
cardinals & bluejays & robins singing & in winter the snow came blowing
off the lake like giant clouds burying the houses and men tied colored hankies
to car antennas but children switched them so every morning the cursing
& now she was laughing, her head way back as I moved closer & she
put her arms around me & rocked us & I wanted it to last forever,
the two of us, together, always.

Philip Schultz
first published in *Poetry*, vol. CLXIX, no. 3, January 1997
also from *The Holy Worm of Praise*

Marriage

> A lady is brought forward, and after making her bow to
> the audience she retires to the back of the stage....There
> she is caused to rise in the air, to move from side to side, to
> advance and retire, and to revolve in all directions.
>   "Conjuring," *Encyclopedia Britannica*, 11th Edition

First, it was the common magic—
organdy skirt, lace petticoat,
your hair in sunlight,
our tight young skin.
Our act was applauded,
held over, licensed in May.

I grew adept at pulling spring blossoms
out of a glass. Bushels of them lay
around your ankles. I learned the rising cards,
the inexhaustible bottle. A toy bird perched
at the top of my chair, fluttering and warbling.
On a table my brazen head of Orpheus
clanked and answered questions. For encore I drank
a melted mixture of pitch, brimstone and lead
from an iron spoon, the stuff blazing furiously.

With my rings, levers and spindles, gears and hoops,
sockets, springs and bellows, I became famous.
The apparent floating of a woman in empty space
was my best. I covered an iron lever with velvet
matching the background and therefore invisible.
The lever, attached to a socket in your metal girdle,
passed through an opening in the back curtain.
You rose, spinning, fanning the air like a bird.
Then I passed a hoop over your body
and brought you to the floor.

Taking from my pocket a newspaper,
I opened it and laid it upon the stage.
I showed the audience a chair, front and back,
and placed it on the paper. You took your seat,
and I cast over you a piece of black silk.
I shouted, "I'll throw you in the air,"
grasped your waist and lifted you above my head.
You vanished, covering and all, at my fingertips.

Richard Frost
from *Neighbor Blood*

Harmonie du Soir

(Hampton's last concert in Santa Monica)

That ever younger evening sky's pastel accord's
A chord off Santa Monica
Even now, deepening shades of past
Shadings, jazzy, night jasmine's pungent fadings
In up from the Blue Virgin's blue
Through blues as interfused as tones in a harmonica
To cobalt blue, to coalfire blue, to Coltrane blue,
Smoky and chuffing, to blooming lavender of jacaranda
Flowers that fail, that fall across lanai, gazebo, and veranda,
Those years before your birth.

A Santa Ana blew...
The stars came out...kept coming out...
Above the dimming earth...
On stage...

The vibraphone solo in "The 'Original' Stardust":
As cocky as cocaine, with each angelic line
Struck off in its constellation,
And then snuffed out, as fine as that cocaine
They use to stanch the pain
Before they break a nose to fix

A broken nose, melody racing out in front, looping around
The orchestra—foxy, teasing, balletic—
Until it's clear that it could go
On forever and so starts
Stopping, begins to
Skip like a heart, or to limp
Like Mother Killdeer in disguise,
To double-hitch down to a kind of foxtrot,
Hunted, haunted, caught,

Danced with by the whole libidinous band
An endless moment, then abandoned,
As it must be, like Valéry's pure poem,
A little lion, or unicorn, until the phallic horn
Flares up like sunset,
Ever so sweetly, compliantly, discretely,
Each gold and gilded sound well worth its silent wait,
To blow the by-then barely, still hardly
Flaming foxbreath out.

There, now: play it at the wake,
From flashes to ashes, dusk to dust,
As though in time with sacring bells and censers swinging—
"Les sons et les parfums tournent dans l'air du soir,"
Dans le beau de l'air du soir…
That's how I'd like to leave you when I must.

Stephen Yenser
first published in *The Yale Review*, vol. 87, no. 3, July 1999

Chitchat with the
Junior League Women

A Junior League woman in blue
Showed me enough panty
To keep my back straight,
To keep my wine glass lifting
Every three minutes.
Do you have children? she asked.
Oh, yes, I chimed. Sip, sip.
Her legs spread just enough to stir
The lint from my eyelashes,
Just enough to think of a porpoise
Smacking me with sea-scented kisses.
The Junior League woman in yellow
Turned to the writer next to me,
Bearded fellow with two remaindered books,
His words smoldering for any goddamn reader.
This gave me time. Sip, sip,
Then a hard, undeceitful swallow
Of really good Napa Valley wine.
My mind, stung with drink,
Felt tight, like it had panty hose
Over its cranium. I thought
About the sun between delightful sips,
How I once told my older brother,
Pale vampire of psychedelic music,
That I was working on a tan.
That summer my mom thought I had worms—
I was thin as a flattened straw,
Nearly invisible, a mere vapor
As I hiked up and down the block.
I rolled out an orange towel in the back yard
And the sun sucked more weight
From my body. After two hours,
My skin hollered...I let the reminiscence

Pass and reached for the bottle,
Delicately because I was in a house
With a hill view held up by cement and lumber.
A Junior League woman in red
Sat with her charming hands
On her lap, studying us two writers,
Now with the panty hose of drunkenness
Pulled over our heads and down to our eyes.
What do you do exactly, Mr. Soto?
And I looked at her blinding
Underwear and—sip, sip—said, Everything.

Gary Soto
from *A Natural Man*

Don Juan
(After He'd Consumed Tons of Lipstick)

After he'd consumed tons of lipstick,
The women,
Cheated of their holiest expectations,
Discovered a means of revenging themselves
On Don Juan.

Each morning,
Before the mirror,
When they've penciled on their eyebrows,
They paint their lips
With rat poison,
They daub rat poison on their hair,
On white shoulders, on eyes, on thoughts,
On breasts,
And they wait.

They show themselves white on balconies,
They search through parks,
But Don Juan, as though forewarned,
Has turned into a bookworm in the library.

He caresses only rare books
And a bevy of paperbacks,
But never anything bound in skin.
Dust on old second-hand volumes
Now seems more refined to him
Than perfume in the boudoir.

So the women go on waiting for him.
Poisoned in all five senses—they wait.
And if Don Juan were to lift his eyes
From his new obsession,
Every day he'd see through the library window
How another loving husband is buried,
Accidentally killed by friendly fire
While kissing his wife
In the line of duty.

Marin Sorescu
first published in *Poetry International*, issue III
translated from Romanian by Adam J. Sorkin

Watching the Men Walk

The man with the gold lighter lights five
tan cigarettes. Anoints the drizzle
with smoke. On his wrist: one watch
at 6 o'clock, one at 9:05.

And then the men walk. They walk
toward a mustard-colored building
where a band of boys sits on the roof
drinking the last of last year's vodka.
I raise my window to hear their toasts. Adieu
to the dregs of their country's potatoes.

The song from their boombox wafts off
into the smoke from five cigarettes
hovering over five new strategies.

The men in black wingtips glance up
at the wet young faces. Nod.
Who among us can help
but tap our toes, though it's a song
about the world's end.

Nance Van Winckel
first published in *Seneca Review*, vol. XXX, no. 2, Fall 2000
also from *Beside Ourselves*

Practice

With studied ease they take their places, withdrawn
as they tune, tensing each timbre into cool accord,
as if unaware of the listeners hushed
in the basement shadows. Like gifted scholars
bent over rare scrolls, who construe impossible
syntax and syllables, the men exchange
notes, offhand jokes, dispute each other's
radical phrasings and interpretations,
absorbed yet giddy as they annotate,
hour after hour, their casual commentary
and practice, more than the music, the pose:
to harden their hearts when the chords turn sweet, to gaze
into each other's eyes alone, they need
wives and lovers, apprentices and friends
there to give steady praise, so that when strangers,
fiercely intent on each improvisation,
rejoice, the men will stiffen and turn inward,
impassive—as if still practicing—on stage.
But now they need to school themselves in the mystic
ways of inattention, attentively
changing a guitar string, rifling through
the fake book, looking past the listeners rapt
outside the circle; almost inured to those who come
night after night to hear them, they solo above
the constant, inarticulate drone of love.

Meg Schoerke
first published in *The Hudson Review*, vol. 55, no. 2, Summer 2002

How to Listen

I am going to cock my head tonight like a dog
in front of McGlinchy's Tavern on Locust;
I am going to stand beside the man who works all day combing
his thatch of gray hair corkscrewed in every direction.
I am going to pay attention to our lives
unraveling between the forks of his fine tooth comb.
For once, we won't talk about the end of the world
or Vietnam or his exquisite paper shoes.
For once, I am going to ignore the profanity and
the dancing and the jukebox so I can hear his head crackle
beneath the sky's stretch of faint stars.

Major Jackson
from *Leaving Saturn*

MAY 21

House, Garden, Madness

Meeting his mouth made it so I had house again.
I called him garden and drew him so, grew
his long lashes like grasses so I could comb
them with my stare. Some evenings a low cloud
would arrive, hang its anxiety over the yard.

Having his mouth at mine again gave me back
home. The walls painted themselves blue,
flowers grew larger than my head, stared
at me with wide eyes through the windows.
I was surrounded. A cloud stretched gray arms.

His mouth and mine again built something back
up with heat. The house was home again, wherever
I lived. The flowers grew fat, fed on weeds
around them. Ladybugs tucked their red luck
beneath petals' chins. The cloud came home again.

His eyes were closed but mine kept swinging open.
I saw him in the garden, surrounded by its light.
The flowers cut their own stalks, handed themselves
over to him in bunches. He kissed their bouquets,
and petals raptured. A cloud lowered, dark with fury.

I pressed my mouth to palm, closed my eyes
to find the garden, then saw: windows shut in fright,
roots drowned, flower stalks broken, their heads dead
in puddles. Startled, I looked around. The cloud
descended, prepared to hemorrhage in my arms.

Cate Marvin
first published in *The Paris Review*, no. 158, Spring, Summer 2001
also from *World's Tallest Disaster*

Pentecost

after the death of our son

Neither the sorrows of afternoon, waiting in the silent house,
Nor the night no sleep relieves, when memory
Repeats its prosecution.

Nor the morning's ache for dream's illusion, nor any prayers
Improvised to an unknowable god
Can extinguish the flame.

We are not as we were. Death has been our pentecost,
And our innocence consumed by these implacable
Tongues of fire.

Comfort me with stones. Quench my thirst with sand.
I offer you this scarred and guilty hand
Until others mix our ashes.

Dana Gioia
from *Interrogations at Noon*

Reflection

For Isaiah Drew

Back when I used to be Indian
I am twenty-six maybe twenty-seven
years old, exhausted, walking the creek
that bends through the hills
down into the clattering mesquite.
Along the muddy bank
I search for any sign
of my family. Footprints, feathers,
blood. A smoldering campfire
sours in my nose. Mojados.
Yellow pencil shavings curl
in the warm ash. Poetas.
A circle of Sun floats
and spreads upon the water.
I step in.
Murky bottom rises
over my boots, swirls
and swallows up the light.
As I kneel to speak
a long, black bird bursts
from my throat.

Mark Turcotte
first published in *Poetry*, vol. CLXXVI, no. 2, May 2000
also from *Exploding Chippewas*

The River

I waded, deepening, into the dark water.
Evening, and the push
and swirl of the river as it closed
around my legs and held on.
Young grilse broke water.
Parr darted one way, smolt another.
Gravel turned under my boots as I edged out.
Watched by the furious eyes of king salmon.
Their immense heads turned slowly,
eyes burning with fury, as they hung
in the deep current.
They were there. I felt them there,
and my skin prickled. But
there was something else.
I braced with the wind on my neck.
Felt the hair rise
as something touched my boot.
Grew afraid at what I couldn't see.
Then of everything that filled my eyes—
that other shore heavy with branches,
the dark lip of the mountain range behind.
And this river that had suddenly
grown black and swift.
I drew breath and cast anyway.
Prayed nothing would strike.

Raymond Carver
from *All of Us: The Collected Poems*

Flowers and Water

The Social Biology of the Vespucci

whose name derives from *vespa*, which has nothing
to do with scooters, although some of the cousins
were said to spin their wheels, and which has nothing
to do with vespers or the evening star,
though there were some stars among them:
    Simonetta,
for example, Marco's bride, the breathing
pulse of *Primavera* and the living
Venus, in Botticelli's version
vibrant with light, only to be, soon after,
out like a light. DaVinci walked beside
her coffin. All Florence was in love with her.
But any entomologist will tell you
the truth about the *vespa*, all ten
thousand varied tribes of opportunists:
how males pick up females at the usual
watering spots lush with flowers, how workers
cluster about the queen, who can never
safely turn her back on all the biting,
stinging, slender-waisted pretenders
vaunting love on the wing. As for Amerigo,
it was natural, his fascination with bodies
of water spilling their outlines
across old charts, fantasias, their ruffled
bays and inlets curling up the vellum
beaches like flourishes on a page
of calligraphy. Natural to pay
a gonfalonier's ransom for a cartographer's
rendering of the Mediterranean's breadth
and depth. Natural that later, living in Spain,
he shifted his opportunistic mind westward
across the swelling ocean toward peninsulas

and trees and birds and people never yet
possessed by European tongues. As for
America, our heroine, she inherited
all the waspish ways, scooting from flower
to flower, country to country, lover to lover,
and ending up in Ogdensburg, a brutally
normal American town on a waterway,
where she walked a careful path between the roses
and hollyhocks behind the garden wall,
having, as they say, made her bed
and learning to accept love where she found it.

Nancy Vieira Couto
first published in *Shenandoah*, vol. 51, nos. 2–3,
    Summer/Fall 2001

Glossolalia

Rae Anne Redfield
is dying for me

to convert to Pentecostal
Christianity,

so one summer day
she prays in tongues,

her voice a plant
forcing out blooms:

cinnamon spikes,
bees in the nightshade,

a foxglove fugue.
My parents' patio

turns hot as lungs,
unsticks from the grid

of level lawns,
and veers into a garden

overrun with wilderness.
I'm fourteen and close

enough to touch Rae Anne's
braids, her bangs,

her birch white hair part.
How could I not feel

Christ's knuckles rap
hard on my heart?

Angela Sorby
from *Distance Learning*

MAY 27

On the Sixth Day the Word Is Taken from Me

because I did not love it enough
    and let it grow bitter in my mouth
because I loved it too much
    and ate and ate and found it sweet

because I killed it while it was still living
    and wrapped it round my throat
and bade it keep me warm

it kept me warm
    when it should have been a window
I threw open to the cold

because I feared the cold
    mistook it for absence
and so missed
    the starry field

Lisa Beskin
first published in *jubilat* 2, Fall/Winter 2000

Judy

If it comes down to choosing sides,
choose Judy. She dies like nobody
else. Besides, her father
owns the theater.
Saturday before the matinee he makes deals,
bags coins in his little office
over the arc light projection room with its empty eyes.
He sits up there owning, a bald thought
in the brain of the building, rolling change.
Let the line outside get long. This place,
Palace, is ours: lobby, mezzanine,
WOMEN, MEN—partners, with Judy there we have it all.
She's everything we ever wanted in an outlaw
—quick draw, wears her sidearm cross-ways, low
and loose, tied at the knee with real leather—not
some older brother's sneaker lace.

She knows this place.
If she weren't so good at dying she might even win.
But she is so good at dying.
Gut shot, she digs her fist in her stomach,
twists her own breath loose,
pulls herself up by the marble table with the dried
arrangement, drags her leg down the hall,
falls back against the gold mirror.
You move in to take her, dead or alive.
In the stand-off, behind her in the glass
you see your hat brim around her face
as though you were behind her,
facing yourself beyond her lolling tongue:

(You have had terrible dreams like this, only you were the one at the end of the hall, and who or what that
    was with hat brought your mother to you with water and light.)

She grips the gold frame, swings
herself against the wall like a door opening,
and now you see exactly how you look
ready to plug yourself.
She rolls into the balcony, then...then
over! Over the balcony! Game over?
No. Below she's taking your shots again,
coughing row by row. She takes you with her
as she goes down against the sandy white arroyo of the screen.

Is that dying, or what?

Her old man's bumping around
behind the eyes, loading the reels. This is the last killing
before the doors open
—the final death of the day except the ones we live
through on the screen. They are free.
Si, mis compadres. See gringos?
If Judy doesn't play, nobody plays.

Paul Allen
from *American Crawl*

The Musician Talks about "Process"

(after Anthony "Spoons" Pough)

I learned the spoons from
my grandfather, who was blind.
Every day he'd go into the woods
'cause that was his thing.
He met all kinds of creatures,
birds and squirrels,
and while he was feeding them
he'd play the spoons,
and after they finished
they'd stay and listen.

When I go into Philly
on a Saturday night,
I don't need nothing but
my spoons and the music.
Laid out on my knees
they look so quiet,
but when I pick them up
I can play to anything:
a dripping faucet,
a tambourine,
fish shining in a creek.

A funny thing:
When my grandfather died,
every creature sang.
And when the men went out
to get him, they kept singing.
They sung for two days,
all the birds, all the animals.
That's when I left the South.

Rita Dove
from *On the Bus with Rosa Parks*

Public Broadcast

Sunday, late. The winter dark already coming down.
Inside the woodshed door, an early FM tuned to Bangor.
Half as old as the backyard oak he's felled—felled,
fitted, split—an old man mad for music lugs the chunks in.
He turns the volume up, up full: an opera he never saw
rises through light snow and marshals its triumphant march.
He marches, lifting stiff knees into highstep, marking
his own bootprints, shooting his victorious fist
against a stand of second growth ranked naked
against the sky. He lets the music take him as
he assumes the music: entering the city gates
he feels the blaze of banners, the shine on breastplates
and the women's hair. He marches near the column's head,
in his just place. The sun on the lead car is hot,
the horses sweat with victory, a victory
he hasn't felt in fifty years. Measure upon measure,
the music pumps him higher. He marches, marches,
through his deep backyard. The chorus soars:
the women's voices open every street, their smiles
are wide with glory, their lips already moist.

Philip Booth
from *Lifelines: Selected Poems, 1950–1999*

Listener of Bats

There, done. I watched it once again,
   —at four fifteen today,
   on the last day in May—
sunrise. Day's sudden juncture

so predictable: what is lit first
   —and always the longest:
   skies, steeples, roofs—
and what will be lit at noon only,

when all shadows, for an instant, recoil.

Bitter-sweet hour, dawn
   —for the listeners of bats,
   shufflers of night—
when darkness pulls back, yes,

but light comes too fast, then arcs
   —with day's bane
   of locusts, traffic, rain—
flares down everything,

and all shadows stretch, then recoil.

At dawn: may I die
   —during those mingling,
   willing hours—
when colors are tender

and lazily blend,
   —when waves braid
   their light in the sea—
and there is time

before all shadows, for an instant, recoil.

Leave, slight as a bat's whir
   —when night recants
   but day is not ablaze—
and before the cicadas

jab their relentless jeers
   —*cheater, cheater*
   cheat, cheat—
I'll go then: at dawn. Silent, slow:

the way a shadow recoils.

Laure-Anne Bosselaar
first published in *AGNI*, no. 53
also from *Small Gods of Grief*

june 1

Selections from Vectors: Aphorisms and Ten-Second Essays

1. It's so much easier to get further from home than nearer that all men become travelers.

2. Of all the ways to avoid living, perfect discipline is the most admired.

4. Say nothing as if it were news.

5. Who breaks the thread, the one who pulls, the one who holds on?

6. Despair says, *I cannot lift that weight.* Happiness says, *I do not have to.*

7. What you give to a thief is stolen.

8. Impatience is not wanting to understand that you don't understand.

9. Greater than the temptations of beauty are those of method.

10. Harder to laugh at the comedy if it's about you, harder to cry at the tragedy if it isn't.

11. Patience is not very different from courage. It just takes longer.

13. I could explain, but then you would understand my explanation, not what I said.

14. If the saints are perfect and unwavering we are excused from trying to imitate them. Also if they are not.

15. Easy to criticize yourself, harder to agree with the criticism.

16. Tragic hero, madman, addict, fatal lover. We exalt those who cannot escape their dreams because we cannot stay inside our own.

17. Every life is allocated one hundred seconds of true genius. They might be enough, if we could just be sure which ones they were.

18. Absence makes the heart grow fonder: then it is only distance that separates us.

19. How much less difficult life is when you do not want anything from people. And yet you owe it to them to want something.

20. Where I touch you lightly enough, there I am also touched.

22. Laziness is the sin most willingly confessed to, since it implies talents greater than have yet appeared.

23. If you reason far enough you will come to unreasonable conclusions.

24. The one who hates you perfectly loves you.

25. What you fear to believe, your children will believe.

27. The road not taken is the part of you not taking the road.

28. We invent a great Loss to convince ourselves we have a beginning. But loss is a current: the coolness of one side of a wet finger held up, the faint hiss in your ears at midnight, water sliding over the dam at the back of your mind, memory unremembering itself.

29. If I didn't spend so much time writing, I'd know a lot more. But I wouldn't know anything.

30. The wounds you do not want to heal are you.

32. If I didn't have so much work to keep me from it, how would I know what I wanted to do?

33. My deepest regrets, if I am honest, are not things I wish were otherwise, but things I wish I wish were otherwise.

34. I lie so I do not have to trust you to believe.

35. Opacity gives way. Transparency is the mystery.

James Richardson
edited by Paul Muldoon
first published in *Ploughshares*, vol. 26, no. 1, Spring 2000

june 2

A Man Gets Off Work Early

and decides to snorkel in a cool mountain lake.
Not as much to see
as in the ocean but it's tranquil (no sharks) floating
face down into that other world.
The pines' serrated shadows reach
across the waters
and just now, below him, to his left,
a pickerel, long and sharp and...*whappa whappa
    whappa,*
louder, behind, above him, louder,
whappa whappa whappa....Two weeks later,
20 miles away, he's found,
a cinder, his wetsuit
melted on him, in a crab-like position
on the still warm ash
of the forest floor
through which fire tore unchecked,
despite the chemicals,
the men with axes and shovels,
despite the huge scoops of lakewater
dropped on it
from his friend, the sky,
on whom he turned his back.

Thomas Lux
first published in *Poetry International*, issue III

june 3

Bringing My Son to the Police Station to Be Fingerprinted

My lemon-colored
whisper-weight blouse
with keyhole closure
and sweetheart neckline is tucked
into a pastel silhouette skirt
with side-slit vents
and triplicate pleats
when I realize in the sunlight
through the windshield
that the cool yellow of this blouse clashes
with the buttermilk heather in my skirt
which makes me slightly queasy
however

the periwinkle in the pattern on the sash
is sufficiently echoed by the twill uppers
of my buckle-snug sandals
while the accents on my purse
pick up the pink
in the button stitches

and then as we pass
through Weapons Check
it's reassuring to note
how the yellows momentarily mesh
and make an overall pleasing
composite

Shoshauna Shy
first published in *Poetry Northwest*, vol. XLII, no. 1,
    Spring 2001

june 4

Tuesday, June 4, 1991

By the time I get myself out of bed, my wife has left
the house to take her botany final and the painter
has arrived in his van and is already painting
the columns of the front porch white and the decking gray.

It is early June, a breezy and sun-riddled Tuesday
that would quickly be forgotten were it not for my
writing these few things down as I sit here empty-headed
at the typewriter with a cup of coffee, light and sweet.

I feel like the secretary to the morning whose only
responsibility is to take down its bright, airy dictation
until it's time to go to lunch with the other girls,
all of us ordering the cottage cheese with half a pear.

This is what stenographers do in courtrooms, too,
alert at their miniature machines taking down every word.
When there is a silence they sit still as I do, waiting
and listening, fingers resting lightly on the keys.

This is also what Samuel Pepys did, jotting down in
private ciphers minor events that would have otherwise
slipped into the dark amnesiac waters of the Thames.
His vigilance finally paid off when London caught fire

as mine does when the painter comes in for coffee
and says how much he likes this slow vocal rendition
of "You Don't Know What Love Is" and I figure I will
make him a tape when he goes back to his brushes and pails.

Under the music I can hear the rush of cars and trucks
on the highway and every so often the new kitten, Felix,
hops into my lap and watches my fingers drumming out
a running record of this particular June Tuesday

as it unrolls before my eyes, a long intricate carpet
that I am walking on slowly with my head bowed
knowing that it is leading me to the quiet shrine
of the afternoon and the melancholy candles of evening.

If I look up, I see out the window the white stars
of clematis climbing a ladder of strings, a woodpile,
a stack of faded bricks, a small green garden of herbs,
things you would expect to find outside a window,

all written down now and placed in the setting
of a stanza as unalterably as they are seated
in their chairs in the ontological rooms of the world.
Yes, this is the kind of job I could succeed in,

an unpaid but contented amanuensis whose hands
are two birds fluttering on the lettered keys,
whose eyes see sunlight splashing through the leaves,
and the bright pink asterisks of honeysuckle

and the piano at the other end of this room with
its small vase of faded flowers and its empty bench.
So convinced am I that I have found my vocation,
tomorrow I will begin my chronicling earlier, at dawn,

a time when hangmen and farmers are up and doing,
when men holding pistols stand in a field back to back.
It is the time the ancients imagined in robes, as Eos
or Aurora, who would leave her sleeping husband in bed,

not to take her botany final, but to pull the sun,
her brother, over the horizon's brilliant rim,
her four-horse chariot aimed at the zenith of the sky.
But tomorrow, dawn will come the way I picture her,

barefoot and disheveled, standing outside my window
in one of the fragile cotton dresses of the poor.
She will look in at me with her thin arms extended,
offering a handful of birdsong and a small cup of light.

Billy Collins
from *The Art of Drowning*

june 5

My Wife's Therapist

My wife's therapist is explaining how counterproductive anger is.
There's a difference between asserting oneself and aggression, she says.
Flying into tirades can cause others to withdraw, and then we can't negotiate
      With them anymore.
She illustrates her point.
I have to get into a new office, right away, she says.
Yeah, I agree, this place is a mess.
Fixing her hair with both hands, she continues:
At the meeting to sign the new lease, the other party makes impossible demands
      And suddenly walks out, slams the door, leaves.
I want to blow up, Angelo, but I don't.
Do I know what her response should be? She asks suddenly.
I shake my head.
She doesn't scream fuck you or kick ass, I bet.
I examine my feelings, Angelo, and then I cry. She leans toward me:
The realtor will set up another meeting later in the week and I'll get to try again.
My wife is breathing deeply so I know she is being moved.
Do I understand how this example is useful?
Sure. Definitely. It's clear to me.
How do I feel about it? What changes can I make in myself to show what I've learned?
I stand up, smack my head, and grasp everything she's been leading me to.
I'm transformed by her analysis.
I grasp her hands in my hands:
      Ann, would you like me to go over there and fuck with them for you?
      I could yell and curse. I could make them treat you good.
      I could scare the piss out of them.
No, she says, crossing and uncrossing her legs. Let's begin again.
      Anger is hurtful. Anger is bad.
Understand?
I nod my head.

Angelo Verga
first published in *The Massachusetts Review*, vol. XL, no. 3, Autumn 1999
also from *A Hurricane Is*

june 6

Six, Sex, Say

Do you think they wanted sex? asks the naïve girl in the film
    about a femme fatale who betrays
just about everyone stupid enough to get involved with her,
    but since they are in New Zealand
it sounds like, *Do you think they wanted six?* which is another
    question altogether,
and I know if I were doing drugs I would think this was
    possibly a key to unraveling
the mysteries of the universe, because six is *cease* in French,
    which could mean stop
to one of another linguistic persuasion, as in cease and desist,
    though it could mean six
and desist, and you don't have to study the kabbala to know
    numbers are powerful, or how to explain
a system invented by Phoenician traders to keep track of
    inventory being used by Einstein,
Dirac, Bohr to describe the mechanics of the universe, and
    even the Marquis de Sade in his long exile
in the Bastille and other dungeons invented a numerical
    code to hide his hideous imagination
from the thought police in that particular patch of hell. *Six,*
    he might cry, but what would he mean,
especially if addressing his pregnant Italian mistress, because
    six is *s-e-i* in Italian,
pronounced *say. Say what?* you might exclaim. *Girlfriend,*
    you don't need drugs, and you're absolutely right,
a conclusion I came to myself rather quickly, because I'm
    crossing the Alps now on Psyche's wings,
and in German its *s-e-c-h-s*, or sex again, in other words, sex
    of one, half a dozen of another,
which for not-so-unfathomable reasons recalls Rembrandt's
    etching of his friend Jan Six,
who later became mayor of Amsterdam, a bustling port in
    those days, and visited by one of the last ships

to leave Japan before it closed itself to the outside world, and
    Rembrandt buying the final shipment
of Japanese paper in the West for two hundred years. I see
    him in his studio, counting each lovely sheet,
Jan Six perhaps in the next room smoking a pipe, and I don't
    know what six is in Dutch,
but it's taking its place in the girdle of sixes circling the
    globe, the satanic triple-six,
the two sixes in my college telephone number, the hidden
    sixes in every deck of cards.
Two plus four, three plus three, chant the six-year-olds
    of the world,
all their sixes adding up to something, or why would the
    psychic have told my friend
he would never have any money until his address added up
    to six, because six is the money number,
the mysterious key to regeneration, if not the alpha then the
    omega, and I who am living
at 15 quai de Bourbon know one and five are six, cease, sex,
    say, and I'm in the money, if the money
is Paris and I a fool walking her golden streets.

Barbara Hamby
first published in *The Southern Review*, vol. 37, no. 1, Winter 2001

june 7

Epithalamion for Sarah and Tony

Her veil, his tie—
They do, and undo
What has not been

Undone. Deer pause
Below their window,
On the sill sparrows

Alight, the wilds
Uncoil and listen in.
Even the mountain

Leans all night down
To discover their
Discovery.

All night it listens
For the wind lifting
The sheets, the lake's

Low murmur lapping
The bed. All night
The mountain leans

Closer and presses
An ear to every
Sound. The mountain

Leans closer, down,
And down, and soon
Levels, becomes

The bed they lie in.
And they become
The mountain, rising

Above the mountain
That listens in.

Jeff Mock
first published in *The Iowa Review*, vol. 27, no. 2,
    Summer/Fall 1997

june 8

The Big White Dress

I will sew you a self
of moon-cloth,
color of angels

and aristocracy.
The shape will buoy you
till your head is an icon,

your hands twin flame
above the weeping guests.
What are nebulae

to this radiance?
The big white dress
floats up it knows

the clouds are its
correspondence,
the sky its bed.

I let it go,
work of a hundred hands
from a hundred ages.

Draping and tatting,
forbidden stitch,
our eyes made dim by it,

our spines bent
over lace, a thread loop,
such frailty—

like a huge bell of chalk,
made only to marvel at.
All that we know is beaded

in clusters and strung
on the spidery lines
between motifs,

and we ask nothing.
We do not ask
for the bloodspot,

for innocence blind
as a sheet, for shy
obeisance.

The linen is
laid for your path,
sheer as a blaze.

The dress incarnates a day,
the day we are trained for.
There is a song

at the end of it,
there is ascension.
Even your hair

will flower
and your pupils reflect
the mass of corollas you clasp.

Lisa Rosenberg
first published in *Shenandoah*, vol. 49, no. 1, Spring 1999

june 9

Little Elegy

Even the stars wear out.
Their great engines fail.
The unapproachable roar
and heat subside.
And wind blows across
the hole in the sky
with a noise like a boy
playing on an empty bottle.
It is an owl, or a train.
You hear it underground.
Where the worms live
that can be cut in half
and start over
again and again.
Their heart must be
in two places at once, like mine.

Keith Althaus
first published in *Grand Street*

june 10

Living Together

Of you I have no memory, keep no promise.
But, as I read, drink, wait, and watch the surf,
Faithful, almost forgotten, your demand
Becomes all others, and this loneliness
The need that is your presence. In the dark,
Beneath the lamp, attentive, like a sound
I listen for, you draw near—closer, surer
Than speech, or sight, or love, or love returned.

Edgar Bowers
from *Collected Poems*

june 11

Socrates

from Travels with Oedipus

for Kurt

Ah, the glory that was Greece!....excrement in the street and houses without windows. I wanted to teach you about Truth, which began as an idea rubbing its jaw against a rock but ended up too tiny to shed its skin. *Gnothi seauton*! (Know Thyself!) What a laugh! "Good means intelligent." "Virtue means wisdom." And what of Socrates? The bugger had a booger in his nose the first time we saw him; still they followed him, happy as hoplites. He seduced you, too, with endless questions, scraps of reasoning. Then the Games—the agora looking like a homecoming weekend for dead philosophers, everyone talking in riddles. "Come home with your father, " I said, and you answered, "What is father?" "Stop the nonsense," I ordered, and you asked, "What is its essential quality?" So I challenged Socrates to a wrestling match, but you took his place. Father and son. Mano a mano. What a testicular idea!....I'm leaning on a cypress, dressed in a loincloth, anointed with olive oil and dusted with white powder, my love handles and skinny legs a nightmare for any self-respecting bronze mirror. I'm led to a muddy pit, where you're squatting, all lathered and powdered like me. Lots of slapping, pushing, and sliding until I'm disqualified for face-biting. On my knees, blinded by a noonday sun, I'm barely able to spy Socrates as he approaches. "There's the story about a father," he laughs, "who swore he'd remain on earth as long as one son had need of him. Two days later, they found him hanging from an olive tree with an empty wine flask over his head."

Peter Johnson
first published in *The American Poetry Review*, vol. 30, no. 5, September/October 2001
also from *Miracles and Mortifications*

june 12

The Accomplice

This poem isn't an intricate theory years in the making.
This poem can speak only for this poem.
This poem will tell you it's not what you think.
This poem is nothing more than a series of coincidences.
This poem can't help but attract the occasional crackpot.
This poem is offered in full compliance with the Freedom of Information Act.
This poem is not anything like the Official Version.
This poem is holding something back.
This poem is covering up.
This poem may be afraid of worldwide panic.
This poem is no secret prototype the government is testing.

This poem has a lot of powerful friends behind it.
This poem is something you'd be happier not knowing.
This poem is murder on reliable witnesses.
This poem is counting on your complete cooperation.
This poem can put you at the scene of untold crimes or
this poem is your iron-clad alibi, depending.
This poem doesn't want anything to happen to you.
This poem hopes you get the message, although
this poem has no explicit message of its own.
This poem can't promise it will bail you out.
This poem won't even remember you.
This poem is well aware of the statute of limitations.

This poem means what it says.
This poem means anything you need it to.
This poem has seen things hard to believe.
This poem is all you have to believe.
This poem has implications.
This poem couldn't possibly be.
This poem is so good it ought to be illegal.
This poem is the only hard evidence recovered.
This poem has your prints all over it.
This poem has recently been discharged.

This poem is not a disgruntled loner acting spontaneously.
This poem has been seen consorting with other known poems.
This poem has confederates in top-floor windows all over the city.
This poem never goes by the same name twice.
This poem has no highly trained Russian look-alike.
This poem never received specific instructions.
This poem has nothing better to do.
This poem can hit you where you live.
This poem seldom misses at this distance.

This poem has its story down cold.
This poem doesn't want to have to say it more than once.
This poem has never seen its share of the money.
This poem is just the patsy.
This poem laughs at the Witness Protection Program.
This poem wants immunity before it starts naming names.
This poem isn't taking the fall for anyone.
This poem has you exactly where it wants you.

This poem you think you're getting to the bottom of right now,
this poem that's taken you into its confidence,
this poem that's made you an accomplice-after-whatever-the-fact,
this poem suggesting in so many words that it's always been on your side:

this poem doesn't make those kinds of mistakes.
This poem will give you up every time.

David Clewell
first published in *Boulevard*, vol. 12, no. 3, Spring/Summer 1997
also from *The Conspiracy Quartet*

The Long Marriage

The sweet jazz
of their college days
spools over them
where they lie
on the dark lake
of night growing
old unevenly:
the sexual thrill
of Peewee Russell's
clarinet; Jack
Teagarden's trombone
half syrup, half
sobbing slide;
Erroll Garner's
rusty hum-along
over the ivories;
and Glenn Miller's
plane going down
again before sleep
repossesses them...

Torschlusspanik.
Of course
the Germans have
a word for it,
the shutting of
the door,
the bowels' terror
that one will go
before
the other as
the clattering horse
hooves near.

Maxine Kumin
from *The Long Marriage*

june 14

They Said I Was a Crying Bride

Mr. and Mrs. Clemente Ríos—
Had anything ever sounded so evening and elegant,

Words from centuries of behaving. These were quiet
Words, but sitting on the lap of Uncle Thrill,

Whispered to me in church by Cousin Hand:
As I helped to cook in the kitchen on a Sunday,

My hands were full of salt, but in me
I was full not of bones but of feeling,

A scaffolding of my shape
Made with all the little pins they put in new shirts.

It was one thing to look at the outside of my hand
But something else to look on the inside,

Mr. and Mrs. Clemente Ríos—
It was a marriage into this family

On the outside—salt, something regular,
Just a wedding, like air and like water, something

Regular and quiet in this way
To the world which made its rules.

But in me was a deeper shore
On whose edge I stood

Looking out toward the farther inside.
I could see Clemente sometimes

In a soaring boat. When he came to me
He was wet, some of that ocean

Falling from so much of itself through my eyes.
It was not unhappiness.

Had I a mountain terrain
Inside myself, rather than an ocean,

Were he a sawyer and not a mariner,
Then the water would be something else,

Something that had clung to him from the trees.
Pine needles instead would fall from my eyes,

Pine and sap, scent and june beetles.
It was only luck that this was not the case,

That instead of flying, instead of shouting,
Instead of all the things that could have

Come from my eyes, the water being water
Was so easily explained as tears.

Albert Ríos
first published in *Quarterly West*, no. 47,
    Autumn/Winter 1998–99

Portrait

There is in his daughter's gaze
A solemnity so elegant
It must seem to some
The very definition of love

Though her profile guards
Any true window to emotion
Any genuine reflection of
Her understanding of her father's

Objective protective despair
As her beauty is shielded
By white & her lips in their easy
Parting draw back

From any kiss now
She is watching in the distance
Of the chapel a whole narrative
Beginning to assemble

One which finds the breath
Of the huge organ an unholy
Accompaniment its
Bellows moaning heavily over

What just a moment ago
The virginal & clear morning
Had promised to unveil forever
Yet which (now) the white day

Seems so certain to withhold

David St. John

first published in *The Kenyon Review*, New Series, vol.
    XXI, no. 2, Spring 1999

june 16

The Deep Pool

I want you to plunge into my life
as if you were diving into a deep

pool in the sea   let nothing be
hidden from you   hold your breath

and swim underwater to explore
every crevice in the rock and

the coral   make your way through
the undersea vegetation question-

ing the strange creatures which
you may encounter   let the fish

gossip with you about me   ques-
tion the giant squid and the

poisonous sting ray   they can
tell you much about me (some of

which you may not like to hear)
let nothing be hidden   you must

know me as I was before you came.

James Laughlin
from *The Love Poems of James Laughlin*

june 17

2 Ways of Crossing the Creek

Just this side of the reservation
over Big Rapids Creek,
there is a fine bridge built by
the CCC in the thirties.
You know the kind:
careful work by proud men
who were ruined by the times.
Stone and wood, it was
a pretty thing and
heavily used by the traffic.

Half-a-mile down in the woods
I come across 6 Indian men
who have felled and trimmed
a big tree and are tying ropes
around its 2 remaining limbs
which they throw to one who
stands on the other side.
Then they all walk the
half-mile to the bridge,
cross over and down to where
the man with the ropes waits.

I sit there and watch, even push
and tug at the limbs as they
strain and heave the tree
across the rapid creek, then
after 2 hours of sweat they
walk across it, big smiles
all over their bronze faces.

I ask them,
Why go to all this trouble
when there's a fine bridge near?

They look at me curiously
and hand me a beer.
They shake their heads and
laugh but do not speak,
as if a man who needs to ask
is already too far gone, as
if he is the kind of man who
would build a bridge when
a log would do.

Red Hawk
first published in *The Kenyon Review*, New Series, vol.
    XX, no. 2, Spring 1998

june 18

Shadblow

Because the shad
are swimming
in our waters now,

breaching the skin
of the river with their
tarnished silvery fins,

heading upstream
straight for our tables
where already

knives and forks gleam
in anticipation, these trees
in the woods break

into flower—small, white
flags surrendering
to the season.

Linda Pastan

first published in *The Georgia Review*, vol. LV, no. 2, Summer 2001

june 19

Landscape Over Zero

it's hawk teaching song to swim
it's song tracing back to the first wind

we trade scraps of joy
enter family from different directions

it's a father confirming darkness
it's darkness leading to that lightning of the classics

a door of weeping slams shut
echoes chasing its cry

it's a pen blossoming in lost hope
it's a blossom resisting the inevitable route

it's love's gleam waking to
light up landscape over zero

Bei Dao
from *Landscape Over Zero*

Bed

I used to sleep in a bed my father made
from a ponderosa. When it died, leaning the last
of its red crown toward the house, he called a sawyer
who came and with careful wedges
laid it safe across the yard. My sisters and I
first straddled, then balanced on top of it,
while my father stared it up and down in silence.

I was sitting in the living room the day my mother
helped him bring up the pieces from the shed.
She created an air of suspense around it.
I heard his machine tools in my bedroom
and when it was time for me to come look,
I saw a bedspread of brown and green flowers
surrounded by blond wood.

There wasn't a night I didn't run my fingers along the grooves
where the bark had been stripped and the wood sanded.
Also the knot, its smooth swelling and withered center.
I grew the length of the bed.

My father naps in it when I'm not home.
No saggy springs to hurt his back
and in the winter he can hang his hand
over the side where the heat comes out.
The Douglas fir beyond the eaves looks in
when he stops reading and places the book
down, pages split, the frame holding his place.

Kendra Borgmann
first published in *Grand Street*

june 21

Cognac

Sometimes I sing so pretty
I like to break my own heart.
　　　—Jimmy Durante

Each summer I would coddle a bottle of cognac
like a birth-blind calico,
then wedge it behind the cabinet's highball glasses
rather than among the stumped
veterans of mash, clear church bells of Finnish vodkas
and swan-necked, elegant slips
of sage and flame liqueurs, so that, reunion over,
we might retrieve it alone,
the two of us, and sip blunt amber that sandpapered
our throats into intimate
speech. We slumped, string-snipped marionettes,
　　　onto chintzy
cushions, heads humped together,
to resume dissection of longtime spouses, elsewhere
asleep despite suspicions,
our feral children, and the longing glimpsed in simple
gestures of close friends even
as they'd sponged glasses or rearranged half-drained
　　　bottles.
Our bottle squatted, muffled
telephone, genie-less lamp, allowing dialogue
its course—our voices bearing
their sad, sexual embassies, their torqued pleasures,
　　　their
"mystic current of meaning."

Each summer our too-brief encounter—solstice
　　　weekend—
distilled itself into mulled
smoke, brassy phosphor, cognac we prodded
　　　toward dawn till
the stories had been consumed,
their light absorbed in slow, deliberate sips toward
　　　depths
cross-channeling forever-
foreign flesh, our bodies drifting inexorably
toward final rigidity
as we'd kiss, almost chaste, then sleep, tongues
　　　swollen with false
fire, annual ritual,
cognac seeping into dreams, into the bearable
future still flush with desire.

Michael Waters
first published in *Chelsea 67*

Journey

Get the word and go.

The river is waking:
the train breaks morning open over water.
Fleets of sleek sailboats bob at anchor.

Steely sheen. The green of the far shore
splashed with light. White
blouses of women
touching their fragrant patient bodies.

A tall bird bends
to its shiver-image
in water, refreshing itself
before flight. The river

runs down to salt, and the sun
of the summer solstice
transforms water
to one wide flash of glass.

Mortuary after mortuary
of spent cars, ghosts
of tenement windows
flapping plastic; the city
suddenly lapping my ankles
with soot and clamour

till the plane pushes up
through clouds, climbing
with streamlined heavy effort
towards the rarer medium:
we're leaving earth

and leaping into the clear
blue dome spread over. Below us
a firmament of cloud
fashions a soft nest
for sunlight, bulky crests
of almost otherworldly weather,

nothing but radiance and shade
stretching as far
as the eye can see, a picture
of speechless peace, a world
that's not our world
yet we've come into it

as into some kingdom of tranquillity
where all our tears will be—
as they say—wiped away,
although this very minute
I might imagine

something still anchored
in her remains, as if
waiting for this face
to bend over her final face,
this firstborn voice to say

the word, any word, and let her go.

Eamon Grennan
from *So It Goes*

june 23

Pause, Pause

Praise to the empty schoolroom, when the folders
are stowed and the sighing desktops close.

Praise to the sixteen-hour silence
after the last chairleg complains against the tiles.

There are tracks in the snow on the sidewalk,
ice salting into the bootprints. Snow clots fall

like good advice from the branches.
See the plaid skirts ticking into the distance?

The bookbags swaying to the footfalls?
Praise to the sun. It sets like a clocktower face,

oranges over, grows. Praise,
praise to the classrooms, empty at last.

One by one, the door-bolts click
and the lightbulbs shudder to a close.

The chairs dream all askew. Praise to the empty
hallway, the pause before the long bells cry.

Kevin Prufer
from *The Finger Bone*

june 24

Conversation with the Sun Bittern

It preens on a root at the edge of the *igarapo*.
Light lights its lower mandible and brick-red eye.

I say, "why am I talking to you?"
"I don't know," it says, and spears a snail. Its head
is striped, its back mottled.

I tell it about the drawer with the false bottom in
my mother's desk.

I tell it about the letter I haven't finished, to a
person who gave me some diamonds.

"I know all that," it says, and watches a minnow in among
the mangrove roots.

"You know what you must do," it says, "you must stop…"
"Breeding miniature horses," I say.
"They are useless," it says.

I watch it lift one foot, and then the other. A drop
of water glistens on the tip of its bill.
"I know," I say, "but sometimes I am afraid."

Talvikki Ansel
first published in *My Shining Archipelago* (Yale Series of Younger Poets, vol. 92)

june 25

Highway 5

We take the direct shot
instead of the coastal route,
knowing what we're missing,
not being able to have
everything, of course.
None of that entanglement:
fantastical ruffling of bays
and inlets, little houses
with slammed doors, gravel
driveways, faces with
three-days' growth of beard.
This bleached line sings
like an aria, not part of
the general narrative.
Like a neutrino, beamed
through everything without
flinching. Ah, to travel
light as light, to hold to
the straight and narrow idea,
to take the wheel and—
as if it were a museum
cross section of a giant redwood—
draw a straight line
from the center: "Magna Carta
Signed. Columbus Discovers
America. Civil War Begins."

There goes our personal
will, petty prejudices,
elegantly tossed off behind
like Isadora's scarf.
There goes this difficult language
dashing like wild horses
into its heaven of metaphor.
Where we're headed, the setting
sun's a long-stemmed rose
held out before the 18-
wheelers: THE END, backlit
pink, a campfire in the dark.

Fleda Brown
first published in *Poetry,* vol. CLXXX, no. 2, May 2002

june 2 6

Ecosystem

1

That somber greens—ferns, conifers, cycads—flittered
with fruit and bloom

That earth's face pinked, reddened, honeycombed glow

That angiosperm came to outnumber gymnosperm

That they seduced insect, bat, and bird, flaunting colors
and smelling good

That they multiplied, hybridized, colonized east to far,
north to near, valley to peak

2

That brush crowded out burr oak and big bluestem grass

That weed evicted sweet brown-eyed Susan

That buckthorn unseated cream gentian and violet bush clover

3

That there had been prairie-fringed orchid, Indian grass,
large-leafed aster

That there had grown starry campion and bottlebrush grass

That there had flown great spangled fritillaries, Edwards' Hairstreaks

That Cooper's hawks, eastern bluebirds, Appalachian browns
    had manned the trees

    4

That what was mis-taken reappeared

That flowers strummed in the trees

    5

That they made it and made it, new, now, and again

That it is possible, possible, spreading, and so

Anna Rabinowitz
first published in *Barrow Street*, Winter 2001

Fiduciary

the relationship between
    blackbird and fencepost, between
the cow and its egret, the field
    and wildflowers overrunning the field—
so little depends upon their trust.

    Here, in God we trust
to keep our cash and thoughts in line—
    in the sky, an unexplained white line
could be the first of many omens.
    But this is no country for omens,

the line as chalky as the moon,
    bleak and useless as the moon
now rising like a breath of cold air...
    There is gullibility in the air.

Randall Mann
first published in Poetry, vol. CLXXX, no. 2, May 2002

june 28

Peonies

In the yard, peonies burst their white hearts,
scalloped edges unfolding only for themselves.
Their simplicity, the blade of it, cuts the morning.

In this Brooklyn of yards haloed in razor wire
and laundry flapping like flags of surrender,
resin smoke drifting up to these windows,

traveled shadows from a smoker's lungs,
I watch the police helicopter menace the neighborhood,
its engine hooking together manifold locks

and keys. Even now, in the face of this sickening,
there is forward movement, American needs
forcing my hand, each day a dull pearl

strung on a weakening line. The last time I saw you,
I held my hand over you while you slept, imagining heat
rising in green and red, as in a photograph of heat,

your body giving up its one treasure. There
is such savagery in this neglect—muscle strain,
fluid failure, the flesh receding

from bone until we are left with the indelible
print and fracture, our cells snapping
in a survivor's brain like grainy pictures,

the only way we'll last. I brought you peonies—
pink, like a shell, like a heaven, a mouth,
an infant, an infinity, a crisis, an end.

Mark Wunderlich
from *The Anchorage*

Giorni

Gather the pears of St. Peter before the first *vespa* begins to suck
out the white juice, and gather the *nocciole* on St. Philibert's day,

hence their other name, before something I can't see bores small
holes into the brown shells. The long cords of the families continue to

unravel, on one end a weight down an old well, green snakes at the bottom.
Gather cabbages when their outer leaves are large enough to wrap

a child in, or when one leaf can be floated in a bucket of water with a honey
jar on top. The recipes get longer when I want them shorter, shorter when

I want them longer. The moon is waxing and now what should I be gathering?
Gather the *pomodori*, *sempre*. Snap them off their thick green stems and eat,

the heat of them in your hands. Make a fist of your hand, make a hand of your
fist. What's the first stop after death, or the next stop? I remember the years

I spent, cumulatively, below zero, frozen families. Then thawed families, gathering
for some reason, and then leaving, saying *tanti auguri*, and may there be one

hundred of these days. The sun gathers the darkness somehow because each
day here I sense two minutes less of light. Exactly two, as if someone holds

up two fingers and someone else in the control room nods. Gather the *melone*,
small and sweet, hundreds of seeds in the wet center. Think of the seeds

the families have sown, have scattered. It has been all of us here who have
gathered, even casually, such as, I gather that you're in a hurry, I gather that

this is the last time we'll see each other alive. It is I, talking, speaking correctly,
writing one last word followed by another last word. I somehow need to

gather darkness around me like the shield I want to be carried home on.
When we gather, we recognize what we've gathered. And all the days,

more than the one hundred, more than the thirty thousand we've been allotted,
all these days repeat *this is us, it is you, here, it is I, here, sono io.*

Edward Kleinschmidt Mayes
from *Works and Days*

....
giorni: days
vespa: wasp
nocciole: hazelnuts
pomodori, sempre: tomatoes, always
tanti auguri: best wishes
sono io: it is I

june 30

Seasonal Ramble

Genoa salami on a bagel? Why not
offend two cultures at once? Three
if you count a few of my relatives.

Ah, time seems to fly when you get up at 4.
Stocks uncharacteristically took their cue from bonds
and tumbled throughout the afternoon.
Not that I could have done much to stop them
as they fluttered down through the recessional air
to the economic floor;

for there are two kinds of people in the world
and I assumed I was one of them—
another notch to loosen in the belt of impressions
while slowly, not too slowly for me, of course,
but not quickly enough, perhaps, for the impatient Future,
I master the art of losing my hair—

in conjunction with which I pause,
for yet another birthday—renewal? or just one more step
up the ladder whose last rung will be gone.
No one actually called me
but my fax gave me a series of beeps,
and Groggy and Feral, two of the household gnomes
I employ for such purposes,
brought in the two videotapes I ordered.
But five minutes into *Your Personal Destiny Revealed*
and the screen just went blank. I hope
the tape was defective,
if you know what I mean.
However, once I started watching *Ferocious Biblical Scenarios*

I was hooked. Instead of a tangle of prophecies, admonitions,
and theological posturing,
exciting events jumped out,
while into the room wandered my know-nothing
teenage stepson. Splat
went David's stone against his forehead;
my stepson, the Philistine, was dead,
an anachronistic victim of the media.

But let me introduce some of the rest of the "family":
my theoretical older brother, Andrew,
who personified himself as a hurricane
and tore through the family fortune;
my great-aunt Beulah, who, though not an actual
force of nature,
could win numerous awards
for inducing perspiration in others
and who would be happy to trumpet your failures
like bugles in the public domain,
where bystanders would be cut dead within seconds
of saying anything funny. And Uncle Henry,
who received the Teflon Star with Bulbous Clusters Removed
for distinguished but baffling conduct
in a lifetime of domestic skirmishing.

But don't stretch out on a basaltic scarp of genealogical fantasy
and imagine that you're really alone,
or think that "being alone" is a synonym for enlightenment.

Confused as to who is actually speaking,
and using such terms as "basaltic scarp,"
I sneak up to the attic and raid my Uncle Bob's
ever-diminishing matchbook collection for illumination.
He himself was an invention of my grandfather's cousin,
last seen by humans in the late Chalcolithic,
somewhere between Indiana and Utah,
indulging in ground-breaking obscurity,
a fictitious characteristic he nonetheless
seems to have passed on.

I take another media break, The Disaster Channel,
in time to see terrified golfers fleeing bolts of lightning,
mashies and niblicks flung away
like weapons cast down by the Edomites,
it's almost a ferocious biblical scenario,
before switching over to the Esoteric Network
to watch the Revelations of the Week in Obscure Tableaux
dissolve into patternless sensors.

Speaking of coming apart, it's time to see what fate
will unveil for me in the tableaux of the coming year:

YOU WILL HAVE A *VERY* PLEASANT EXPERIENCE.
YOU CAN BREEZE THROUGH *MOST* OF THE DAY.
YOU *SHOULD* BE ABLE TO MAKE MONEY AND HOLD ON TO IT.

YOUR LOVE LIFE *WILL* BE HAPPY AND HARMONIOUS.
IF YOU'RE THE ONE THAT'S MUMBLING INCOHERENTLY,

QUIT IT.

And no doubt there will be more such premonitions
to illuminate the scenes with misdirection,
though that will remain private,
though perhaps not only to me.

THERE IS A TRUE AND SINCERE FRIENDSHIP
BETWEEN YOU BOTH,
my fortunes conclude,
SO TAKE A MINT AND KISS YOURSELF GOODNIGHT.

Tony Towle
from *The History of the Invitation: New and Selected Poems 1963–2000*

JULY 1

Jeep Cherokee

You've never known
a single Indian
who wasn't painted
onto a football helmet
or branded in chrome
on a tailgate,
but there you go,
off mashing the landscape
like some edge-city explorer,
flinging yourself toward
new worlds beyond the driveway,
Lewis and Clark
with a seat belt.
Go ahead, you trampling trooper,
you goose-stepping little
Godzilla, you shining beast
of raging fashion,
riding the big teeth
of your tires as if you
would ever follow a dirt road
anywhere but to a car wash.
This is America,
and you're free to drive
anything you can buy
but I will tell you:
Hitler would love this car—
a machine in which
even the middle class
can master the world,
purchase their way through peril
safely as senators.
This is a car for
a uniformed strongman,
a one-car motorcade

through a thatched village
of strangers.
This is the car that will
replace Prozac.
This is the car that Barbie buys
with mad money
after the date with Angry White Ken.
This is the car every KKK member
wants to drive after dark.
This is the car that makes it safe
to be hateful in public.
Go ahead. Climb in. Look
at yourself, way up there
on the bridge of this
thick-windowed ship of enterprise.
Everybody knows
the only way today is to
buy your way through,
be bigger, be better,
be a bully, be a barger,
be sure you're safe from the poor,
bustle your way through
each day's bombardment
with the muscle of royalty.
You've got the power
to bring back the monarchy
four fat tires at a time.
Go anywhere. You're entitled.
You have squasher's rights.
Onward! Accelerate,
you brawny bruising winner,
you self-saluting junta on wheels.
you reclaimer of gold-bricked streets.
Democracy is for people

stuck in small cars
and God has never ruled
through traffic laws.
Get used to the feeling
of having your way.
Each broad cut of the steering wheel
is your turn at conquest,
the power-assisted triumph
of the me
in heavy traffic.
You are rolling proof
that voting is stupid,
that the whole damn machine is fixed
before it leaves the factory,
that fairness is a showroom,
that togetherness is for bus riders,
that TV has the right idea:
there is just you in a small room
on the safe side of glass,
with desire spread out before you
like a ballroom without walls,
and you will not be denied,
you've got the moves and the view,
you don't need government, unions,
bank regulation, mercy,
the soft hands of strangers.
You've got 4-wheel drive
and a phone, you've got
the friendship of a reinforced chassis,
you've got empathy for dictators
without knowing it,
you've got freedom from rear-view mirrors,
you've got wide-bodied citizenship,
you've gained Custer's Revenge:

caissons packed with children and soccer balls
coasting across the plowed prairie,
history remodeled with one great
blaring of jingles and horns:

Hail Citizen King!
Hail the unswerving settler!
Hail the rule of logo!
Hail Jeep Cherokee!

Bruce A. Jacobs
first published in *The Beloit Poetry Journal*, vol. 50,
    no. 4, Summer 2000

JULY 2

Needlework

Sometimes fate takes
a needle's path through cloth,
looping in and out,
retracing its own stitches,
twisting like a serpent.

In a Moorish seraglio
at Tordesillas, later a convent,
Phillippe, le Bel, kept one woman only,
Juana, his wife, Juana, la Loca,
in a cell with no windows
for forty-nine years.

Daughter of Ferdinand and Isabella,
mother of the Emperor Charles V,
she never stood beneath
the throne room's coffered ceiling,
never drew through her fingers
Phillippe's gift, red-violet tapestries
stiffened with gold.

Here one day Pedro the Cruel
would install his young mistress
and their daughter begin
the long chain of white-robed nuns.

Thyme climbed the hillside then,
as it does now. Sparrows flitted in dust,
scattering anywhere fear sent them.
Within her stone walls
Juana walked off from herself
into flowers and ferns,
past statues with their mouths open.

Each day was a union of light and sense,
her needle stammering through cloth
as trumpet vines vied for her attention
with the bright eyes
in the butterfly's orange wings.

Elaine Terranova
from *Damages*

JULY 3

History

In Boston, a tongue of red paint traces the city's history, from Massacre to Tea Party to Faneuil Hall. We didn't listen. We were busy composing our own republic: delivering fiery speeches of popcorn to mobs of pigeons in the Common, pledging allegiance in the green glow of the Aquarium's piranha tank. In the North End some traitor shouted, *Not in front of Paul Revere's house, youse! You'll raise him from the dead!* The red line led into our hotel, through our room, up the bedsheets. Here history lifted her hips. Here the rebels put their maniacal plan into motion.

Joel Brouwer
first published in *AGNI*, no.53
also from *Centuries*

JULY 4

Immigrant Picnic

It's the Fourth of July, the flags
are painting the town,
the plastic forks and knives
are laid out like a parade.

And I'm grilling, I've got my apron,
I've got potato salad, macaroni, relish,
I've got a hat shaped
like the state of Pennsylvania.

I ask my father what's his pleasure
and he says, "Hot dog, medium rare,"
and then, "Hamburger, sure,
what's the big difference,"
as if he's really asking.

I put on hamburgers *and* hot dogs,
slice up the sour pickles and Bermudas,
uncap the condiments. The paper napkins
are fluttering away like lost messages.

"You're running around," my mother says,
"like a chicken with its head loose."

"Ma," I say, "you mean *cut off*,
loose and *cut off* being as far apart
as, say, *son* and *daughter*."

She gives me a quizzical look as though
I've been caught in some impropriety.
"I love you and your sister just the same," she
     says.
"Sure," my grandmother pipes in,
"you're both our children, so why worry?"

That's not the point I begin telling them,
and I'm comparing words to fish now,
like the ones in the sea at Port Said,
or like birds among the date palms by the Nile,
unrepentantly elusive, wild.

"Sonia," my father says to my mother,
"what the hell is he talking about?"
"He's on a ball," my mother says.

"That's *roll*!" I say, throwing up my hands,
"as in hot dog, hamburger, dinner roll...."

"And what about *roll out the barrels*?"
     my mother asks,
and my father claps his hands, "Why sure,"
     he says,
"let's have some fun," and launches
into a polka, twirling my mother
around and around like the happiest top,

and my uncle is shaking his head, saying
"You could grow nuts listening to us,"

and I'm thinking of pistachios in the Sinai
burgeoning without end,
pecans in the South, the jumbled
flavor of them suddenly in my mouth,
wordless, confusing,
crowding out everything else.

Gregory Djanikian
first published in *Poetry*, vol. CLXXIV, no. 4, July 1999

JULY 5

Lion's Teeth

When others more decorous
are bent on composing, crafting
the trousseau (a thousand hands
preparing petals, another thousand
embroidering spores), I admire the indecent
burst of the dandelion, the straight-up
bloom so soon after snows.

Well before the cocktail hour,
she is freshly dressed, her cheeks
pollen-powdered, her feet squeezed
into the well-broken earth. And when others
are just showing an after-dinner blush
(a tendril just beginning its unpinnings)
she's waving her fourth-of-July,
baring her lion's teeth.

True, she flashes her underside white
to the wind sooner than might be
thought proper, but she does enjoy the music.
And true, she might go to seed
before the night is through, but
I admire what becomes of her:
bald bones, milk-sweet spine.

When others hold back their burst
allowing only one white petal
to show from under the shawl, I can't help
but wish that I too could seduce
that solo from the sun. A dizzy dance
out back. Can't help but watch her steps,
listen as she calls to him:
Faster
Hotter.

Rebecca Hoogs
first published in *Poetry Northwest*, vol. XLII, no. 2,
    Summer 2001

JULY 6

Seven Horizons

It is an old story: the oppressed
Become oppressors, the conquerors
Are conquered, the grass rises from
Their bones, and the rat is totem.

The archeologist of mounds
Studies the seven horizons of death
And discovers endless repetition,
Civilizations wearing out their plumes

And dying under their tin cans:
A shoe in the ashes, a set of false teeth,
A shattered hand, a cistern full of heads
Of broken jocks and forgotten movie stars.

Here in Flushing I let the rain
Wash away my rotting selves,
The rubble of what I was, the thick
Deeps of silence among the ruins,

The seven layers of abandonment
No archeologist will ever read.

Stephen Stepanchev
from *Seven Horizons*

JULY 7

Flight

The summer night is flying
by, rattling windows where light
is alive. Bats are shadows,
brilliant flickers in a mist
of insects, and bumblebees
circle the hyssop. The air
thickens. Directly above
us now a small plane crosses
the horizon of the half
moon on its way to the sea.

This is a night even deer
might soar. We believe they are
searching for a wind somewhere
within the thicket of wild
rose, hazel, and blackberries.
We believe the dark whisper
of grasses to be an owl's
wingprints, the drift of oak leaves
an echo of shifting tides
from beyond the Coast Range.

As silence glides in gentle
spirals back to the earth, first
the sheen, then the shock of all
we have seen comes clear. This is
the moment we know pure flight
has little to do with lift
or drag and much to do with
dreams. It is the moment we
turn together to begin
our own powerful ascent.

Floyd Skloot
first published in *Chelsea 60*
also from *Evening Light*

JULY 8

I Used to Go to Church

When my doctors thought
I was dying
I saw my father
slumped over
in a painted chair
in 6 A.M. sunlight
wearing faded paisley
boxer shorts

Before I was sure
if I should call
out to him
he got up
& moved through the room
looking at everything
picking up photographs
of my friends
cupping the mug
I'd used for tea

His hands ran
along the edge
of the dining table
as if the objects
he touched
could tell him
the few things
he wanted to know
about my life

My old man
opened a window
& the wind rushed in
bringing birds

Pigeons perched
on his outstretched arms
& on his head

Each one cooed
a single note
but the sounds mingled
together
like a chorale
of bell ringers
& my father
he did nothing

to stop it

G. E. Patterson
from *Tug*

Copyright Renewal Under the Texaco Star

The sass pumping my gas
Is flashing a come-hither tattoo—
Kokopelli, the gigolo flute player
(After some Anasazi petroglyphs).
And you know
The way it peekaboos into view
When her arm eclipses the blaze of the windshield,
A five-color icon, conga dancing through that tan line,
And the way the waist of her oversized, orange jumpsuit
Grabs ass when she roll-casts the air hose
Out of the way of my going,
Lug sole boots by R. Crumb
Zippering the tarmac,
Walk-away wink,
You just know
How Susanna burned those elders down.

Jeffrey Dye

first published in *The Threepenny Review*, 76, vol. XIX, no. 4, Winter 1999

JULY 10

Pole Boat at Honey Island

The way he pushes deeper
into everything I hate—the heat rising
like wet crepe from silt and muck
to fill our lungs with its rotten breath.

Listen to the grunting armadillos
pad the tule pond on tiny feet.
Listen to the owl croon
in the loblolly.

I want to be brave, to bathe
myself in the humid night,
to cross the irradiant lawn
under magnolias,

those creamy-faced babies
perched in evergreen leaves,
to float through dives,
sick-smelling bayous full of turtle,

yellow-capped night heron,
to let the air penetrate at last,
the miasma that sends women to attics,
sets them scratching walls like mice,

rocking, humming with no release.
But I am afraid. I have danced
the sad slippers. I have placed
a hand on blind branches,

felt it flame with fire ants.
My lover's body like water snakes,
his sweat the odor of crawfish,
boiled. As he poles deeper

into the gauzy night—water swims
beside kerosene. So too as peepers
fill their bugle pouches—
like voices in an asylum,

an orchestra of cracked reeds,
throbbing sacs of chameleon—
we strum our giddy throats.
We begin to screech.

Sandra Alcosser
from *Except by Nature*

American Manhood

In the dull ache that is midnight for a boy
his age, I heard the sound of him first:
hiss of the pistol-grip hose from the garden
and the clatter a watery arc makes
coming down silver under streetlights,
on the day-warmed pavement of the road.
And though I muttered at first
to be awakened, I stand now in the window
upstairs, naked and alert, the cool breeze
sweet with the blossoms of locusts.

My wife murmurs, stirs. She is a slope of white
in the bedclothes, dunes of softness
below the light from the window
and the single blind eye of the clock.
"It's just Travis," I say, hoping
she'll lapse again into sleep.

I hope she'll sleep because he is a boy,
fourteen, soft yet himself, unwhiskered.
He believes he is the only one
awake, the only one alive in a world
of cruel nights and unbearable silence.
His parents snore, their house is dark.
He crouches on the curb
in just his pajama bottoms, barefoot,
swirling figure eights into the air trafficked
by insects and the fluttering, hunting bats.

Tonight he speaks a language I believe
I must have known, in the time before, those years
when a boy's body imagines the world, the heartbeat
rhythm of water on the road, the riches
coined by streetlights, the smell of the night
that is everything at once, alterable
and contained—all that keeps him awake
long after I've gone back to bed.

But before sleep comes, I listen, until the noise
he makes is my own even breathing, and I
    remember how
the old rented guitar I learned on smelled of music,
how the young married woman across the street
robbed me of the power of speech,
and how I wandered one night the alleys
of the town I grew up in, a brick in my hand,
breaking thermometers, taillights, and windows,
and went home and laughed aloud and wept.

Robert Wrigley
from *Moon in a Mason Jar* & *What My Father Believed*

July **12**

"Even Ornaments of Speech Are Forms of Deceit."

History of the Royal Society

It's 1667. Reason is everywhere, saving
for the future, ordering a small glass of wine.
Cause, arm in arm with Effect, strolls by
in sturdy shoes.

Of course, there are those who venture
out under cover of darkness to buy a bag
of metaphors or even some personification
from Italy, primo and uncut.

But for the most part, poets like Roderigo
stroll the boulevards in their normal hats.
When he thinks of his beloved, he opens
his notebook with a flourish.

"Your lips," he writes, "are like
lips."

Ron Koertge
from *Geography of the Forehead*

A Man of 1794

And like a discarded statue, propped up in a cart,
He is borne along toward the page allotted to him
   in history.

To open his heavy-lidded eyes now would be merely
To familiarize himself with the banal and destined
   route.

He is aware of the mockery of the streets,
But does not understand it. It hardly occurs to him

That what they fear is that he might yet address
   them
And call them back to their inflamed duty.

But this he cannot do; the broken jaw prevents
   speech.
Today he will not accuse the accusers; it is perhaps
   all that saves them.

Meanwhile his head rocks back and forth loosely
   on his chest
With each new jolt and lurch of the endless-
   seeming street:

Impossible to resist this idiot shaking.
—But it is hard after all to sympathize

With a man formerly so immaculate,
Who, after a single night of ambiguous confinement,

Lets go all pride of appearance. Nevertheless,
Under the soiled jabot, beneath the stained blue
   coat,

Are the principles nothing has shaken. Rousseau
   was right,
Of that he is still convinced: *Man is naturally good!*

And in the moment before the blade eases his pain
He thinks perhaps of his dog or of the woods at
   Choissy,

Some thought in any case of a perfectly trivial
   nature,
As though already he were possessed of a sweet,
   indefinite leisure.

Donald Justice
from *New and Selected Poems*

JULY 14

Concrete Seascape

oceanoceanoceanoceanocean
oceanoceanoceanoceanocean
oceanoceancanoeoceanocean
oceanoceanoceanoceanocean
oceanoceanoceanoceanocean

William Harmon

first published in *Blink*, vol. 1, no. 2, September/October 2001

Aunt Lily and Frederick the Great

After the war, she painted her walls
a French blue, pale as the watered
blue silk of her eyes, filled her rooms
with cream and gold-leaf chairs,
and when she raised her porcelain cup
with pinky arched and blew the word
"Limo-o-o-gges" across the lip,
that made a tender wind, as if a host
of cherubs rafted through the room.
Mad for all things French,
She'd never read Voltaire,
went straight from the Academy
of Typing in the Bronx to work
for Mr. Hyman at the J.D.C.
In 1945 she went to Paris—ah, the city
was a shambles then, American cigarettes
were currency, her Yiddish
far more useful than her French
for work among the refugees. History
was hell, she learned, but life
moved on. She purchased
silver fruit knives, teacups, pastel
figurines, and tottered home on platform
wedgies to attend the rattle and attack
of morning trucks along Third
Avenue and to receive us kindly
when we came to call—in short,

to lead a life not *sans souci*
(for there were deaths,
and loneliness), but of her own
design. You'd never guess
King Frederick and my aunt
would have so much
in common. Both were short,
bilingual, stubborn, confused,
enlightened in some ways, benighted
in others, tyrannical, clever, benevolent,
fierce. Like Frederick, she flourished,
like Frederick, she died. She was tiny
and great and is buried in Queens.

Jean Nordhaus
first published in *The Gettysburg Review*, vol. 12,
no. 3, Fall 1999

JULY 16

Siren

In your think tank you're Olympia,
all languid length and skin and two red roses
budding in the suds; or you're unhappy, a
sea fury frozen in your fountain poses.
And then a fine rime settles on the water,
hides you almost, Susannah, soaped to gleaming,
but wise from birth to what the elders taught her,
that though the tongue be stone the spirit's scheming
heat and action, craves to be
swimming with you into infinity—
as on those evenings when I hear you run
your bath and put your hair up in a bun
and sigh, and sink into your second home,
and then you call me from the other room.

Jonathan Galassi
first published in *The Yale Review*, vol. 88, no. 1, January 2000
also from *North Street*

Woman Holding a Fox

Buried inside, page three, below the fold,
a woman crumpled on fresh dirt begins to get the gist:
that she has lost the use of her left leg, that when she tripped
        her hip gave out. Shock explains
this all to her, a self-assured young doctor mouthing, Rest.

The reason for the break, a rabid fox
that came at her when she stepped out for half a cigarette.
Age seventy-nine, the paper said; she hadn't toppled far,
        merely down her few fronts steps,
but late enough that no one finds her till the following day.

And here's the eerie part. Just when she thinks
to drag herself down to the curb, the twisted fox comes back.
In hours her arms are bitten blue, waving her one defense.
        Her glasses lost in tufted grass,
she hears it thread the underbrush before she sees it leap.

At two o'clock, a nurse toggles the lamp.
Something for the pain. Since after dark, the fox has come
to look on her as prey, the way he circles then descends.
        This is no dream, she tells herself.
Yet it had seemed unreal from the initial streak of red:

a comedy at first, a photo-op,
then something else, an eye-white flash our unsuspecting trust
shields us from until the outward show no longer jibes.
        She's landed in her garden row,
her Marlboro still smoking on the carefully weeded path.

Beyond the gate a sunset has begun,
the swatch of sky above her roof dyed jacaranda-blue.
These are things she sees as she assumes things can't get worse.
        But then they do. When it returns,
she clasps it to herself. Somehow she's managed to affix

small hands around its muzzle and bared teeth.
All night she feels it panting and enraged, then weirdly calm.
So off and on for hours until someone spots her there.
        A neighbor comes, she knows that now.
But on the sedge she hadn't guessed that it would end so well.

      As for what crowds her head: a single thought
repeated in contrition, while the same minute extends,
infinitely regressing between mirrors set opposed.
        Music's playing down the hall,
carried on a crack of light that shows the door ajar.

      It's nearly dawn. I have not killed the fox,
my arms barely keep him hemmed, my fingers have gone limp.
Across the lawn an amniotic slick of dew gives off
        a silver sheen and sudden cold.
I'm glad you happened by, she wryly croaks when he appears.

      Before he batters in the hissing fox,
he asks her why she simply didn't let it run away.
I know this creature pretty well by now. She shows her skin.
        It's true, she understands the fox
and wonders if she hasn't always known that he was there,

      known it when her first child was born,
and known it, too, the day her husband died three years ago.
At any rate she knows it now, will always keep him close
        in her embrace from day to day,
up to a time when memories of these no longer serve.

David Yezzi
first published in *New England Review*, vol. 20, no. 3, Summer 1999
also from *The Hidden Model*

JULY 18

Letter after a Year

Here's a story I never told you.
Living in a rented house
on South University in Ann Arbor
long before we met, I found
bundled letters in the attic room
where I took myself to work.
A young woman tenant of the attic
wrote these letters to her lover,
who had died in a plane crash.
In my thirtieth year, with tenure
and a new book coming out,
I read the letters in puzzlement.
"She's writing to somebody *dead*?"

There's one good thing
about April. Every day Gus and I
take a walk in the graveyard.
I'm the one who doesn't
piss on your stone. All winter
when ice and snow kept me away
I worried that you missed me.
"Perkins! Where the hell
are you?"

        In hell. Every day
I play in repertory the same
script without you, without love,
without audience except for Gus,
who waits attentive
for cues: a walk, a biscuit,
bedtime. The year of days
without you and your body swept by
as quick as an afternoon;
but each afternoon took a year.

At first in my outrage
I daydreamed burning the house:
kerosene in pie plates
with a candle lit in the middle.
I locked myself in your study
with Gus, Ada, and the rifle
my father gave me at twelve.
I killed our cat and dog.
I swallowed a bottle of pills,
knowing that if I woke on fire
I had the gun.

        After you died
I stopped rereading history.
I took up Cormac McCarthy
for the rage and murder.
Now I return to Gibbon; secure
in his reasonable civilization,
he exercises detachment
as barbarians skewer Romans.
Then Huns gallop from the sunrise
wearing skulls.

        What's new?
I see more people now. In March,
I took Kate and Mary to Piero's.
At the end of the month ice dropped
to the pond's bottom, and water
flashed and flowed
through pines in western light.
The year melted into April
and I lived through the hour
we learned last year you would die.
For the next ten days, my mind
sat by our bed again
as you diminished cell by cell.

Last week the goldfinches
flew back for a second spring.
Again I witnessed snowdrops
worry from dead leaves
into air. Now your hillside
daffodils edge up, and today
it's a year since we set you down
at the border of the graveyard
on a breezy April day. We stood
in a circle around the coffin
and its hole, under pines
and birches, to lower you
into glacial sand.

                When I dream
sometimes your hair is long
and we make love as we used to.
One nap time I saw your face
at eighty: many lines, more flesh,
the good bones distinct.

It's astonishing to be old.
When I stand after sitting,
I'm shocked at how I must stretch
to ease the stiffness out.
When we first spoke of marriage
we dismissed the notion
because you'd be a widow
twenty-five years, or maybe
I wouldn't be able to make love
while desire still flared in you.
Sometimes now I feel crazy
with desire again
as if I were forty, drinking,
and just divorced.

Ruth Houghton had a stroke.
Her daughter sent me the album
of photographs Roger took
in his documentary passion ?
inside and outside our house,
every room, every corner ?
one day in September 1984.
I howled as I gazed at that day
intact. Our furniture
looked out of place, as if vandals
had shoved everything awry.
There were pictures on the walls
we put away long ago.
The kitchen wallpaper shone
bright red in Roger's Kodacolor;
it faded over the years
as we watched, not seeing it fade.

Donald Hall
from *Without*

Miss Chang Is Missing

We know it's to San Francisco
or New York—she couldn't have stopped
anywhere in between, and she requires
a coast. It's her taste for seafood
and the smell of salt water, even
industrial ocean. She couldn't

have been abducted; she would have
karate-chopped the guy's pistol,
snapped his partner's neck. She wouldn't
have run away—in spite of herself
she's the Buddha
through and through; she dissolves

ill humor with her eyes. Nor
has she eloped; she doesn't like men
as much as she likes lemongrass prawns
with black pepper, and marriage
in the only world she knows
doesn't suit her. She once talked

about relatives in Hong Kong, but
they must have perished years ago
and her Chinese was broken anyway.
Not *was*—she isn't gone for good.
She often leaves town on short notice,
just never this short. She left

a syllable on a client's machine:
way, which could have been *wei*
the Chinese telephone greeting
or the beginning of *wait*, or
way do you think you're going
as she sometimes said. It must

be tough to have an accent
in both languages. The neighbors
think she intended to come back
that night; she hadn't taken the trash
to the curb, the cat came looking
for food, and she couldn't have vanished

into thin air. But she was
oriental in a way most Asian people
aren't, somehow immaterial and bound
to outlast the trees, the house,
her body—one could get in trouble
for saying it, but anyone who met her

would agree. She was the only woman
who really was that creature hovering
at the edge of the movies: dark-haired,
dark-eyed, supernatural, ginseng-
scented, otherworldly. Likely to one day
walk off the earth and into the sky.

Adrienne Su
from *Middle Kingdom*

Larson Arson

Andreas and Carl Larson were the thug twins.
They lit up the wolf at the door,
burned things down.

We would see them in night cars, Andreas so
    handsome
we called him the ace of face, and Carl
with a thousand dollars of black leather
running over his body
like the tender hands of his girl.
We booked their doom, called them
silver skeletons riding, were surprised
they burned and burned, and lived to tell.

Larson Arson was on the job
when Andreas saw the gas jet and Carl didn't
and had just time to torch the rags and grin and say
Is everybody toasty?
when Andreas was blown through the wall like a
    knife,
every pore, tooth, and hair burned clear;
every bone in his body broken;
not enough left to bury.
Carl was thrown through an open window
into the thickest flowering bush in town.
He stepped down as though from his mother's palm
and walked past his molten double
without missing stride.

Carl gave up fire. He said he didn't
want to die roasting like a pig in hell.
People love human brands
snatched from the burning, and from that day
Carl was the darling wherever he went.
Roads smoothed themselves before him,
landscapes bloomed before their time.
Old rooms of fire
gilded his new skin of reformation.
Old rooms of smoke, those thumbs on the throat,
were glamorous sandalwood at the banquet.

Margaret Benbow
from *Stalking Joy*

When My Car Broke Down

I was somewhere in Utah or Wyoming,
somewhere in the high inhuman deserts,
in the thin blue flame of wavering air,
bluffs of red earth scorched and

stratified on the horizon. I had stopped
to admire the desolation, to smoke
a cigarette and consider that ten thousand
years ago this was all under water,

that strange fish would have swum
through the space my eyes now occupied;
before that ice, and before that
something else again, unimaginably alien.

The Buddhists say first thought best thought,
but my first thought when I saw the steam
billowing up from under my car was:
if I just keep driving, maybe it will go away.

After all, I was moving three thousand miles
not to "escape" my problems but to put
a nice distance between them and me.
A problem has to be fierce to travel that far.

My second thought was to stare at the engine
for a while. I leaned over and looked
down into it as into the bowels of a ship
or the cranium of some fantastic beast.

And recalled how my father tried to teach me
about cars. Mostly he had me hold
the light for hours and mostly I studied
the back of his head, turning over the words

he said and knowing even then I'd never
understand. The blood would drain
from my arm and I'd prop it up
with my one free hand to keep from

caving in or betraying my halfheartedness.
Even then I was hopelessly afflicted
with the disease of the Wandering Mind.
Even then I was dreaming myself

across magical landscapes, just like this,
and learning all he had to teach me
about standing rooted to one spot,
wishing I were somewhere else.

John Brehm
first published in *Poetry*, vol. CLXX, no. 5, August 1997

JULY 22

In a City

In an eastern city where I won't return
there is a winged stone light and huge
lightning strikes this winged stone
I close my eyes to remember

in my city where I won't return
there is heavy and nourishing water
the one who gives you a cup of this water
gives you the faith you will still return

in my faraway city that has gone
from all maps of the world there is bread that can nourish
throughout life black as the faith you will see again
stone bread water and the presence of towers at dawn

Zbigniew Herbert

first published in *The Kenyon Review*, New Series, vol. XXIII, no. 3/4, Summer/Fall 2001

translated from Polish by John and Bogdana Carpenter

JULY 23

Under the Big Top

near Grand Island, Nebraska, July 23, 1913

I. Heat Lightning

Fields of flax and sweetcorn flash under a half-moon
climbing the trellised treeline. Distant clouds tremble
each time the horizon flares, and the mare's hipbones

glisten as if sun-lit. She snorts, shakes her bridle,
but Ted's mother tightens the reins, cooing what seems
almost a love-song over the throb of their wheels

against wagon ruts, grass swishing the axletree.
He shuts his eyes and listens: peepers, cicadas,
wind in the cottonwoods. When he rouses from sleep,

they're nearing the fairgrounds. Kerosene bulbs, abuzz
with June bugs, swing from the tentpoles. A light drizzle
has begun to fall, and Ted watches the shadows of boys

sway toward the bigtop, lamps bobbing like thistles.
A nighthawk calls, faint as a distant train whistle.

II. Porch

L.C. lets the door slap, lifts the whistling kettle
from the stove with a dishtowel. Granary patched
with tinscrap, cobs ground and slopped for the cattle,

evening has crept in like the dull ache in his back.
He blows steam from his cup, watching out the window.
Soon his boys will come following the foot-path

over the ridge. Single-file and nodding like cows,
they will drop their tools, jog to the night-cooled river,
and shed their sweat-crusted clothes, strung from the willows,

till the moon is high overhead. The four others
jaundiced in their cribs, before they even had names.
Mostly what he remembers is the scent of cedar,

clawhammer, sixpenny nails, the chuck of the plane.
He remembers the rattling cart, digging their graves.

III. Field-work

Sunset. Knee-deep in corn. Wallace driving the spade.
Down the row, Lynn in silhouette squats to knock dirt
from the lacy roots of cocklebur and bindweed,

then stands, wiping his hands on the tail of his shirt,
its thin denim, touched with the deep rust of dusk
and clay. But all is bleached white by the time they work

the last groove, stooped under a half-moon, amid husks
rustling, dark trees rocking at the top of the ridge.
In the distance, the night-train kicks clouds of white dust

into the air, rumbles over the wood-frame bridge,
so the moon shivers on the face of the river.
Now, his spade still, the whistle sounds like a pigeon

roosted high in the rafters of the old houses; firs
rise like bedposts into a canopy of stars.

IV. Center Ring

Under the canopy—snapping like a tattered flag—
the wirewalker shoulders her balance. It wobbles,
sagged at each end, but her feet creep down the rope rigged

between the tallest poles. The tent-walls mottle
with lamplight and shadow, dumb-show of elephants,
tumbling clowns, spinning like sun through a milk-bottle.

Goldie steals a glimpse of the others. Eyes round
with fear, their stares are fixed on a woman, standing
arms wide on a sway-backed, sequin-studded stallion,

but then the horse stops, mid-air, its rider dangling
like the wirewalker between sky and earth: the hiss
and sizzle of the struck post, the thunderclap, screaming

and sawdust, people running for the flame-lit tracks
where caged animals howl at the edge of darkness.

V. The Platte River

Storm-gales howl in the darkness, whipping treetops side
to side. Rain streams from Bob's hat brim. Huddled here
at the far edge of the woods, his unsteady steed

stamping the underbrush into black mud, he stares
across the acreage, where corn rows sink in the glut.
Last spring, he aimed the drafthorse like a rifle—ears

solid as a sight—at the pine grove across the Platte.
Without bit or blinders, he cut each furrow, straight
as new corduroy. Now hailstones beat green stalks flat.

Ditchwater swells and gushes over the floodgate.
He turns up the roadway to check for their carriage,
pushing against the wind until he finds a break

and stays his horse like a sentry atop the ridge.
The river climbs its banks, tearing planks from the bridge.

VI. Chapman Bridge

Loose planks bob and disappear downriver. Reins hitched
to the truss, Catherine inches out onto the deck.
The dark water gushes through knot-holes in the bridge,

surges over her boots, dashing her face and dress
with mud churned by the current. She pushes her foot
forward, feeling for gaps, shaking—she thinks—like legs

on a wire. Far-off, thunder cracks like splitting wood
and she sees the girl fall through fire, the burning tent,
hears the trapped elephant squawl like a wailing child.

Then, through the rain, she sees the bent brim of Bob's hat.
He yells *stay where you are* then *take hold of my arm*.
When they clear the bend, the boys rush from the milkshed:

Wallace, stripping wet quilts, hoisting Ted in his arms,
while Lynn runs the team toward the dim light of the barn.

VII. Hayloft

Lynn leads the horses through the barn's sliding door,
down the lamplit feedway to their stalls. His hair clings
to his forehead and his wet overalls sag, but he moors

them to their stanchions, brushes each down, then cleans
with a hoof-knife the hard clay clotted to their soles.
Wind rattles the bare rafters. On the roof's thin tin

rain hums like a snare. By now, they must be nestled
in dry quilts, warm in the glow of the stove. Their soft
hands must throb, cupping mugs of black-tea, but Lynn scales

the ladder into the dark reaches of the loft.
He crawls over damp bales and unbolts the hay-door.
Here, above thrashing pines and wind that just won't stop,

he counts breaths between flare and crack, until the storm
moves on, flashing across fields of flax and sweetcorn.

Ted Genoways
first published in *The Virginia Quarterly Review*, vol. 77, no. 1, Winter 2001
also from *Bullroarer: A Sequence*

Fear And Fame

Half an hour to dress, wide rubber hip boots,
gauntlets to the elbow, a plastic helmet
like a knight's but with a little glass window
that kept steaming over, and a respirator
to save my smoke-stained lungs. I would descend
step by slow step into the dim world
of the pickling tank and there prepare
the new solutions from the great carboys
of acids lowered to me on ropes—all from a recipe
I shared with nobody and learned from Frank O'Mera
before he went off to the bars on Vernor Highway
to drink himself to death. A gallon of hydrochloric
steaming from the wide glass mouth, a dash
of pale nitric to bubble up, sulphuric to calm,
metals for sweeteners, cleansers for salts,
until I knew the burning stew was done.
Then to climb back, step by stately step, the
        adventurer
returned to the ordinary blinking lights
of the swing shift at Feinberg and Breslin's
First-Rate Plumbing and Plating with a message
from the kingdom of fire. Oddly enough
no one welcomed me back, and I'd stand
fully armored as the downpour of cold water
rained down on me and the smoking traces puddled
at my feet like so much milk and melting snow.
Then to disrobe down to my work pants and shirt,
my black street shoes and white cotton socks,
to reassume my nickname, strap on my Bulova,
screw back my wedding ring, and with tap water
gargle away the bitterness as best I could.

For fifteen minutes or more I'd sit quietly
off to the side of the world as the women
polished the tubes and fixtures to a burnished purity
hung like Christmas ornaments on the racks
pulled steadily toward the tanks I'd cooked.
Ahead lay the second cigarette, held in a shaking hand,
as I took into myself the sickening heat to quell heat,
a lunch of two Genoa salami sandwiches and Swiss
        cheese
on heavy peasant bread baked by my Aunt Tsipie,
and a third cigarette to kill the taste of the others.
Then to arise and dress again in the costume
of my trade for the second time that night, stiffened
by the knowledge that to descend and rise up
from the other world merely once in eight hours is half
what it takes to be known among women and men.

Philip Levine
from *What Work Is*

The Visit

We were at the camp, it must have been
some afternoon that summer
when your Aunt Ruth came back
from her stroke, because her mouth
looked skeptical, almost provocative,
as if she had suddenly achieved the role
of the great lady she'd spent a lifetime
preparing for. And I remember how,
with this new dignity, she turned
to Uncle Herb's thought about the good
taste of beer on a hot day as if
he weren't wearing Bermuda shorts
and wing-tipped shoes at all,
but a loincloth. How could he
have known that she meant, if he waited
a few respectful minutes, just one
would be OK, and what was more,
(the porch had got so hot, even
with the breeze), Aunt Ruth would feel
compelled to have one too? So,
what Herb came back with was beers
for everybody, even Ruth's 80-
year-old sister, do you remember,
the one who was shrinking and said Oh,

because she liked the cheese
your mother brought out or the small flowers
on the TV tray or the wind that threatened
to blow her wide hat off? It didn't,
of course, and when Ruth said No, no, no,
Herbert, we knew he could go on telling
what they did when they were younger,
because it had turned out to be
one of those wonderful days which had nothing
quite to do with wind or words. So Herb
just sat there, his white legs happy
to be free of pants, and talked—was it
about the wildest party, or how fast they drove
in his new car afterward? And while
they said they couldn't stay, they stayed
until the last light rose into the tops
of the trees around us on the lake,
and the wind suddenly stopped,
and even Aunt Ruth said how nice
it had got. Perfection
is what almost doesn't happen.

Wesley McNair
from *The Town of No & My Brother Running*

JULY 26

A Madeleine

For me, it's a bit of cool hide
from an orange, a continent
torn from a pulpy planet,
held to the light and squeezed
until its cratered field
bursts with little geysers,
citrine explosions.

Hold it to my nose
and I go Proustian:
there's the twenty-acre grove
my parents owned, the stucco house,
and the whole family
gathered under one light,
a ripe fruit as yet unpeeled.

George Bilgere
from *Big Bang*

JULY 27

Trapeze

To float you must float from within.
You must not feel attached

as you brush past the body you loved,
an arm past an arm, an almost weightless vapor.

Don't ask questions anymore. Don't hear
his seismic voice. Fractures thread the floor;

time will energize their creep
until you're caving through his ceiling.

It's all a matter of containment,
held-in breath, the hidden table. Keep in mind

that dreaming up means waking down,
so keep your swing in limbo. Don't aim high:

Where air turns thin, the ear tears open
with a secret's restless heat,

surrendering its recess—the details of explosion
fizzling in a tree, remembered now and then,

but not so well, by something on and off,
like fireflies—when pressure mounts beneath it.

Larissa Szporluk
from *Isolato*

July **28**

Shall I Compare Thee?

According to early Icelandic law it was a serious offense to
address a love poem to a woman, even an unmarried one.

Love prefers the least contact to the greatest distant joy.

If I loved the moon I would not praise
the varied light she casts from night to night,
nor tell her how much she fills the dark and somewhat
    speckled sky
when she is not there, when memory only
    lifts her above the horizon, pulls her
above me where I lie and wait.

If I loved the earth at twilight,
when mountains are soft contours in the dying light,
when the lake lies silver and still and I wade deeper,
    beyond the shallows, until
I am buoyed, afloat and surrounded by her touch,
I would not call her a woman.

Oh no, each thing I praised I would be sure to say
was only what it was, was not what my body
most desired, the other half of my torn self,
was not what I need most when my spirit
wishes to speak without words.

I would say nothing to the woman I loved,
not even in what I write, because I would not
    have others know how she is all
they could want, would not want even
the smallest syllable to lie between us.

T. Alan Broughton
first published in *The Southern Review*, vol. 37, no. 3,
    Summer 2001

JULY 29

What Can Stop This

What can stop this

I found a pleasure

I found an easy faith

One is senseless

One never shakes

What can stop this

It makes no difference anymore

What I choose

Or if I choose to walk to St Augustine

To the sea beach driving

A green orange over the sand

With a stick singing

The sympathy of friends is pleasant **VIOLINS**

But it makes no difference anymore **TROMBONE**

Donald Revell
first published in *New American Writing*, no. 17, 1999
also from *Arcady*

JULY 30

Asylum

The fish are the first to return:
the moorish idol, the black surgeon,

the trumpet and lesser scorpion, the angel
seemingly radiogenic, the goatfish

with its face of spikes. Whole phyla converging:
the devil rays in fluid sheets, the leatherbacks,

hawksbills, their shells reticent as maps.
On the atoll: the golden plover, the kingfisher,

egrets and honeyeaters
nesting like an occupation. And the flowers:

the flame trees, the now forgotten, the wait-a-bit
all drawn to what we desert, a preserve

where the chinese lantern's elliptic seed
is bone-smooth, cesium-laced.

Quan Barry
from *Asylum*

JULY 31

Mansion Beach

1

I count the rays of the jellyfish:
twelve in this one, like a clock to tell time by,
thirteen in the next, time gone awry.

A great wind brought them in, left them here
to die, indifferent time measured by whirling moon
and sun, by tides in perpetual fall and rise.

Englobed, transparent, they litter the beach,
creatureless creatures deprived of speech
who spawn more like themselves before they die.

I peer into each and see a faceless
red center, red spokes like a star.
They are, and are not, like what we are.

2

At noon, in the too bright light, watchful,
looking too hard, we saw the scene turn dark
and lost the children for a moment, waves

crashing around them. Shadow blended with shadow,
the sun inside a cloud, and then the children
were restored to us, our worst fears a hallucination.

All afternoon their castles, poor and proud,
rose and fell. Great civilizations were built,
came to an end, the children mighty lords, their castles

only as small as we are to the stars and starry structures.
The day was infinite for them, time stretching
to the farthest horizon, the sun their overlord.

But how to reconcile these summer days washing away
with our need to commemorate, to hold onto?
They knew. And so they sang a song tuneless and true,

admitting no fixed point, no absolute, words
overheard and blurred by great winds blowing in,
a rhyme or round for a time such as we live in:

The world is made, knocked down, and made again!

3

This is the moment of stasis: gulls stall
above the burned-out mansion on the bluff,
gone for thirty years, and cairns rise up,

stone balanced on stone. By evening, the beach
is empty, my shadow a long-legged giant leading me
past small battlements to the day's masterpiece:

a dripping castle, all towers and crenellation,
tall as a child, made by many children, flying
three-pointed flags that wave hopefully in the wind.

Closer, I see the moat, the courtyard's secret
pool in which, macabrely, red jellyfish float,
death and potentiality entwined forever.

A crab small as my fingernail, dead,
perfect in every detail, with hairlike spinnerets
and claws, guards the open castle door from entry

as night begins to fall and shadows dark as ink
wash in to stain the beach. Shivering, I think,
O sentry, who would enter here?

4

Traveling once, I stood under the open sky
inside a great unfinished cathedral.
Stonemasons, there for generations, clung

like ants to thin scaffolding, carving
griffins and saints, the rising spires and portals
dripping like hot wax, and birds flew

freely in and out of lacy walls, like angels
thrown down from heaven. Gaudy and grand,
it was a vision of eternal mind. Its maker,

dead for a long time, had left no finished plan,
design, but work went on, days turning
into years, the century coming to a close.

In disbelief, I touched each twisting vine
and leaf, marveling at what had been done,
and what was yet to be, and wished,

as I wish now, O let it never be complete!

Elizabeth Spires
from *Worldling*

AUGUST 1

Hostess

One of the guests arrives with irises, all

funnel & hood, papery tongues whispering little
rumors in their mouths, and leaves

his white shoes in the doorway
where the others stumble
on the emptiness when they come. He

smiles. He says, "I'm
here to ruin your party, Laura," and he does. The
    stems

of the irises are too
long and stiff for a vase, and when

I cannot find the scissors, I slice
them off with a knife

while the party waits. Of course, the jokes

are pornographic, and the flowers

tongued and stunted
and seductive, while
in the distance weeds & lightning

make wired anxiety of the night. But I'm

a hostess, a woman who must give
the blessing of forced content, carry
a cage of nervous birds

like conversation through my living room, turning

up the music, dimming
the lights, offering more, or less, or something
    else

as it seems fit, using
only the intuition
of a lover's tongue, a confessional poet, or
a blind woman fluffing up her hair. It is

an effort, making pleasure, passing
it around on a silver platter, and I'm

distracted all night
by his pale eye

like a symbol of a symbol of something
out of logic's reach forever, until

the soggy cocktail napkin
of my party ends
with this guest carrying
an iris around the kitchen in his teeth, daring me

to take it out with mine. Perhaps

a hostess should not laugh
too hard, or dance
at her own affair. Frolic

is for the guests, who've now
found their coats and shrugged them on. I hear

someone call "Good-night"
sullenly to the night, disappointment
like a gray fur lining

in her voice. Someone

mentions to this guest
that his shoes have filled with rain, suggests
suggestively he wear

a pair of my
husband's shoes home when he goes. Of course,
   of course, one

of the godmothers has always
come to the christening for revenge. She
leans over the squirming bassinet and smiles
and sprinkles the baby with just
a bit of badness. In his

white smock, he
is prettier than we imagined
he could be, but also
sneaky, easily
bored, annoyed
with the happy
lives of his dull friends. When

he grows up he'll go to parties just
to drink too much, to touch
the women in ways that offer

favors he can't grant. The women

will roll their eyes behind
one another's necks. The men

will bicker about the wine. And
after the party, and the storm, in the after-

quiet, the hostess will find
herself standing
a long time on the patio
alone, as I
stand tonight, after
the party, in the still, small song of embarrassment
and regret, aeolian

in my white dress, the wind

feeling up
those places again while I
smoke a cigarette, which fills

my whole body with the calm that comes
just after the barn
has burned to the ground, and the farmers' wives
in nightgowns stand

around in moonlit air, their
breasts nearly exposed, their
swan-necks warm. Perhaps

it was the wine. When I
passed him in the hallway by the bathroom, I

thought I heard him say, "Laura, I want

to ruin your life," and, trying to be polite, I said,
   "That's

fine." I said, "Make yourself at home."

Laura Kasischke
from *Fire & Flower*

The Field

Once I left the room
of the boardinghouse
I dreamed, I saw at the end
of a long fallow field

the derricks and cranes
like spider-woven filament
against the bay
curdling in the sun.

The clods of earth
beneath my shoes
crumbled at each step
and reeked of ammonia,

that friable breaking up
like a quavering voice
leaping to attack,
laddering up and down

a dissonant scale
so pure, so atonal
that it shivered all through me
as if I were a tuning fork

vibrating through
the far-echoing afternoon.
On and on my feet
kept moving, the softly

combusting clods
cushioning each step
as before me the field spread
always larger and more still,

the dream taking me
wherever I would go,
my black shadow
plunging and lifting

like a plough—
until I was borne up
by the buoyant exhaustion
of my path down

the furrows that flowed out
like a never-ending note
floating on the breath
of a singer whose eyes shut

and who feels himself lifted
past the spotlit hall
into a solitude beyond
appeal or recall.

Tom Sleigh
from *The Dreamhouse*

AUGUST 3

Swept

When we say I
miss you what
we mean is I'm
filled with

dread. At night
alone going
to bed is
like lying down

in a wave. Total
absence of light.
Swept away to
gone.

Hayden Carruth
from *Scrambled Eggs & Whiskey: Poems 1991–1995*

AUGUST 4

Sinking

He takes night as a kind of medicine,
swallowing it with a buck and shiver.
Sometimes a drowning must come from within

and spread stealthily out toward the skin
with the drowsy patience of a fever.
He takes night as a kind of medicine,

his blood expanding as the moon goes thin—
its liquid light is something to savor.
Sometimes a drowning must come from within,

where it works like the fingerprint of gin
on the breath of an unfaithful lover.
He takes night as a kind of medicine

and relishes its pliable calfskin
smack, hoping it will blunt him forever.
Sometimes a drowning must come from within.

Finished waiting for the end to begin,
he's a thought in the mind of the river.
He takes night as a kind of medicine—
sometimes a drowning must come from within.

Mark Bibbins
from *Take Three: 3*

Demas, in Love with This Present World

2 Timothy 4:9–10

What you've heard is true—I've gone to Thessilonika.
I've taken a room above the agora with a view
of the harbor and wake too early to merchants' voices,
bleatings of every sort, and carpets being beaten.
The innkeeper and his wife bring bread—they are kind,
and their daughter is pretty, though she has a withered hand.

At night I watch the fishing boats come in to shore,
hung with many lanterns. The men pull up their nets
and sort the catch in shifting light; they sometimes sing
a song about the moon seducing an old sailor
and drink a bit and fall asleep wrapped in their robes.
Later someone puts the lights out one by one.

In between, the days are slow, and I think of you often.
I know what some are saying, that I loved my father
and his estate more than truth and our way of life.
It wasn't the inheritance that called me back,
and I won't return to the assembly or his house.
Demetrius is here, asleep beside me as I write.

He has thrown one of his warm legs over me
in a dream, and two pears with a jar of wine wait
on the table for when he wakes. I wish you understood
how it feels to fear the truth while also loving him.
I still believe this present world is passing away,
but now it is impossible to rejoice with you.

Sometimes when I walk outside the city gates
and look up into the mountains, toward Rome
where all of you are waiting, I want to come back—
but it doesn't last. I walk home through the colonnade,
listening to the temple priests and fortune tellers,
the eastern caravans selling cedar, pearls, and linen.

The innkeeper's daughter greets me at the door,
the weak hand cupped to her breast. She has been
praying to a small bright god in the corner
of her room, for health and peace, as she has been taught.
I will go upstairs and place my arms around the loved
and living body of one who owns no household gods,

who confesses no world but this. We will watch
the sky turn dark and wait for the fishermen to light
their lamps and disappear across the invisible sea.
I pray to the God I remember, whom I love and fail
to love, knowing words are all I have to bind
us to each other, knowing they are passing too.

Kristin Fogdall
first published in *Poetry*, vol. CLXXVI, no. 4, July 2000

The Intrusion of Ovid

Brother Ovid, my classical leanings run thin
tonight, alone with weepy music and food
less interesting than the politics of mollusks.

Catullus and his exploits in the front yard
with the maid and one of his pale girlfriends
puts me to shame, so it's to you I turn

for good company. It helps that you're dead.
Your book shuts without protest
unlike my front door or someone's mouth

when I'm tired of intrusion. The stars
blur the perfect darkness of the night.
The moon muddies the shore where I go

to think of its distant urgings. The crickets
themselves should learn to dream
in silence, without singing to the large world

of loneliness. You, yourself, trample
the sadness I lushly tend like a garden
and tell me to come in from the rain,

to laugh while I can, to get more sleep,
good advices all, and at this window
in which is framed the world that's mine

and once was yours, I'm inclined to listen,
to put you down and shut my eyes
because pain is ancient, and therefore classic,

as you are and I am not.

Paul Guest
first published in *The Iowa Review*, vol. 31, no. 1,
    Summer 2001
also from *The Resurrection of the Body and the Ruin of
    the World*

AUGUST 7

The time comes when you are facing him

The time comes when you are facing him
as by accident, as by sheer inadvertency.
You had been running from each other
in opposite directions, avoiding what
had to be done and now have run
the roundness of the globe to come
smack up against each other
from opposite directions.

There is no escape from growing up
and becoming a man, taking your father's
life—his fortune, his will, his pride
and place—and setting him on one side
off the road he is blocking. He stays
where you have placed him, filled
with shame for himself and hatred
and a desire to die at once or to kill.
He dies slowly. You helped him to it,
and it will be so written and read
and remembered, with horror in it
because it is the one way that sends
a man to become religious and heartbroken
and fearful, filled with the mystery
of himself.

He turns to his own children
for justification, their need for bread,
clothes and shelter, and his pride
as a man capable of acting. The rest,
while waiting to act, is prayer,
and it is like the moment before going
into battle.

David Ignatow
from *At My Ease: Uncollected Poems of the Fifties and Sixties*

AUGUST 8

Elegy in August

Sleep, little sister, far from pain.
Water smooths out stones in the river
As memory calms the chaos
You left behind. Rest easy, sister,
Your babies are older than you ever were.
Even the stain will fade
When none are left to remember
The calls for help you never made.

After burning, blackberry bushes
Struggle up through ash, and love, resilient,
Blooms in all seasons, even for you
Who suffered and could not tell what was right
As you hurled yourself, suddenly
Spiraling upward to darkness or light.

Robert McDowell
from *On Foot, in Flames*

Summer Afternoon in Solon, Iowa

Cats, contagious with sleep, bake
on the back porch, and the Wasp Service
has arrived to inspect each grid
of the screens. Disguised as a weedlot,
the prairie—gouged, shorn, parceled out—
breaks into wildflowers and hums
at a pitch an octave above
the ordinary bliss of bees,
while behind the house, rusty train

tracks that stretch toward Nebraska
have lost their perspective
in the wing-winnowed air:
a vapor of hovering dragonflies
fanned to a glare by rising grackles,
glittering trajectories
as beetles drop into the world
like meteors armored in the mineral
gleam of a cosmic explosion.

Now, with green apples casting long shadows
that drench the grass; here,
on the rickety back porch held together
by the tangled twine of morning glories,
a fly composes a sonata for the glass
harmonics of a windowpane
beneath which violets are arranged
in a stately row along the sill.
Each flowerpot contains its own horizon.

Stuart Dybek

first published in *The Gettysburg Review*, vol. 11, no. 4, Winter 1998

The Dancer

Say you came once as a dragonfly,
a one-inch serpent-twig, the suspended "I,"

its double pair of barely air-dried wings
sewing one moment to the next. Quietness

makes it clear: it's not an exact equation,
the weight of clouds and the dusty mirror

of the pond. The nymphs are always hatching.
Something is always disturbing the surface,

changing the leeway: future perfect, past
imperfect, this green ocean of air in between.

Margaret Holley
from *Kore in Bloom*

The Precision

There is a modesty in nature. In the small
of it and in the strongest. The leaf moves
just the amount the breeze indicates
and nothing more. In the power of lust, too,
there can be a quiet and clarity, a fusion
of exact moments. There is a silence of it
inside the thundering. And when the body swoons,
it is because the heart knows its truth.
There is directness and equipoise in the fervor,
just as the greatest turmoil has precision.
Like the discretion a tornado has when it tears
down building after building, house by house.
It is enough, Kafka said, that the arrow fit
exactly into the wound that it makes. I think
about my body in love as I look down on these
lavish apple trees and the workers moving
with skill from one to the next, singing.

Linda Gregg
from *Things and Flesh*

AUGUST 12

Monsoon Song

Dark birds flutter at my fingertips
drawn to the lantern in my skin

like dragonflies to vacant water.

Silvered in a houri moon
foxes stalk the summer cane.

James Cordeiro
first published in *Chelsea 67*

AUGUST 13

A Sunday Dinner

1
Mosquito and tick
on that island of mud, centipede, fly, scorpion, lice,
all breed of bug, as she told it,
but mostly mosquitoes—yellow clouds smoking off
the mangrove swamps—and so with exhaustion and hunger
the long hazy weakness of malaria.
Or if you were lucky
you only starved, dug in with your pound of captured rice
for the green flares on parachutes
and Banzai screams charging from the jungle.
Water was there
at your feet, in whatever hole was handy.

He wasn't so lucky, my uncle.
When he could sleep
he snatched it on his back in a floorless tent,
oozed down in mud and the waves of chill and convulsive fever,
for hours grenades going off
in his brain and hot colors swimming,
sizzle and shell thud, and the jungle growing tongues—
obscenity in broken English, suck
of boots in mud
or the horrible suck and wheeze of the wounded,
and sometimes up from the beach
those silky horns and clarinets—
Dorsey, Miller,
Goodman—then the sad honey voice
of Tokyo Rose...

2

They wouldn't talk, she said, pointing with her knife.
Not my uncle, not my father
lost on those waters for fifteen months
and his family on their prayer-bones nightly
at the altar of Oakdale Baptist.
                              And that dread
of memory? A fear of eternity,
that onslaught of past into future?

No rice on the table for years...
green beans, peppers, yellow corn, okra, not much
that didn't come from his garden.
No, they wouldn't talk, though once in early marriage
on a corner of their bed,
he held her hand for almost an hour

in a story of men on their knees in the mud,
mouths open for the wafer,
and tried to describe the sweetness on his tongue
when he understood finally
no troops were coming.

3
So until the end
this is as close as we can come to 1942, to Guadalcanal
and that Friday the 13th of stars and no moon,
the fragrance of tropical flowers and sweet gases
of decaying flesh,
as clearly as we can see the searchlight
he caught from his hill as it stabbed across the sound
to target the bridge of the cruiser *Atlanta*,
where my father and his gun crew
were already spinning turret number six
as the first shells blasted out that light
and the ocean caught fire
with flares and the big guns spitting,

and as close as we can hold him, who watched
through fever with his unsaid thoughts,
which we can't know
until the end, and lived to see
fresh troops hit the beach,
so that years later he could meet my father,
who had floated all night near death
in that water, and never mention the war,
though he would marry the man's sister
and scratch out a living on used cars and cattle
and ponder his happiness,
and share with her once his first glimpse of peace
when tumbling through a night between drifts of sleep,
over crackle of tide and insect, groan
and scrap of prayer, a moment neared stillness
as a cockatoo screeched
between sniper fire.

David Bottoms

first published in *Poetry,* vol. CLXXII, no. 4, July 1998
also from *Vagrant Grace*

AUGUST 14

**bio / *autography*
(or, 18th-century multiculturalism)**

found in africa / *dawned in freedom*
raised in boston / *rose in slavery*
schooled in greek / *grew in god*
published in england / *died in poverty*

        —*for phillis wheatley*

Evie Shockley
first published in *Blink*, vol. 1, no. 5,
    March/April 2002

AUGUST 15

Syntax

She walks to a table
She walk to table

She is walking to a table
She walk to table now

What difference does it make
What difference it make

In Nature, no completeness
No sentence really complete thought

Language, like woman
Look best when free, undressed

Wang Ping
from *Of Flesh & Spirit*

AUGUST 16

Out-of-Body Experience

This time I'm wide awake, and
it's as vivid as pissing or
eating an olive—no dream or

near-death coma, no transcendental
levitation—just me, at fifty-
nine, playing in what I will soon

decide was my final softball game,
stretched out in horizontal flight
a foot above the ground, diving

headfirst for a sizzling liner,
but suddenly aware that my body,
like a drag-chute in tow, is still

back there somewhere, just starting
its dive, even as the ball passes
clean through my phantom glove of

desire and sings on by into the out-
field. Then, finally, here comes
the old life-sack, snapping back

onto me like a rubber suit, and
we're rolling over one another
in the grass, whispering tenderly

about maybe one of those getaway
weekends, to put a little juice
back into our long, tired affair.

Jim Crenner
first published in *Seneca Review,* vol. XXIX, no. 2, Fall 1999

Hearing Loss

Only the most obvious questions
were asked her, how she felt
or if she'd slept, and even these words,
before they reached her, wavered free of meanings
as if a wind were in them. Friends and family
came close and called to her
as they would call down a well, peering
into some darkness their own altered voices
might rise out of. In time,
even the echoes faded, until
any moment's simple music—
a bird singing, her grandchildren laughing—
faltered before her, trembling
somewhere in the very air she breathed.
She felt sounds she was hardly conscious of
before: the deep-freezer's door hummed
when touched, and the dry heartbeat
of an old clock ticked lightly into her fingers.
Her son, old himself, would lean over her
trying to make her understand an hour
was all he could stay, it was Sunday
or Monday, or a particular silence
was the silence of rain,
and on the long drive out here
the wet road whispered him home.

Waking alone,
dawns so quiet she hears
leaves breathing light, or drifting
alone through days unchanging as smooth water,
she can almost believe the life she remembers
is life. Lovers on the television screen
know only the words she gives them, birds
in the trees sing her memories
of their song. She answers the softest knocks
at her door, surprised each time
that no one is there, she listens intently
to mirrors, stands at a window
bringing the wind inside. Until,
in the muted light of late afternoon
she lies resting, resisting
sleep like a small child
who has stayed up too long, who half dreams
the arms that hold her, the room full of voices
and laughter, but cannot bring herself wholly
into the world where they are.

Christian Wiman
from *The Long Home*

AUGUST 18

To the Days Lost in August

with a line by Philip Booth

Summer is over on the island.
Pleasure boats are cradled.
The schooner that hauled tourists
to the archipelagoes
is dry-docked in Camden.
Neva's has closed for the season,
the *New York Times* gone back
to the mainland. At Fisherman's Friend,
lobster by the pound is off the menu.
No one picnics on Caterpillar Hill.

Summer is over on the island.
Orion's retreated higher.
Fog, thickening, salty, closes in.
Birches are past their yellow,
maples their red. Winds
back around Northeast,
argue with hemlocks,
petition the hackmatacks.
Acorns become brisk business
in the leaves, needles. Winesaps,
thick with bees, distill.

Any morning, a first frost
will glaze the cabbages,
chicory, and aster, the salt hay
not baled in silos.
Squalls will flood the pilings.
No boats, for days, will put off.
The talk over mended traps and rakes
has turned to tarpon, marlin,
to the days lost in August.
Hopes for revision, a few
rekindling days out of season, dwindle.
The sky ebbs into gray,
darker than the water,
darker than the woodstove's spirals.

Deborah Cummins
from *Beyond the Reach*

Letter to Ko

In the market of Totora
a scribe had set up
his ancient Underwood
on a plank table.

He offered to write a note
that would reach you
there, in Karia,
in the high granite valley
where you lay in fever.

The price was a night's sleep
or the light of the eye.

I bargained:
if it requires a miracle
then it is not love.

Then I dictated the letter
stating my terms:

a small house,
a well and fig trees,
beehives and clean linen
for your hand in marriage.

He held the paper
straight into the candle flame
and let it twist
and dissolve inwards,
like a soul looking for itself.

He dropped it in distaste
just before the live ash
scalded his fingertips
and I paid him.

It was that hour of evening
when the passes become visible—

snowcaps flickering in desert heat,
absentminded as the daylight moon,

and no road,
no other life,
no sign.

D. Nurkse
first published in *The Virginia Quarterly Review*, vol. 73,
        no. 4, Autumn 1997

Bravura Lament

For Berryman

He would tell you the grass this spring was a pale
imitation of the deep lushness of the year gone by.

He would say the notes from the reed of Charlie Parker
stirred him to a longing no longer soluble,

a kind of dampness leaving him for days at a time,
inconsolable. Although he would not be remembered

as a brave man, those who knew him well would say
what he lived at the end was akin to bravura lament.

Of the constellations that summer he would locate
only the brightly conspicuous stars of Ursa Major,

his head back, his eyes vacant but focused light years
down that starry road, his grizzled mouth slack

and mindless, like a turkey's in a downpour swiveled up,
drowning while showered by the fluid blow of keen insight.

Daniel Halpern
first published in *Poetry*, vol. CLXXIV, no. 5, August 1999
also from *Something Shining*

Sky

I like you with nothing. Are you
what I was? What I will be?
I look out there by the hour,
so clear, so sure. I could
smile, or frown—still nothing.

Be my father, be my mother,
great sleep of blue; reach
far within me; open doors,
find whatever is hiding; invite it
for many clear days in the sun.

When I turn away I know
you are there. We won't forget
each other: every look is a promise.
Others can't tell what you say
when it's the blue voice, when
you come to the window and look for me.

Your word arches over
the roof all day. I know it
within my bowed head, where
the other sky listens.
You will bring me
everything when the time comes.

William Stafford
from *The Way It Is: New & Selected Poems*

One Filament against the Firmament

Most days Group V. practiced on seeing through
Prisms because of the way they bend the light
They are considered the first marker of advanced
Sight tests had been conducted on them all as
Children these ones could examine a dewdrop
Perched on a furred leaf & not cry when it fell to
The ground had no more data to give though later
The books would be buried to give us something new
To discover God could not be a matter of spaceships
The way must be found through the mind &
The eyes are distractible as the Leader discovered one night
In a stairwell when one lightbulb overhead managed
To distract him from the sky outside he decided
That finding beauty pointless might actually be the
Point at something & then see past it became
The first lesson to lessen attachment to things put
Here to distract us of course there were detractors
Who thought the fingers or tongue would work just
Fine lines of personality scar the fingertips though
& tastebuds cannot belie their bias only the mind
& the eyes could absorb indefinitely pupils practiced
Not shrinking at the sun it was an honor to go blind

Trying to ignore the tiny creatures that float across
Our eyes was a task that drove hundreds crazy because
It didn't make sense that something tiny & see-through
Could lure the gaze away from the Taj Majal or a Monet
Which they practiced in front of because of the lovely
Colors & affection for them were eliminated later as were
All forms of luxury like being able to see your family
Across the breakfast table they all disappeared one by
One day everybody woke up alone & couldn't find
Each other & they all would have died from standing
Still there was one girl who hadn't been able to stop loving
The word marshmallow & one boy who still had a favorite
Color slowly seeped back into the world & a new group
Formed to research why it had left but it never became clear

Matthea Harvey
from *Pity the Bathtub Its Forced Embrace of the Human Form*

Colophon

More than the beetles turned russet,
sunset, dragging their shield, more than
the crickets who think it's evening all afternoon,
it's the bees I love this time of year.

Sated, maybe drunk, who've lapped at the hips
of too many flowers for one summer but
still must go on hunting, one secret
closing, another ensuing, picking

lock after lock, rapping the glass,
getting stuck in a puddle of dish soap,
almost winter, almost dark, reading far past
the last paragraph into the back blank page,

acknowledgments, and history of type.
I think when my head finally cracks
out will come one of those ravening scouts
autumnal with hunger beyond any sipping,

swallowing, beyond the hive's teeming
factory's needs. I think maybe then,
when I'm dying like a bug in a puddle
of dish soap, I'll be relieved,

my wings wet capes and not working,
antennae slicked back and not working,
eye that sees the ruby above going out,
eye that sees the ruby within getting brighter

as I drag myself to a tomato ripening
on the window sill, reddest, softest
island of my last planet, last aureola,
stinger waving and useless. I'll wait then,

while air from the north rushes gulf air,
a tree indicating wildly, each leaf woke
in orange outcry. It won't be suffering,
exactly. Rain coming, then gone, a chill

that means all my barbarous kind are alone
and perishing, our unrecognizable young
buried and waiting, bodies of fire becoming
bodies of air. I don't think there's any way

to prepare.

Dean Young
from *First Course in Turbulence*

Bees Stumble

The old-world machinery of beework
is an arguing with azure odds. The guys land, weave,
grab; headlights go dusty.
Some bees stumble—the knights are drastic. They go to ride.
What you didn't see was the system.
They send a stiff, dark thread down to mine,
stinking, hydraulic,
and withdraw it minutely. The flower throbs,
selfish, quirky. The bourse goes wild,
youngsters yell, cells are cracking,
and the big, mild farmers of our lives
divvy up the take,
harpists, moronic,
left-footed.

Molly McQuade
from *Barbarism*

AUGUST 25

Maculate Beauty

To speak of maculate beauty, it is this:
      my son's head as he stands in the shower,
his body stippled by the water's hiss
      as the gold is slowly silvered over—

I don't mean vermeil, which is silver gilded,
      but silvered gold, which further age will bring,
beauty being heightened by the unyielded
      advance out of its own diminishing,

just as Delaune designed parade armor
      magnificent in all its decorations
(Python's gilt scales, Daphne's gilt pubic hair,
      Apollo's rays) for Henry II of France,

and the first steel, embossed, blued, gilt, then silvered,
      came to resemble nothing it had been,
overbuilt in the rich chase, grown so fecund
      it seemed a profligate beyond invention,

privileged to vision for a moment—or as
      a ferry slows, approaching the gray chute
of boards, and rubs them screaming into splinters,
      and in that narrowed place of creaming salt,

plants stand revealed, briefly shiver and drip,
      their roots a pink of such delicacy
it cannot have come from the turbid wallop
      and gasp of brine: but has, being maculate beauty.

Karl Kirchwey
first published in *New England Review*, vol. 19, no. 4, Fall 1998

Poison, 1959

Sixteen wasps against a fallen apple, hissing green,

*

bejeweled & dappled. A child can bend

*

to their seething, astonished as they drain

*

the sweet fermenting juices. But insecticide

*

can change them utterly & the child can briefly

*

consider God, now incarnate as himself,

*

God-of-Pillar-of-Smoke-from-Heaven-DDT

*

(in those days the poison of choice) & He sprays.
   Strafed

*

they mutate, strafed they still. & what child

*

does not covet many eyes, to weave & hover,

*

weave & sting, to expel like breath miraculous
   paper & build

*

for himself a palace wondrous strange & infinitely
   chambered?

*

Of many eyes the world is the made. Infinite are its
   wishes

*

& its sibilant wings. Therefore they each must perish.

David Wojahn
first published in *New England Review*, vol. 21, no. 2,
   Spring 2000
also from *Spirit Cabinet*

AUGUST 27

I am peeling four pink grapefruit

to make sorbet with campari, for a party,
removing the bitter white pith,
but I am also eating so many sweet fleshy globules
that the I who is doing the work
is clearly not the I swallowing the fruit.
Soon there's no hope of sorbet for six,
only enough for two; one of us
boils the rind and sugar into syrup,
freezes the small mound into dessert.

The self who hops to conclusions
like popcorn, who falls in love on the basis
of a bare arm, the self always
drunk with the pleasure at hand, shares a body
with the woman who has been true to one man,
who even at midnight when the other I wants
only to roll into bed, is reaching for chocolate and
   eggs,
melting and separating, envisioning the faces
of her guests at the first mouthful of mousse,

dark as the heart of a faithless wife.

Natasha Sajé
first published in *Shenandoah*, vol. 48, no. 1, Spring 1998
also from *Bend*

AUGUST 28

Death by Fruit

Only the crudest
of the *vanitas* set
ever thought you *had* to get
a skull into the picture
whether you needed
its tallowy color
near the grapes or not.
Others, stopping to consider
shapes and textures,
often discovered that
eggs or aubergines
went better, or leeks,
or a plate of string beans.
A skull is so dominant.
It takes so much
bunched up drapery,
such a ponderous
display of ornate cutlery,
just to make it less prominent.
The greatest masters
preferred the subtlest *vanitas*,
modestly trusting to fruit baskets
to whisper *ashes to ashes*,
relying on the poignant exactness
of oranges to release
like a citrus mist
the always fresh fact
of how hard we resist
how briefly we're pleased.

Kay Ryan
first published in *Partisan Review*,
   vol. LXVII, no. 3, Summer 2000
also from *Say Uncle*

Aguacero

These downpours of my Cuban childhood
when my father loved to smoke a cigarette
on the patio of the house in Havana
and watch as the sheets of rain bent against
the tin roofs of the shacks in the neighbor's
yard, the way drops hung from the wire
mesh of the chicken coops and fell one
by one on the dirt, dampening, darkening
as they fell, and he would remove his shirt
after a long day's work feeding the zoo
animals and he would sit on his makeshift
hammock, lean back, blow smoke up
at the rafters, and he listened to all that rain
as it fell on everything. He imagined
it was raining all over the island, his island,
and the sound of it drumming on the plantain
fronds rose all around him like the clamor
of thousands of cattle birds scattershot
into the heavens, and when he closed his eyes
he dreamt of a man, his hands buried deep
into fertile earth, seeding a son, a wife,
in new life from which so much hardship
sprouted in this life, in the next, exile
a possibility dripping from his fingertips—
then the song of bullfrogs calling home the night.

Virgil Suárez
from *Banyan*

AUGUST 30

Ant Farm

One summer day
I took a kettle of steaming water and flooded an anthill, watched as balled black bodies
floated down my brewed Nile and dried in the sand looking sugared, cinnamon-crusted.
I should have baked them into cookies and become famous for indecipherable
irresistible taste, a certain *je ne sais quoi.* Or thought to serve them poached. This
annihilation was not annihilation; the ants did not suffer and were turned into sugar beads
and their floating was serene. I didn't know there'd be few

survivors; I expected in insects stamina a backbone obfuscates,
keeping vertebrates upright and vulnerable, subject to arrogance, breakage,
ravages, paralysis, the ideal immobility of food, facilitating admonishments to eat
until bones are picked clean, not only piranhas eating their instinct, but families
in public: Red Lobster, Bill Knapps, Kentucky Fried, countless rib joints, clean
as ivory; meals conclude with skeletons. I admire teeth, the cutting

of the first one long before there can be any controlling of the bowels, a first pair
center front, vegetarian before that fulfillment; meat's indigestible until the fontanels
seal fate. Fetus eats as if entirely an embryonic flower, through root and stem called cord.
In the slits fanning around the navel like the possibility of petals
are dark slivers reminiscent of ants without their legs and my first boyfriend's
delight. I killed them

although I had an ant farm sitting by my bed, such a narrow world it was, pressed
between sheets of Plexiglas no bigger than standard issue composition paper on which
I took notes on their progress that in my notebook never was, for I kept looking
at them from my perspective had I been as restricted; they could not open the world,
reach for stars though their tunnels longed to be telescopes.
Could not use a mirror's condolences to double their impression of space, so busy, busy,
carrying on their drudgery to distract them from escaping, even an ant queen
who could not fly away to mate with a marked man, but one day, her wings

were discarded, as they should be after the nuptials, at the opening to a tunnel, like a set
of tiny lips, white such as what, at the time, I thought happened, the bleaching, if arsenic
was kissed, but it happens too when there's too much confectioner's sugar
on what is consumed, and usually, when consumption takes place, there's too much
something, what, of course, varies so that sooner or later, everything has a turn being vice.
Outside, trophallaxis keeps ants going, reciprocal feeding, exchange of chemical

stimulation, workers (wingless, infertile females denied or uninterested in sex) tend
the young, feeding them honeydew from raids on aphids and giving other luscious stuff
of their own feeding to larvae whose surfaces secrete a substance more luscious that
these females crave, and thus, work even harder for the high, the all-consuming high,

the paradisiacal reward although these busy ants are neither saved nor unsaved nor
concerned. A group of lactating women assemble in a suburban park, get high together as
their babies nurse. Feelings some of them

don't get from spousal intimacy. Some fancy ants are living honey pots, workers,
through whatever awareness is possible in formic nervous systems, who know
themselves sublime as they are fed unbearable quantities of honeydew, and they must
wonder whether or not they are deserving of overwhelming pleasure though none
complain, accepting a blessed fate that nevertheless restricts their options. Then these
females, rather ideally nunnish, gorged to a real inedia, lose their ant form, becoming
butterballs round as the cosmos and becoming the cherubic sustainers of the colony,
releasing sweet drops as needed yet remaining full, complete. Diva ants.

The boyfriend who lived near water let ants crawl along his arms, then he would flick
them off, quickly kicking his leg, trying to catch them in his pants cuff. He became good
at this. Too good to forget.

There are close to five thousand species of ants, among them the Cameroonian
stink ant capable of producing a sound audible to humans, especially to women
full of milk who are so sensitive to crying, a frail decibel makes milk flow just as our

desperation is supposed to touch God to the point that he can't help but dispense
remedies, sometimes in code, to what has become his own misery. The stink ant feeds
from the rain forest floor and in just trying to survive, which is when everything happens,
during attempts at survival, sometimes inhales a fungal spore that survives in the ant's
brain, reproducing and controlling, using the ant as its slave wagon for transport to prominence
at the top of a fern, a pinnacle like a spear and the ant that knows of its disgrace,
despite the takeover of its brain, clamps its mandibles to the spear so that it seems
impaled, sort of an act of hara-kiri, and dies as the spore now flourishes, consuming
the totality of the dead meat; death graciously allows for less grievous consumption, more
open relish, and in two weeks, the time it takes for a woman to miss a period after
fertilization, a spike with a tip orange as sunset begins to emanate
from the former head of the ant, and upon reaching an inch and a half of success,
triggers fireworks, an explosion of spores descending from the heights and looking

for a sponsor. There's an ant like this in Florida where you could be in love, foolish,
getting pregnant in grass on which some of these dead ants are fastened by their jaws.
I was told not to eat watermelon seeds, that vines and snakes would grow within me, so
after eating them, I took Castoria, the whole bottle of that gentle laxative for children,

although I knew, for the color betrayed it, that Castoria was made by liquefying ants,
that ants were farmed just to purge.

Thylias Moss
first published in *The Kenyon Review*, New Series, vol. XX, no. 1, Winter 1998

Ancestored-Back *Is the Overpresiding Spirit of This Poem*

If only somebody would drill with a finger-long rig down
into my skull, and saw a tiny circle out of its bone,
so pools of acid antsiness and angst can steam away;
so all of the great in-gnarling, all of the bunched-up
broodiness can breathe; and so at least the day's
accumulated ephemera, its fenderbender squabbles,
its parade of petty heartache can evaporate in writhes
of sour mist—this spatting couple, for example,
in the booth across the aisle as I'm chowing on a burger
and their every more-than-whispered perturbation is,
this afternoon, a further furrow worked into my mind....
You know I'm kvetching metaphorically. But literalist
Amanda Fielding, wielding a scalpel and electric drill,
bored a hole in her skull in 1970, filming that self-surgery,

·

and zealously thereafter promoting the benefits of this
third eye, finally "running for Parliament on a platform
of trepanation for national health." The operation
was successfully conducted in the Stone Age (72%
of the skulls we've found reveal that the patients far survived
that crisis moment), and the Chinese medico Thai Tshang Kung
(150 B.C.) was said "to cut open the skulls of the sick
and arrange their brains in order." A Roman physician's
effects from the second century A.D. include a trepanation kit
in bronze, its tooth-edged bit and driving-bow
as finely produced as any machine-tooled apparatus
a surgeon in 1996 would wish for—when the bow unfolds
it's as intricate in its simplicity as a line of true haiku.
I've read a book whose major pleasure is its breathlessness

·

in gasping at the ancientness of various devices,
flushing toilets(!) condoms(!) hand grenades(!) — the book
is a grove of invisible exclamation points. These
green glass beads like rain-splats on a leaf
—4,000 years ago. Bone dice, the same. The ribbed vault
in this early Gothic church is a masterly hollowing-out
of space—but houses of *literal* ribs, of mammoth bones,
were sturdy dwellings 15,000 years ago. Rhinoplasty(!)
soccer(!) odometers(!) "Butter" (a favorite sentence)
"spread everywhere, once it was discovered." Though we don't know
poot about the urgent stirrings in our own hearts
or the dreams irrupting nightly in our own heads,
we've been diagramming stars on plaques
of tortoise plate and antler, we've made sky maps,

•

from before we even understood the link of sex
to birth. And if our coin-op slot machines
can be ancestored-back to that Greco-Egyptian
contrivance of Heron of Alexandria (by which
a dropped-in-place five-drachma bronze piece
starts the portioned flow of a worshiper's ablution-water)...
if *ancestored-back* is the overpresiding spirit
of this poem...we *are* the progeny of stars,
we *are* their original core-born elements
in new recombination, densed and sizzled into
sentience and soul. I can't imagine the interior tumult
driving Amanda Fielding and her followers, but
I'm not surprised our smallest human units were created
in explosion, speed, and void. My friends

•

are not the kind to drill their heads and rid themselves
of troubles by decanting. Even so, I've seen them consider
their restless faces in the mirror and wish for *some* release.
Our daily dole of woe is unrelenting. In this burger joint,
in the Booth of a Thousand Sorrows across the aisle,
they're arguing still. Outside, the snow provides each tree
with a clerical collar—this couple is arguing. Outside,
the setting summer sun makes each tree a flambeau
—this couple is arguing, they'll never stop, their joys
have been prodigious and their anti-joy will balance this
or more, the hands with which they make their hard points
in the air are hands of oxygen and nitrogen and argon
older than dust or salt. It's midnight. How
emphatic we can be. How long they've been at it.

Albert Goldbarth
from *Troubled Lovers in History: A Sequence of Poems*

september 1

The Search for Baby Combover

In Paris one night the doorbell rings,
      and there's this little guy, shaking like a leaf
and going "uh-uh-uh-UNH-ah!" and his eyes get big
      and he raises his hands like a gospel singer
and goes "UNH-ah-uh-uh-uh-UNH-uh-ah!"

and for just a fraction of a second I think
      he's doing the first part of Wilson Pickett's
"Land of a Thousand Dances" and he wants me
      to join him in some kind of weird welcome
to the neighborhood, so I raise my hands a little

and begin to sort of hum along, though
      not very loudly in case I'm wrong about this,
and I'm smiling the way old people smile
      when they can't hear you but want you to know
that everything's okay as far as they're concerned

or a poet smiles in a roomful of scientists,
      as if to say, "Hey! I'm just a poet!
But your data's great, really! Even if
      I don't understand it!" And by the time
I start to half-wonder if this gentleman wants me

to take the you-got-to-know-how-to-pony part
      or means to launch into it himself, he gives
a little hop and slaps his hands down to his sides
      and says, "PLEASE! YOU MUST NOT MOVE
THE FURNITURE AFTER ELEVEN O'CLOCK OF THE NIGHT!"

so I lower my own hands and say, "Whaaaa...?"
        And he says, "ALWAYS YOU ARE MOVING IT WHEN
THE BABY TRY TO SLEEP! YOU MUST NOT DO IT!"
        And now that he's feeling a little bolder,
he steps in closer, where the light's better,

and I see he's got something on his head,
        like strands of oily seaweed, something
you'd expect to find on a rock after one of
        those big tanker spills in the Channel,
so I lean a little bit and realize it's what

stylists call a "combover," not a bad idea
        on the tall fellows but definitely a grooming no-no
for your vertically-challenged caballeros,
        of which Monsieur here is certainly one,
especially if they are yelling at you.

But I'd read an article about AA that said
        when your loved ones stage an intervention
and go off on you for getting drunk
        and busting up the furniture and running out
into traffic and threatening to kill the President,

it's better to just let them wind down
        and then say, "You're probably right,"
because if you're combative, they will be, too,
        and then your problems will just start over again,
so I wait till Mr. Combover—it's not nice, I know,

but it's the first name that comes to mind—stops shaking,
          and I say, "You're probably right," and he raises
a finger and opens his mouth as if to say something
          but then snaps his jaw shut and whirls around
and marches downstairs, skidding a little

and windmilling his arms and almost falling
          but catching himself, though not without
that indignant backward glance we all give
          the stupid step that some stupid idiot would have
attended to long ago if he hadn't been so stupid.

The next day, I ask Nadine the *gardienne*
          qu'est-ce que c'est the deal *avec* the *monsieur*
qui lives under *moi*, and Nadine says his *femme*
          is *toujours* busting his chops, but *il est* afraid
of her, so *il* takes out his *rage* on the rest of *nous*.

There's something else, though: a few days later,
          Barbara and I see Mr. and Mrs. Combover
crossing the Pont Marie, and she is a virtual giantess
          compared to him! Now I remember once hearing Barbara
give boyfriend advice to this niece of mine,

and Barbara said (1) he's got to have a job,
          (2) he's got to tell you you're beautiful all the time,
and (3) he's got to be taller than you are,
          so when I see Mrs. Combover looming over her hubby,
I think, Well, that explains the busted chops.

Not only that, Mrs. Combover looks cheap.
          She looks rich, sure—Nadine had told me *Monsieur*
is some *sorte de* diplomat *avec* the Chilean delegation—
          but also like one of those professional ladies
offering her services up around the Rue St. Denis.

But who are they, really? "Combover" is one
          of those names from a fifties black-and-white movie;
he's the kind of guy neighborhood kids call "Mr. C."
          and who has a boss who says things like, "Now see here,
Combover, this sort of thing just won't do!"

He's like one of Dagwood's unnamed colleagues—
          he's not even Dagwood, who at least excites
Mr. Dithers enough to be fired a couple
          of times a week, not to mention severely beaten.
Only Dagwood is really in charge. Everything goes his way!

Despite cronic incompetence, ol' Dag keeps
          the job that allows him his fabulous home life:
long naps, towering sandwiches, affectionate
          and well-behaved teenaged children, a loyal dog,
and, best of all, the love of Blondie.

Blondie! The name says it all: glamorous but fun.
          Big Trashy Mrs. Combover is not glamorous,
although she thinks she is, and no fun at all.
          She is the anti-Blondie. Her job seems to be
to stay home and smoke, since we're always smelling

the cigarette fumes that seep up though the floor
        into our apartment day and night. And he says
we're keeping Baby Combover awake when we move
        the furniture, which we've never done, but then
we've never seen Baby Combover, either. Or heard him.

Baby Combover: the world's first silent baby.
        Barbara has this theory that, after a life
of prostitution, Mrs. Combover has not only repented but
        undergone a false pregnancy and imaginary birth.
Therefore, the reason why Baby Combover is silent

is that he is not a real baby who fusses and eats and
        wets and poops but is instead a pillowcase with knots
for ears and a smiley-face drawn with a Magic Marker and
        a hole for its mouth so Mrs. Combover can teach it
to smoke when it's older, like eight, say.

Now I know what they fight about: "You never spend
        any time with the baby!" hisses Mrs. Combover.
"I will—when he's older and can talk!" says Mr. Combover.
        "Here I am stuck with this baby all day long!
And those horrible people upstairs!"

And he says, "Oh, be silent, you...prostitute!"
        And she says, "Quiet, you horrible man—
not in front of the child!" Maybe it's time
        for a call to the police. Or the newspapers.
I can see the headlines: OU EST LE PETIT ENFANT COMBOVER?

I feel sorry for him. With parents like this,
        it would be better if someone were to kidnap him.
Or I could take him back to America with me,
        I who have a wife who loves me and two grown sons.
Why not? We've got all this extra room now.

We'll feed him a lot and tickle him;
        there's nothing funnier than a fat, happy baby.
And when the boys come home to visit,
        they'll take him out with them in their sports cars:
"It's my little brother!" they'll say. "He's French!"

The neighborhood kids, once a band of sullen mendicants,
        will beg us to let him play with them,
even though he doesn't speak their language.
        Look! There they go toward the baseball field,
with Baby Combover under their arm!

I love you, Baby Combover! You *are* Joseph Campbell's
        classic mythical hero, i.e., "an agent of change
who relinquishes self-interest and breaks down
        the established social order." But you're so pale!
You've stayed out too long and caught cold.

Barbara and the boys gather around his bed;
        they hug each other, and we try not to cry.
Baby Combover is smiling—he always smiled, that kid.
            His little mouth begins to move, and we lean in
and think we hear him say, "Be bwave fo' me."

Back in Paris, Mr. Combover grows a full head of hair.
        Mrs. Combover reaches up to touch it.
He puts down his attaché case and caresses her cheek.
            "How beautiful you are!" he says. It's so quiet now.
Then they hear it: in the next room, a child is crying.

David Kirby
first published in *Five Points*, vol. IV, no. 3, Summer 2000
also from *The Ha-Ha*

september 2

Fiber Optics

On Labor Day the last barbecue smoke
        had drifted into the branches,
and Public TV showed the legendary strike
                at J&L Steel in Aliquippa,
the cops opening fire
      on the worker's picnic, the men in shirtsleeves running,
the women, some carrying children, falling in the Pennsylvania dirt.

I'm thinking about this,
      driving my new truck down Highway 280,
getting twelve miles to the gallon on the company credit card
           with a storm coming in from the west.

We're working nights and week-ends pulling wire
      into the ceilings of Silicon Valley,
moving our ladders just ahead of the drywall crews
      with their knives of adhesive,
          their radios blasting Metallica,
the carpet gang in the finished wing
          spreading beige-colored glue on the floor,
nobody talking, hurrying along in the midnight glare of the heat lamps.

Impossible anyone here would strike,
      though we're comrades of sorts,
            and hungry for something,
listening to rain pound the glass doors
      of this palace paid for
by venture capitalists, whose appetite nobody questions.
      Inside it's a hardware bonanza: boxes
of galvanized fasteners overflow onto the Visqueen tarp
           that covers the stairs like a membrane.
Somebody squats by the telephone switch,
wiring teflon patch bays into brilliant steel racks,
      and testing each pathway
           the delicate voltages follow.

Everybody wants to work, the more hours the better,
especially the young ones, snowy with gypsum dust, wolfing their lunch
      on a stack of new two-by-fours
while the overtime keeps piling up
                        like valet parking behind the first tee
where the owners and union reps, weekday afternoons
                gather to discuss trade.

Outside the trenches and conduits slowly fill with water
and two of us crouch in a low cement box,
                adjusting the filament cable,
the fiberglass link that feeds the big hubs.
And nobody's wondering about Karl Marx or the poems of Cesare Pavese.

We're trying to stay down out of the wind
and close up the resin-filled splice case
      so the ghostlight signal can travel across,
sending its neuron-flickering code
                as fast as a man can think.

Joseph Millar
from *Overtime*

september 3

Job No. 75-14

for Ron Boyce

Drive stakes, shoot grades,
get a big Cat to scalp and scrape and gouge:
contour the site for proper drainage.
Berm and swale.

Rough-grade it then, with
a blade, and hope
it don't rain. Set hubs,
haul in base rock, grade it again, then
pave it with a thick crust of blacktop
to make a parking lot.

              I'm building
a new Safeway, in West Salem,
for some religious millionaire,
and we will all buy our groceries there.

"Well, tomorrow's Friday," I say
to the guy who looks like Jesus driving stakes
and rod-hopping for me,
and he says "Yeah, then two!
and then five and then two and then five..."

Seven being a magic number
and the earth having a thin skin,
we make motions to bow
ceremoniously, but instead, a couple of
unmasked accomplices, confederates
on a losing planet,
we look at each other
and grin—

                which means: "to draw back the lips
so as to show the teeth
as a dog in snarling,
or a person in laughter or pain."

Clemens Starck
from *Journeyman's Wages*

september 4

Benefit Picnic, Cigar Makers' Strike, August 1884

I'd seen a head or two a club had done with—
    its skin distended across a swollen globe
        of purple-orange and blue, even the holes
            for eyes and nose and mouth puffed shut,

indistinct as those imagination grants
    the full moon, a trick of wishfulness
        that what we see is really human, soon
            to speak to us. Not a word.

Still, when I got there, stung by briars
    and low-slung branches, my chest heaving
        for air like the old man I am, when they
            flipped over the body so what was the face

was facing us, I dropped to my knees and retched.
    His black wool jacket, white collar and tie,
        the bit of brown hair not bloodied—all
            belonged to Louis, our son. In the dark

behind the dance floor, while I flounced about
    with his wife, her sallow skin almost pink
        in the gaslight, hired men had yanked him
            from the privy and into the woods, had played

the company tune upon his skull one two three,
    one two three. He'd thought me odd
        to worry so. "This is America!" he'd said,
            as if the words were holy. Now this blessing.

By then the women came running, dress hems
    in hand, their petticoats a ghostly presence
        hovering above the blond grass. One scream
            brought forth a chain of screams receding

like some hysterical human telegraph,
    until it reached the bandstand, and music
        stopped as a heart in mid-beat, an awful
            metaphor I'll admit to, even now.

It's strange what the mind does to keep sane.
    I thought to cry, to blubber in public,
        was man's worst shame. I refused to give in.
            It was one stateliness I'd maintain

for us both, after the stinking mess I'd made
    upon seeing the mess they'd made of him.
        Instead, I spent the minutes thinking of
            what to tell his wife and mother, how he'd

died a martyr for a decent wage, as if
    that romantic tale might make his death
        less brutal, as if a special heaven
            were reserved for union men clubbed

by church-going bosses. It was a stupid lie—
    though half-true, and so absorbing in its
        own naive way, I hardly heard the voice
            behind my head, "Father, I'm all right."

I lurched around to see Louis, clutching
    a whiskey bottle he and friends had drained
        behind the grandstand. Even his drinking
            seemed salvation, arisen from the grave

he'd never entered. Such joy I felt
    embracing my drunken Lazarus, such joy
        in my heart, while in my gut a bitter pot
            brewed, bilious and soon to spill—for whose

son was this, splayed dead in the Johnson grass?

Kevin Stein
from *Bruised Paradise*

Sunday Shopping

For Joe

Not for me today the *vox angelica*
Nor the *vox humana*. The telephone is dead.
Through the door I can see his coat
Lying as he left it on the other bed.

Ordinary cloth shabby with wear,
Out at the elbow, long out of style,
From the way it gathers itself, plainly
It has been his for quite awhile.

Just when it was he held the heathered tweed
Up to himself for simple suit and size
And turned to me for my assessment,
A lurking smile in his hazel eyes,

I cannot tell: but it was long ago.
We went home from the store together,
Dazzling and dawdling our way through
High bluffs of blue September weather.

Sunday became our day—great, soft music,
Bantering talk and laughter—the more
Made so because we said love lasted.
He never left his coat with me before.

Not for me today the *vox angelica*
Nor the *vox humana*. On the other bed
The frayed coat lies. Spring hawks fret
Above the Sabbath mountain. The telephone is
    dead.

George A. Scarbrough
first published in *Poetry*, vol. CLXIX, no. 4, February
    1997

september 6

Influencing Factors

I am dating a woman whose brother is a Trotskyite.

I was dating a woman with an angel tattoo anchoring her back
to the sky but she dropped me. Or, rather, she drifted.

Alone, I started skipping meals;
I read myself into the work of Simone Weil,
thin and plagued with headaches.

(I was in there among the others operating a line
of future, repackaging the past. We stamped the bags
with the wrong date code; we sent them on anyway.)

I remember the headaches I used to get
when I worked midnights in a factory.
Two workers had died there fifteen years before
I dusted the ledges and swept the floors. Some nights
I thought I felt them in the sifting room
gently pushing me forward in circles.
I went on break early, taking aspirin with my coffee.

I am dating a woman whose brother is a Trotskyite.

When I try to imagine a worldwide revolution of proletariats
I can't get past the clockout room, the guys jostling,
punching each others' arms, telling jokes
before the click of the hour.

I was dating a woman with an angel tattoo anchoring her back
to the sky but she dropped me. Or, rather, she drifted.

Factory angels don't wear white
or embarrass the working class with trumpets.
They sneak in, looking over your shoulder
while you go through the motions.
Then they wander off, sadly shaking their golden heads.

Karen Helfrich
first published in *AGNI*, no. 46, 25th anniversary issue

september 7

Burial

Like a sister who borrows
a blouse without asking,
the earth slipped

the ring from my finger
as I worked the soil
our first married spring

when your leaving
was a seed planted
beneath my knowing.

I dug among roots,
white tendrils, my emptied
hand snaking deep.

Months later
when the seed sprouted
there was nothing

left of you to remove.
The bare finger
wore the shape

of absence, pale
ring of flesh the sun
was slow to touch.

Rebecca McClanahan
first published in *Shenandoah*, vol. 47, no. 1, Spring
    1997
also from *Naked as Eve*

september 8

Not for Burning

I come across your old letters,
the words still clinging to the page,
holding onto their places patiently,
with no intention of abandoning
the white spaces. They say
that you will always love me,
and reading them again, I almost
believe it, but I suspect that
they are heretics, that later,
in the fire, they will deny it all.

Then I remember something I once
read (my memory is filled with voices
of the dead): that it is a heretic which
makes the fire, and that I am more guilty
than your words, poor pilgrims who trusted
the road you sent them down and kept
severely to the way. I forgive them;
I let them live to proclaim freely what
they thought would always be true.

Joyce Sutphen
from *Coming Back to the Body*

Euripides' Cave

In Pericles' city, cold marble nights,
Protagoras, Socrates, pacing beside me,
ideas like stars arcing, or steadily blazing, or
    falling.
Mornings of papyri, mounting in rolls.
Reports of the War.

Afternoons, the agora, democracy's
broil. Men tricked out in the old dried skins
of politics, masculine voices
braying the many tongues of money,
reports from the War.
Believers bellowing gods like crowds at the races
urging their runner on with noise.
So many signs to interpret—and I
with an eye for significance:
which citizen is rich, whose ignorance will kill,
whose wife is back at home, unclasping
another man's warm gold necklace.

And all through the days of the sun,
the glare of the theater, rising around me.
Tiers of men hoarding their careful prizes,
bearing down on my actors,
surrounding my circle of chosen words
with ceaseless mutter and drone.

There's a simple boat I can row
to Salamis.
In a cave I call mine
I fire my light.
In Salamis I wait for the women in silence.

Late sun falls on the stones of the entry,
on the one sail in the dark blue Gulf.
It is so quiet, I hear Andromache crying.
Phaedra's whispers, Medea breathing
before she screams.

Elizabeth Seydel Morgan
first published in *Poetry*, vol. CLXXIV, no. 6,
    September 1999

september 10

The Busses

From our corner window
rainy winter mornings
we watch the yellow school busses
nudging their way down Park
moistly glowing, puddled by the rain.

Stopping at doorways here and there
where children climb aboard
they merge into the traffic's flow
and dwindle from our sight.

We watch—then turn away,
and when in changing light
we look again, we see a stream
dark and serene in China,
down which sleek goldfish dart and gleam.

Frederick Morgan
from *Poems for Paula*

september 11

Arguments of Everlasting

My mother
gathers gladiolas: the little tubes
shout and clamor: a poppling
of unstoppled laughter: the guileless leaps
and quiet plosives
of the fountain when it is working: when
mechanics and meaning are flush
and untroubled. Not like
my brother's stammer: speech and its edicts
broken by that intruder
between tongue and tooth: something
winged: of insect color.
                My mother
gathers gladiolas. The gladness
is fractured. As when
the globe with its thousand mirrors
cracked the light. How
it hoarded sight: all the stolen perspectives
and the show of light
they shot around us: so that
down the dark hall the ghosts danced
with us: down the dark hall
the broken angels.
                What keeps
the grass from slipping? The steep
grass? Like my brother
it imitates the stone's arrest: *this done*
this done and nothing
doing. In the face of the wind
it plants its foot
and fights its own going:
a travelling line
of adamance.

My mother,
the doves are in full cry
this morning.
The leaves are heavy
with silken grieving: soft packages
of sorrow: cacophonies
of sighing. It is a pretty
thing, a pretty thing,
the light lathered like feathers,
and the day's spendage
beginning. The flag unspools its furl
above the school,
pulsing out and out: a wake
of color on the air:
blue: red: blue:

and how white the sky is. How white.

Brigit Pegeen Kelly
from *Song*

september 12

At the Opening of Oak Grove Cemetery Bridge

Before this bridge we took the long way around
up First Street to Commerce, then left at Main,
taking our black processions down through town
among storefronts declaring *Dollar Days!*
Going Out of Business! Final Mark Downs!
Then pausing for the light at Liberty,
we'd make for the Southside by the Main Street bridge
past used-car sales and party stores as if
the dead required one last shopping spree
to finish their unfinished business.
Then eastbound on Oakland by the jelly-works,
the landfill site and unmarked railroad tracks—
by bump and grinding motorcade we'd come
to bury our dead by the river at Oak Grove.

And it is not so much that shoppers gawked
or merchants carried on irreverently.
As many bowed their heads or paused or crossed
themselves against their own mortalities.
It's that bereavement is a cottage industry,
a private enterprise that takes in trade
long years of loving for long years of grief.
The heart cuts bargains in a marketplace
that opens after hours when the stores are dark
and Christmases and Sundays when the hard
currencies of void and absences
nickel-and-dime us into nights awake
with soured appetites and shaken faith
and a numb hush fallen on the premises.

Such stillness leaves us moving room by room
rummaging through cupboards and the closet space
for any remembrance of our dead lovers,
numbering our losses by the noise they made
at home—in basements tinkering with tools
or in steamy bathrooms where they sang in the shower,
in kitchens where they labored over stoves
or gossiped over coffee with the nextdoor neighbor,
in bedrooms where they made their tender moves;
whenever we miss that division of labor
whereby he washed, she dried; she dreams, he snores;
he does the storm windows, she does floors;
she nods in the rocker, he dozes on the couch;
he hammers a thumbnail, she says "Ouch!"

This bridge allows a residential route.
So now we take our dead by tidy homes
with fresh bedlinens hung in the backyards
and lanky boys in driveways shooting hoops
and gardens to turn and lawns for mowing
and young girls sunning in their bright new bodies.
First to Atlantic and down Mont-Eagle
to the marshy north bank of the Huron
where blue heron nest, rock bass and bluegill
bed in the shallows and life goes on.
And on the other side, the granite rows
of Johnsons, Jacksons, Ruggles, Wilsons, Smiths—
the common names we have in common with
this place, this river and these winter oaks.

And have, likewise in common, our own ends
that bristle in us when we cross this bridge—
the cancer or the cardiac arrest
or lapse of caution that will do us in.
Among these stones we find the binding thread:
old wars, old famines, whole families killed by flus,
a century and then some of our dead
this bridge restores our easy access to.
A river is a decent distance kept.
A graveyard is an old agreement made
between the living and the living who have died
that says we keep their names and dates alive.
This bridge connects our daily lives to them
and makes them, once our neighbors, neighbors once again.

Thomas Lynch
from *Still Life in Milford*

Tryma

A tryma is a nutlike drupe.
No one in your playground is likely to respond
to such an observation in any reasonable way, but
you can always explain that a drupe has a single endocarp,
which is true but not, perhaps, helpful.

A pneuma is, by extension, a breathlike trope?
That, we may agree, would be horsing around, but
a drupelet, which is a small drupe, as, for example, the pulpy grain of the blackberry,
would have, logically, an endocarplet.
When it rains, as it may from time to time,
I can imagine you running through the meadow exclaiming,
"Ah, see the droplets on the drupelets!"

You will be an exquisite child,
or, rather, are already but you will proclaim it
in such a way as to defy the world.
And will they call you on the carplet?
Defy them, defy them.

The trauma of the tryma
is with us always, as are the poor
in spirit, who will stare at you blankly
or in resentment ask,
"Wha'? Who?"
Answer them smartly and tell them
the wahoo is a kind of Euonymous
(which is a good name)
with arillate seeds.
Tell them your grandfather said so.

If that doesn't work, and it won't, you can take some comfort
from knowing that the false aril originates
from the orifice instead of the stalk of an ovule,
as in the mace of the nutmeg, which is an arillode.

It follows, I suppose, that a true aril is a false arillode,
although people seldom say so,
but never let that stop you.

David R. Slavitt
from *PS3569.L3*

Cartoon Physics, part 1

Children under, say, *ten*, shouldn't know
that the universe is ever-expanding,
inexorably pushing into the vacuum, galaxies

swallowed by galaxies, whole

solar systems collapsing, all of it
acted out in silence. At ten we are still learning

the rules of cartoon animation,

that if a man draws a door on a rock
only he can pass through it.
Anyone else who tries

will crash into the rock. Ten-year-olds
should stick with burning houses, car wrecks,
ships going down—earthbound, tangible

disasters, arenas

where they can be heroes. You can run
back into a burning house, sinking ships

have lifeboats, the trucks will come
with their ladders, if you jump

you will be saved. A child

places her hand on the roof of a schoolbus,
& drives across a city of sand. She knows

the exact spot it will skid, at which point
the bridge will give, who will swim to safety
& who will be pulled under by sharks. She will
    learn

that if a man runs off the edge of a cliff
he will not fall

until he notices his mistake.

Nick Flynn
from *Some Ether*

september 15

The Revised Versions

Even Samuel Johnson found that ending
unbearable, and for over a hundred years
Lear was allowed to live, along with Cordelia,
who marries Edgar, who tried so hard
to do the right thing. It's not easy
being a king, having to worry every day

about the ambitions of your friends.
Who needs a bigger castle?
Let's sleep on it, Macbeth might tell his wife,
wait and see what comes along.
So Antony keeps his temper, takes Cleopatra
aside to say: We need to talk this through.

And Hamlet? Send him back to school to learn
no one ever really pleases his father.
And while he's reading he'll remember
how pretty Ophelia was, how much
she admired his poems.
Why not make what you can of love?

It's what we want for ourselves,
wary of starting a fight, anxious
to avoid another scene, having suffered
through too many funerals and heard
how eloquently the dead are praised
who threw their lives away.

Lawrence Raab
from *The Probable World*

Touch Me

Summer is late, my heart.
Words plucked out of the air
some forty years ago
when I was wild with love
and torn almost in two
scatter like leaves this night
of whistling wind and rain.
It is my heart that's late,
it is my song that's flown.
Outdoors all afternoon
under a gunmetal sky
staking my garden down,
I kneeled to the crickets trilling
underfoot as if about
to burst from their crusty shells;
and like a child again
marveled to hear so clear
and brave a music pour
from such a small machine.
What makes the engine go?
Desire, desire, desire.
The longing for the dance
stirs in the buried life.
One season only,
              and it's done.
So let the battered old willow
thrash against the windowpanes
and the house timbers creak.
Darling, do you remember
the man you married? Touch me,
remind me who I am.

Stanley Kunitz
from *Passing Through: The Later Poems, New and Selected*

september 17

The Dawn of the Navajo Woman

(for Evan)

The Navajo medicine woman gets up early
to greet the sun. So my radio tells me
and so I stay tuned, though you already showed
the way of greeting: simply to hold
this winter the hickory nut brushed free
of snow, the plain prize beneath the season's tree.

Perhaps it's the way your arch fits my instep,
my instep curves over your arch, but we've kept
at it these years, our limbs linking and unlinking
        deep
in the quilting, and still a hunger for skin, not sleep,
leads me on to you, your hand on my breast or
your calm talk of death and the ghosts of our
        ancestors,

all of them gone into the crowded earth. Such
comfort and ease I can almost consider
        becoming mulch
myself. Or ash. And I wonder at how a rush of
        heat can
disperse into something so much bigger than I am
that it leaves me pulsing, ignoring what's beyond,
daring to dispute the frozen ground.

The predawn sky offers an arctic green
below a blanket of flaming clouds. I try to imagine
the devotions of that Navajo woman but get
        only as far
as yesterday when we detoured through a graveyard
seeking, after shopping, a more quiet crowd.
The sun dazzled us: stark trunks thrusting upward

in the polar air, a batch of mallards in a bubbled
pool and all around the bright untroubled
snow. In the granite names I read the luck and
        rhythm
of even this hair's-breadth of a life, your breath
        with mine,
the branches swirling by, and the bobbing
        ducks, their
emerald heads flashing a green and palpable fire.

Terry Blackhawk
from *Body & Field*

Homage to Life

(*Jules Supervielle*, Hommage à la Vie)

It is good to have chosen
a living home
and harbored time
in a constant heart,
to have seen one's hands
touch the world
as an apple
in a small garden,
to have loved the earth,
the moon and the sun,
like old friends
beyond any others,
and to have entrusted
the world to memory
like a luminous horseman
to his black steed,
to have given shape
to these words: wife, children,
and to have served as a shore
for roving continents,
to have come upon the soul
with little oarstrokes
for it is frightened
by a sudden approach.

It is good to have known
the shade under the leaves
and to have felt age
steal over the naked body
accompanying the grief
of dark blood in our veins
and glazing its silence
with the star, Patience,
and to have all these words
stirring in the head,
to choose the least beautiful
and make a little feast for them,
to have felt life
rushed and ill-loved,
to have held it
in this poetry.

Joseph Stroud
from *Below Cold Mountain*

Paradise Consists of Forty-Nine Rotating Spheres

paradise gave me these legs
   for spinning
weep and pray and be joyful
paradise gave me these legs
   to weep and pray and be joyful

when I have fixed each corner
   p l i é relevé spin
I start the silky spokes
    p l i é relevé spin

paradise gave me these legs
   to weep and pray
         I am joyful

  youthful youthful
    paradise gave me these legs
so I spin
   black nights
    blue days
       p l i é relevé spin
my web against the sky

  a perfect circle shakes the stars
mine's a pure imitation
   sung from planets of memory
    spun from threads of dreams
weep and pray and be joyful

  paradise gave me these legs
that's all I need to know
paradise gave me these legs
   for spinning

I have spun
forty-nine webs of silken threads
   my window to the sky

Jane Mead
from *The Lord and the General Din of the World*

Skirts

Women spin and dance in skirts, sleep and wake
in them sometimes, ascend and descend stairs.
Some have walked into the sea in skirts,
which is like tossing a skirt over a man's head,
or pressing his face against the tent of one.
Some woman, maybe wearing a velvet skirt,
embraces another woman—so one skirt brushes
against another. Women wash and wring and hang
skirts up to dry, spray them, iron them, hem them,
slip them over slips, over tights. Once, I confess,
I owned six black ones: rayon, wool, gabardine,
linen, cotton, silk. The wind can blow the bulk
of a skirt between a woman's legs, or wrap her in
a twist, billow underneath so skirls of wind touch
faintly, delightfully. Some women hear skirts
murmuring or sighing, conversing with the flesh
they cover. But most skirts drape in silence, the silence
of slow snow falling, or the hushed liquid glide
of a woman's body through a sunlit pool, the sweet
descent to sleep, or passion, or passion's nemesis,
ennui. A woman's spirit lengthens or widens in a skirt,
magnified by cloth and cut and her stride through
the quickened space. If instead a woman wears
a tight skirt, she feels containment and its
amplification—reduction's power to suggest.
Right now my favorite is a crimpy cinnabar silk
I twist into wrinkles to dry. I wear it walking in
the evenings. I vanish as its folds enfold the sky.

Gray Jacobik
from *The Double Task*

Epith

Here's the little dressmaker
on her knees at your feet,
mouth full of pins:
fixing you in the dummy's image.

Your belled satin shivers like
a goblet of fizzled brut—
You wanted it late in life,
happiness, wanted a little family

but after the kids grew up.
Like a saint on her death pallet,
you longed for an erotic God
but a refined deity—

not some oversexed Zeus
in a see-through raincoat,
spritzing gold coins,
rattling the canopy. No,

at last you've found a groom
born to forget the ring,
the bride's name—
a regular holy ghost.

You forget yourself
with each glittering pin,
each chip off the old rock,
each sip of the long toast

to your famous independence,
negotiated at such cost—
and still refusing to fit.

Carol Muske
first published in *Ploughshares*, vol. 23, no. 4,
    Winter 1997–98
edited by Howard Norman and Jane Shore

september 22

Works and Days

More in number, five
or six at a time
perched atop stiff cat-

tail tufts or calling
from lush caverns in
the willow limbs—more

on the wing, more flash
and blood, more wild song,
who seldom travel

in numbers bigger
than a pair—the red-
wings returning this

spring to the park pond
have surprised us all.
It's supposed to be

a bad time for birds.
El Nino has smeared
California

for months, spreading east
and windward its strain
of killer drought, of

greenhouse-effect storms.
A few blocks away
the factory mill

dusts our own fields with
a mineral mist—
pesticide spills from

the well-water taps.
The honeybees are
dying out and what-

ever food these birds
are used to has thinned
next to nothing: yet

here they are, bright as
bobbers, floating the
rich, brown surfaces.

It's a windless day
of someone's childhood.
Small wonder so many

of us have come
to sun with the red-
wings on the flat bank.

The birds, to see us,
must think all is well,
to see so many

so happy to be
here—, to see so many
more gathering now.

David Baker
from *Changeable Thunder*

september 23

The Code

There was a delicate white mole
in the crook of my mother's elbow
that at the age of two or three
I loved to finger. Lying drowsy
in her lap while she sang, floating off
to sleep at night, I touched the soft
bump erect as a nipple.
Half dreaming I rubbed the morsel,
playing with the soft firmness,
counting its bead, the lone nevus
of comfort and connection like
a telegraph key that sent quick
codes of pulse and nourishing blood
to me at the smallest end of touch.

Robert Morgan

first published in *The Virginia Quarterly Review*, vol. 74, no. 4, Autumn 1998

Incident in a Filing Cupboard

Thank you, she says, *we both needed that*,
as if an intimacy had just occurred between us.
Old so-and-so really blew his top today, I say.
It was always going to happen, she replies.

Unless I've blacked out for a moment or two,
nothing has changed, although I am aware
of an oil-film on my lips, as if I have woken
in the arms of someone entirely unknown.

The female thigh begins a steady atrophy
from the late twenties. *These things happen.*
Male muscle tissue slackens and weakens
from 23. *I always have trouble with figures.*

It's difficult, with both of us seeing people.
One in seven of us doesn't have the father
we think we have. Only 9% of what we say
is understood in exactly the way we mean it.

Where do we go from here? That question!
I offer her a sheaf of processed application forms
like a bouquet. *All these numbers*, I say, as if
the intimacy between us had never taken place.

Roddy Lumsden
from *The Book of Love*

september 25

This Is Not Love's Offering

for a child in the Sudan

Having little to do with Eros
the vulture cranes to feed:
the child of famine recedes
to skin, and the black bird inches
to pierce the web of pulse
playing out on the desert floor.

The bird may not know
the breath of a child, may
be unfamiliar with his sighing.
But soon the two will merge
to prey upon the living
in a photograph.

When the child wakes
to another world, solemn
with the feathers of struggle,
there will be no eyes to receive him,
no camera to record. He will lie
as he was, in the kingdom of birds.

Shaun T. Griffin
from *Bathing in the River of Ashes*

Mentor

for Robert Francis

Had I known, only known
when I lived so near,
I'd have gone, gladly gone
foregoing my fear
of the wholly grown
and the nearly great.
But I learned alone,
so I learned too late.

Timothy Murphy
first published in *The Formalist, A Journal of Metrical Poetry,* vol. 12, issue 1, 2001
also from *Very Far North*

september 27

Fix

There is no caring less
for you. I fix on music in the weeds,
count cricket beats to tell the temp, count
my breaths from here to Zen.
September does its best.
The Alaskan pipeline lacks integrity,
mineral fibers are making people dizzy,
we're waiting for a major quake. Ultra-
violet intensity is gaining,
the ozone's full of holes and

I can find no shade.
There is no caring less.
Without the moon the earth
would whirl us three times faster, gale-force
winds would push us down. Say
earth lost mass, a neighbor
star exploded—it's *if*

and *and* and
but. The cosmos owns our luck.
Say under right and rare conditions,
space and time could oscillate.
I know what conditions
those would be for me.
I'd like to keep my distance,
my others, keep my rights reserved.
Yet look at you, intreasured,

where resolutions end.
No matter how we breathe
or count our breaths,
there is no caring less
for you for me. I have to stop myself

from writing "sovereign," praising
with the glory words I know.
Glaciologists say changes
in the mantle, the planet's vast
cold sheets could melt. Catastrophe
is everywhere, my presence
here is extra—yet—
there is no caring less.

Alice Fulton
from *Felt*

One Petition Lofted into the Ginkgos

For the train-wrecked, the puck-struck,
    the viciously punched,
the pole-vaulter whose pole
        snapped in ascent.
            For his asphalt-face,
his capped-off scream, God bless
        his dad in the stands.
            For the living dog in the median
car-struck and shuddering
        on crumpled haunches, eyes
            large as plates, seeing nothing, but
    looking
looking. For the blessed pigeon
who threw himself from the cliff
        after plucking out his feathers
            just to taste a falling death. For
the poisoned, scalded and gassed, the bayoneted,
        the bit and blind-sided,
            asthmatic veteran
who just before his first date in years and years
swallowed his own glass eye. For these and all
and all the drunk,

Imagine a handful of quarters chucked up at sunset,

lofted into the ginkgos—
    and there, at apogee,
        while the whole ringing wad
pauses, pink-lit,
    about to seed the penny-colored earth
        with an hour's wages—
As shining, ringing, brief, and cheap
    as a prayer should be—

Imagine it all falling

into some dark machine
    brimming with nurses,
        nutrices ex machina—

and they blustering out
    with juices and gauze, peaches and brushes,
        to patch such dents and wounds.

Gabriel Gudding
first published in *The Iowa Review*, vol. 27, no. 2,
    Summer/Fall 1997
also from *A Defense of Poetry*

september 29

The Floating Rib

Because a woman had eaten something
when a man told her not to. Because the man
who told her not to had made her
from another man's bones. That's why
men badgered the heart-side of her chest,
knowing she could not give the bone back, knowing
she would always owe them that one bone.

And you could see how older girls who knew
their catechism armed themselves against it:
with the pike end of teasing combs
they scabbarded in pocketbooks that clashed
against the jumper's nightwatch plaid.
In the girl's bathroom, you watched them
wield the spike in dangerous proximity to their eyes,

shepherding the bangs through which they peered
like cheetahs in an upside-downward-growing grass.
Then they'd mouth the words to "Runaway"
while they ran white lipstick round their lips,
white to announce they had no blood
so any wound would leave no trace, as Eve's
having nothing more to lose must have made

her fearless. What was weird was how soon
the ordinary days started running past them
like a river, how willingly they entered it
and how they rose up on the other side. Tamed,
or god no...your *mother*: ready to settle
with whoever found the bone under her blouse
and give it over, and make a life out of the getting
    back.

Lucia Perillo
first published in *Shenandoah*, vol. 47, no. 1, Spring 1997

Last in before Dark

Some distance in, a life fills
with people,
despite the early departures—
the childhood friends who must be home
before dark and after a while never
come again,
some of the very old
who were at the gatherings once
or twice, tenderly served and seated
to the side, speaking
their other language sparingly
among themselves—
of those who vanish forever
you may keep a likeness—
but after much coming and going
a life begins to fill,
from the tiny nursery downward—
two figures there, wherever
else they may be,
whose shadows over you
began the night
and day, but now there is
no place for a shadow to fall
that doesn't have shadows
or people in it.

The eave's gutter leads the water away
until the flow is too great
and rises and brims over,
pouring down in front of the windows.

Underneath the rain, the rooms
shelter too many in this, the imagined
occasion, everywhere the constant
and occasional loiter together,
near neighbor and honored guest,
each with something particular to do
with you, an old teacher of yours
who was the first to believe in you,
a woman friend of your wife who exasperates
you in just the way your mother
used to and to whom you are drawn,
your four children with their hundred faces,
an array for each encountered
in every room
under a table, in a closet,
behind the drapes,
taking up spaces, secret or ludicrous,
no else could.

Inside a great company
and no one expected,
except perhaps the one
whom it seems urgent,
an emergency, to know.
Somehow a space will be made
for such a one,
and all those milling will stand aside
as if into the room a bride comes.
But soon there seems simply no room
for anybody.

The corridors jam with co-workers,
a few college friends, a second wife,
her relatives, the incidental players
from the third city in your life,
a man from whom you get tickets,
a tennis partner.
For months, even years ahead
the boxes in the calendar
contain these known names,

until everyone else must be turned away
no matter what they might be to you,
what promise they hold.
You no longer look—it's impossible,
where could you put them?
And daily you may
brush by people who might stir you,
even meeting a few:
a young man on a train with whom
you really talk about the book
that you are reading.
Where would you put him?
There appeared to be a space
on the second floor
but your dentist is in it,
whom you sometimes see socially,
and where would you put a young man?
Does he have your number?
Do you have his?
Even now there is someone at your door.

How much rarer even than one
whose entry
cannot be denied
like an awaited bride,
more than the sweetness of
the new friend just in before dark,
is the sweetness of you, yourself,
moving through your crowded house
in late afternoon
after rain,
whose life will not fill,
who will answer the door
and make room.

Jason Sommer
from *Other People's Troubles*

october 1

Humble Herb Is Rival to Prozac

In memory of my mother

An item in *Science Tuesday* happens to catch my eye.
A woman in Germany
(it seems that she is only one of many)
having been drinking several cups a day
of Saint John's Wort brewed into tea
reports *The fear*
that everything good would disappear
has stopped.

Reading this, I seem to see
something shiny, peeling: elderly
Scotch tape, no longer strong enough to keep
the little sprigs in place, maintain the shape
of wild flowers picked and pressed
(though not pressed long enough to be quite flat—
even at five years old I probably
found time too slow:
"Those flowers must be all pressed flat by now!")
and taped into the pages of a smallish spiral notebook,
whose khaki cover
bulges with still bulky flower after flower.

Open the notebook. Turn the freighted page:
buttercup, clover, yarrow brown with age
or else pellucid—fragile either way.
Time has not only thoroughly discolored
the contents of this makeshift album, but
has begun the task of disassembling.
Delicate petals grow
amber-veined and clear;

tough little stalks now show
their pith; the tiny, no
longer yolk-gold tubelets
that form the daisy's eye
have gradually begun to come apart
and one by one escape
the sagging tape,
meander down the page
like stray eyelashes, like fluffs of lint.
Black-eyed Susan, Queen Anne's Lace,
found, picked, pressed, taped, and labelled;
aster, devil's paintbrush, everlasting,
St. John's Wort. Even then
I knew—I think I knew—this last-named flower
was rarer than the others. Knew it how?
Because she showed me the reliably
five-petalled pale gold blossoms. Naturally,
knowing nothing, I had to be taught
every flower's name,
though probably I thought
Solomon's-seal, vetch, mullein, morning glory
were transparently my birthright,
as if all flowers hadn't come to me
through her who guided my unsteadily
printing pencil (1953);
whose disappearance (1992)
never made me fear
that everything good would disappear,
but teaches me, if anything, again
a lesson that each year I must relearn,
the renewable epiphany
of vanishing and then recovery.

The little notebook with my staggering
pencilled captions labelling
every blessed thing,
picked and pressed and anchored to the page,
recording the first summer I remember;
her long full skirts, their cotton prints, the florals
    and batiks,
my clinging at knee level,
or her bending over
or leading me to the cowfield, where clover
and thyme attracted hordes of noisy bees,
showing me where this and that plant grew,
their names, and how to write them,
enlisting me in the whole enterprise
of writing, how to press a summer flat
between the pages of a heavy book—
what storage! what retrieval! what an arc
from something tiny as a daisy's eye
to something vast, too nebulous to hold—
the trail from recollection to invention
blazed and reblazed of necessity,
since memory can take us
only so far before it lets us down.

That bulgy little notebook
vanished years ago
and I no longer care
whether or not I find it.
Probably it's gathering
(even as it turns to) dust somewhere.
But laws of leaf and stem and petal hold:
what seems sheer desiccation
unlocks its stored, distilled
power into this brew,
this brimming mug whose steam
wreathes the lonely air:
Courage. Nothing good will disappear.

Rachel Hadas

first published in *TriQuarterly*, no. 103, Fall 1998
also from *Indelible*

A Deathplace

Very few people know where they will die,
But I do: in a brick-faced hospital,
Divided, not unlike Caesarean Gaul,
Into three parts: the Dean Memorial
Wing, in the classic cast of 1910,
Green-grated in unglazed, Aeolian
Embrasures; the Maud Wiggin Building, which
Commemorates a dog-jawed Boston bitch
Who fought the brass down to their whipcord knees
In World War I, and won enlisted men
Some decent hospitals, and, being rich,
Donated her own granite monument;
The Mandeville Pavilion, pink-brick tent
With marble piping, flying snapping flags
Above the entry where our bloody rags
Are rolled in to be sponged and sewn again.
Today is fair; tomorrow, scourging rain
(If only my own tears) will see me in
Those jaundiced and distempered corridors
Off which the five-foot-wide doors slowly close.
White as my skimpy chiton, I will cringe
Before the pinpoint of the least syringe;
Before the buttered catheter goes in;
Before the I.V.'s lisp and drip begins
Inside my skin; before the rubber hand
Upon the lancet takes aim and descends
To lay me open, and upon its thumb
Retracts the trouble, a malignant plum;

And finally, I'll quail before the hour
When the authorities shut off the power
In that vast hospital, and in my bed
I'll feel my blood go thin, go white, the red,
The rose all leached away, and I'll go dead.
Then will the business of life resume:
The muffled trolley wheeled into my room,
The off-white blanket blanking off my face,
The stealing, secret, private, *largo* race
Down halls and elevators to the place
I'll be consigned to for transshipment, cased
In artificial air and light: the ward
That's underground; the terminal; the morgue.
Then one fine day when all the smart flags flap,
A booted man in black with a peaked cap
Will call for me and troll me down the hall
And slot me into his black car. That's all.

L. E. Sissman
from *Night Music*

OCTOBER 3

Poetry Is the Art of Not Succeeding

Poetry is the art of not succeeding;
the art of making a little ritual
out of your own bad luck, lighting a little fire
made of leaves, reciting a prayer
in the ordinary dark.

It's the art of those who didn't make it
after all; who were lucky enough to be
left behind, while the winners ran on ahead
to wherever it is winners
go running to.

O blessed rainy day, glorious
as a paper bag. The kingdom of poetry
is like this—quiet, anonymous,
a dab of sunlight on the back of your hand,
a view out the window just before dusk.

It's an art more shadow than statue,
and has something to do with your dreams
running out—a bare branch darkening
on a winter sky, the week-old snow
frozen into something hard.

It's an art as simple as drinking water
from a tin cup; of loving that moment
at the end of autumn, say, when the air
holds no more promises, and the days are short
and likely to be gray.

A bland light is best to see it in.
Middle age brings it to flower.
And there, just when you're feeling your weakest,
it floods you completely,
leaving you weeping as you drive your car.

Joe Salerno
from *Only Here*

World Truffle

This time the mycorrhizal infection
at the crooked roots of a hazelnut tree
meets a set of conditions so knotted and invisible
it feels like good will, or magic,
when the truffle begins its warty branches
that grow away from the sun.
This time it doesn't stop with one fairy ring
and dissolute spores, but fingers its way
beneath the turf and under the fence
and past the signs for Truffle Reserve:
Harvest Regulated by the State Forestry Department,
out through Umbria, up the shank of Italy;
it enmeshes the skin of the Alps.
In time its pale filaments have threaded Europe and,
almost as stubborn as death, are probing
sand on one side and burrowing on the other
through the heated muttering bed of the sea.
Its pregnant mounds rise modestly
in deserts, rain forests, city parks;
yellow truffle-flies hover and buzz
at tiny aromatic cracks in Panama and the Aleutians.

It smells like wood smoke, humus and ore,
it smells of sex. It smells like ten thousand years.
It smells of a promise that a little tastes better than all,
that a mix and disguise is best.
Young dogs whiff it, twist in the air
and bury their faces in loam;
tapirs and cormorants sway in its fragrance,
camels open their nostrils for it,
coatimundi and honey badgers start digging,
lemurs bark and octopi embrace.
Humans sense nothing unusual. Yet some of them—
teachers raking leaves in Sioux City,
truck drivers stretching their legs in Ulan Bator—
take a few deep breaths and, unaware,
begin to love the world.

Sarah Lindsay
first published in *The Paris Review*, no. 159, Fall 2001
also from *Mount Clutter*

october 5

Sin

The tree bore the efflorescence of October apples
like the bush that burned with fire and was not consumed.

The wind blew in cold sweet gusts,
and the burning taste of fresh snow came with the gradual dark

down through the goldenrod. The blue and scarlet sky
was gently losing its color,

as if from use.
The towers and telephone poles rose in the distance.

And a decline
of spirit, hearing, all senses; where the mind no longer rests,

dwells, intrigue; and Satan's quick perspective of what lies ahead,
was foretold by the springing back of a bough.

—We'll never know the all of it: nature's manifesto,
the sleight-of-hand in God's light, the invisible,

visible, sinned against, absolved, no matter the enormity
of trying, and Eve's help.

But come just before sunrise and see and taste again
the apple tree coming into fire

—shadow-glyphs on the crystallized grasses,
geese surging above the loblolly pine, the smell of sap—

as if willingly through its long life
it held on to one unclarified passion and grew and regretted nothing.

Carol Frost
first published in *Ploughshares*, vol. 25, no. 4, Winter 1999–00
edited by Madison Smartt Bell and Elizabeth Spires
also from *Love and Scorn: New and Selected Poems*

OCTOBER 6

The Prose Poem

On the map it is precise and rectilinear as a chessboard, though driving past you would hardly notice it, this boundary line or ragged margin, a shallow swale that cups a simple trickle of water, less rill than rivulet, more gully than dell, a tangled ditch grown up throughout with a fearsome assortment of wildflowers and bracken. There is no fence, though here and there a weathered post asserts a former claim, strands of fallen wire taken by the dust. To the left a cornfield carries into the distance, dips and rises to the blue sky, a rolling plain of green and healthy plants aligned in close order, row upon row upon row. To the right, a field of wheat, a field of hay, young grasses breaking the soil, filling their allotted land with the rich, slow-waving spectacle of their grain. As for the farmers, they are, for the most part, indistinguishable: here the tractor is red, there yellow; here a pair of dirty hands, there a pair of dirty hands. They are cultivators of the soil. They grow crops by pattern, by acre, by foresight, by habit. What corn is to one, wheat is to the other, and though to some eyes the similarities outweigh the differences it would be as unthinkable for the second to commence planting corn as for the first to switch over to wheat. What happens in the gully between them is no concern of theirs, they say, so long as the plough stays out, the weeds stay in the ditch where they belong, though anyone would notice the wind-sewn cornstalks poking up their shaggy ears like young lovers run off into the bushes, and the kinship of these wild grasses with those the farmer cultivates is too obvious to mention, sage and dun-colored stalks hanging their noble heads, hoarding exotic burrs and seeds, and yet it is neither corn nor wheat that truly flourishes there, nor some jackalopian hybrid of the two. What grows in that place is possessed of a beauty all its own, ramshackle and unexpected, even in winter, when the wind hangs icicles from the skeletons of briars and small tracks cross the snow in search of forgotten grain; in the spring the little trickle of water swells to welcome frogs and minnows, a muskrat, a family of turtles, nesting doves in the verdant grass; in summer it is a thoroughfare for raccoons and opossums, field mice, swallows and black birds, migrating egrets, a passing fox; in autumn the geese avoid its abundance, seeking out windrows of toppled stalks, fatter grain more quickly discerned, more easily digested. Of those that travel the local road, few pay that fertile hollow any mind, even those with an eye for what blossoms, vetch and timothy, early forsythia, the fatted calf in the fallow field, the rabbit running for cover, the hawk's descent from the lightning-struck tree. You've passed this way yourself many times, and can tell me, if you would, do the formal fields end where the valley begins, or does everything that surrounds us emerge from its embrace?

Campbell McGrath
from *Road Atlas*

A Mayan Astronomer in Hell's Kitchen

—9th Avenue and West 48th Street, New York
October 1998

Above the deli in Hell's Kitchen where the fire erupted,
above the firefighters charging with hoses like great serpents,
above the fingerprints of smoke smearing the night,
above the crowd calling his name with tilted faces,
above the fire truck and its ladder reaching for him,

a man leaned elbows on the third floor fire escape,
bronze skin, black hair in a braid, leather jacket,
with a grin for the firefighters
bellowing at the crowds to *stand back*,
a Mayan astronomer in Hell's Kitchen
watching galaxies spiral in the fingerprints of smoke,
smoking a cigarette.

Martín Espada
first published in *The Threepenny Review*, 80, vol. XX, no. 4, Winter 2000
also from *A Mayan Astronomer in Hell's Kitchen*

OCTOBER 8

Winged Snake Found on a Path

A long time ago, twelve hours from here
by car, on a small bit of acreage with a pond,
I was squatting in my shorts and contemplating
a poisoned, purple bean
when the grownups slapped it from my grasp.

It was hot in the air, in the furrows in the field.
It was cool on the black bottom of the pond,
and a chill rose from the deep
and settled under the trees.
This was known only to children
or to someone without goals.

I left the heat and circled the princely pond.
My head even then was too big,
and filled with trees.
And I almost did not see the winged snake
stretched across the path.
His long bright wings were battered and thin.
I knelt: someone had done him in.
And that was the last one I have seen.

Matthew Rohrer
first published in *Denver Quarterly*, vol. 35, no. 4, Winter 2001
also from *Satellite*

Sleeping with Artemis

I hadn't been that ashamed since
the Spartiate festival of the Hyacinthids,
and it was harder than we thought, sleeping
with Artemis. We brought sandwiches;
she brought arrows and stuck them
fletching up in the sand. We were vastly
unequipped. I looked to the heavens,
like you will, and asked for guidance
and a shield. To no avail. Furthermore,

the wine didn't help like we thought.
She drank it down, cursed our mothers,
and only got reckless, really, popped
the blister on her heel, drew the bow,
and, with both eyes shut, skewered
Crissippus. We scattered like snacks.
I believe it happened in that clearing
by the stream, where much transpired
as of late: two dead last April—the girl

who smoked flowers—that quiet kid who
turned into bark. We should have known
better, with the storied plants along the bank
and the instructive constellations in the sky.
Then she swept out of the hedge like
a jack-knifed lion, a moon on each shoulder,
but you read the report. Indeed, sir,
we felt hairless, the offspring of mice,
when she quoted Hemingway, then turned
the forest to her wishes: leaves dropped

like bombs: branches shook: and where
the hounds came from, no one can tell.
From time to time, picking us apart now
from the stream, knee-deep and eyeing
the rushes for movement, she'd glance down
to her shirt, but it was always someone
else's blood. I remember her teeth
weren't as straight as you'd think.
But something about her was perfect.

Josh Bell
first published in *jubilat 3*, Spring/Summer 2000

OCTOBER 10

Psyche Revised

She could not love him till she saw him clear:
that much she thought she knew. A troubled light
gossiped in whispers from her lifted lamp;
she neared the bed he slept in, not in fear
so much as in resigned need for full sight
of him, such as he might be. He lay damp
and heavy, as if travels through the night
were more than even gods could bear; a cramp
stirred like regret across his breast, his face
sealed in the momentary grasp of bright
visions destined to fail by day. How near
he was, perfected by imperfect grace!
She quenched the lamp, and radiance washed the
    place.
She could not see him till she held him dear.

Rhina P. Espaillat
from *Rehearsing Absence*

OCTOBER 11

The Baby

"Doesn't it break your heart,"
she said to her husband one morning,
"that he's going to die one day?"

(The future, until now a silent letter, was pronounced.)

The new parents resolved to make
the present a migration towards that
original silence, and vain
progress was made, as if they were rowing
a boat across a lake to a restaurant
they didn't know had closed down.

Rex Wilder
first published in *The New Republic*,
    vol. 218, no. 26, issue 4,354, 1998

The Clearing

Always in that clearing
the oaks are black with crows
and I can't be certain
my presence starts it
but something catches like
a fuse, and the branches seethe
until the air grows raucous
with calling crows. First one,
then another, now all
stretch into brief grace
then oar up into a spiral-
ing choir, into such teasing
synchroneity, just approaching
then skirting a pattern.

Far below and minuscule
under that disarming blue
circle of light, I watch them,
charred bits in a whirl-
wind of logic, beyond grasp
of cause or destiny, beyond
delight or grief. Their flight,
I tell myself, has nothing
to do with me, and that widening
echo, even when it falls
together a moment, orchestral,
has nothing to do with me,
though it sounds at times fearsome
and something like a name.

Richard Foerster
from *Trillium*

october 13

The X Files

In search of them—the aliens we don't
know whether we should fear or hate—the stars
look puzzled by the gruesome murder scene.
I want to love them, touch them, but I can't.
The world I live in seems as damned as theirs.
The government denies all knowledge. Soon

the terrible conspiracy begins
unraveling; the aliens we hate
and fear are colonizing us the way
that cancer does. The stars, forever in
the kind of conflict desire can create,
look puzzled when they recognize its face.

We search, we search, for something that we think
is killing us. The cancer in a gland,
the alien with terrible black eyes,
the government whose politicians stink
of some conspiracy. Here is my hand,
Mulder—take me. Here, Scully, is the lie—

destroy it. All of us are aliens
no other understands. The world is full
of stars like me, each one no universe
can hide. Once I was abducted. My sins
were all erased, but they were clinical
in their precision when they stole my voice.

Rafael Campo
from *Diva*

Horses

Setting out on my bicycle alone,
I came upon the horses
drenched in bright sunshine,
yard after yard of blue-black ironed silk,
drawn before stopped traffic.

With white stars on their foreheads
and white bracelets on their legs,
each blood horse wore nothing
but a fine noseband
and a shroud of steam.

I felt lazy and vicious watching them,
with my large joints and big head,
stricken by thoughts of my brothers.
If only the barbarous horsemen
could lead *us* down the path, unestranged.

It smashed in me like water galloped through.
Flinching there on my haunches,
with wide nostrils,
nipping the air as if it were green grass,
how I yearned for my neck to be brushed!

Henri Cole
from *The Visible Man*

october 15

Our Other Sister

for Ellen

The cruelest thing I did to my younger sister
wasn't shooting a homemade blowdart into her knee,
where it dangled for a breathless second

before dropping off, but telling her we had
another, older sister who'd gone away.
What my motives were I can't recall: a whim,

or was it some need of mine to toy with loss,
to probe the ache of imaginary wounds?
But that first sentence was like a strand of DNA

that replicated itself in coiling lies
when my sister began asking her desperate questions.
I called our older sister Isabel

and gave her hazel eyes and long blonde hair.
I had her run away to California
where she took drugs and made hippie jewelry.

Before I knew it, she'd moved to Santa Fe
and opened a shop. She sent a postcard
every year or so, but she'd stopped calling.

I can still see my younger sister staring at me,
her eyes widening with desolation
then filling with tears. I can still remember

how thrilled and horrified I was
that something I'd just made up
had that kind of power, and I can still feel

the blowdart of remorse stabbing me in the heart
as I rushed to tell her none of it was true.
But it was too late. Our other sister

had already taken shape, and we could not
call her back from her life far away
or tell her how badly we missed her.

Jeffrey Harrison
from *Feeding the Fire*

OCTOBER 16

Book

Its leaves flutter, they thrive or wither, its outspread
Signatures like wings open to form the gutter.

The pages riffling brush my fingertips with their edges:
Whispering, erotic touch this hand knows from ages back.

What progress we have made, they are burning my books, not
Me, as once they would have done, said Freud in 1933.

A little later, the laugh was on him, on the Jews,
On his sisters. O people of the book, wanderers, *anderes*.

When we have wandered all our ways, said Raleigh, Time
Shuts up the story of our days—beheaded, his life like a story.

The sound *bk*: lips then palate, outward plosive to interior stop.
Bk, bch: the beech tree, pale wood incised with Germanic runes.

Enchanted wood. Glyphs and characters between boards.
The reader's dread of finishing a book, that loss of a world,

And also the reader's dread of beginning a book, becoming
Hostage to a new world, to some spirit or spirits unknown.

Look! What thy mind cannot contain you can commit
To these waste blanks. The jacket ripped, the spine cracked,

Still it arouses me, torn crippled god like Loki the schemer
As the book of Lancelot aroused Paolo and Francesca

Who cling together even in Hell, O passionate, so we read.
Love that turns or torments or comforts me, love of the need

Of love, need for need, columns of characters that sting
Sometimes deeper than any music or movie or picture,

Deeper sometimes even than a body touching another.
And the passion to make a book—passion of the writer

Smelling glue and ink, sensuous. The writer's dread of making
Another tombstone, my marker orderly in its place in the stacks.

Or to infiltrate and inhabit another soul, as a splinter of spirit
Pressed between pages like a wildflower, odorless, brittle.

Robert Pinsky
first published in *The Threepenny Review*, 85, vol. XXII, no. 3, Fall 2001

This Poem

Let the form be a garden in wild wilderness,
a hyacinth language, a turning in wind
               when marginal influences
disrupt the flow.

Build thought as a bee does,
one concern at a time, a hexagonal symmetry
             deep in the structure;
or explore the foundation

of a derelict house, its cellarhole cracked
by bracken and trees—with daffodils blooming
             alongside the door,
and off in the woods, sometimes

a forsythia. And a carrion beetle to bury
the mouse, the skeletal memories of things
             that are gone;
or hidden, like antlers, deep in the pines

where branches are tossed,
a path to the edge of recorded time, that stops
             at a place
where the language is lost.

Barbara Jordan
from *Trace Elements*

OCTOBER 18

After

In memoriam William Matthews

All long labors, whether for hunger, for duty, for
Pleasure, or none of the above, one day wrap up.
Put down the itinerant's beaten pouch, pluck no fruit further;
Linger over the melancholy taste of *last* on the tongue.
Even a switchblade wit can't sever another stem.

Plenty is a relative measure—if less than paradise,
It's more than enough. The prolific orchard will of course
Continue, other soles trod ladders into the heady
Kingdom of weighted boughs. Insatiable, you might even say
Incorrigible (as though mumbling in winter sleep), the way they can't
Not keep coming back, grasping, tugging, lifting down those
Globes that swell and blush to be handled so.

Jeanne Marie Beaumont
first published in *The Gettysburg Review*, vol. 12, no. 3, Autumn 1999

The Opposite of Nostalgia

You are running away from everyone
who loves you,
from your family,
from old lovers, from friends.

They run after you with accumulations
of a former life, copper earrings,
plates of noodles, banners
of many lost revolutions.

You love to say the trees are naked now
because it never happens
in your country. This is a mystery
from which you will never

recover. And yes, the trees are naked now,
everything that still breathes in them
lies silent and stark
and waiting. You love October most

of all, how there is no word
for so much splendor.
This, too, is a source
of consolation. Between you and memory

everything is water. Names of the dead,
or saints, or history.
There is a realm in which
—no, forget it,

it's still too early to make anyone understand.
A man drives a stake
through his own heart
and afterwards the opposite of nostalgia

begins to make sense: he stops raking the leaves
and the leaves take over
and again he has learned
to let go.

Eric Gamalinda
from *Zero Gravity*

october 20

A Star Is Born in the Eagle Nebula

to Larry Levis, 1946-1996

They've finally admitted that trying to save oil-soaked
seabirds doesn't work. You can wash them, rinse them
with a high-pressure nozzle, feed them activated charcoal
to absorb toxic chemicals, & test them for anemia, but the oil
still disrupts the microscopic alignment of feathers that creates
a kind of wet suit around the body. (Besides, it costs $600 to wash
the oil slick off a penguin & $32,000 to clean an Alaskan seabird.)
We now know that the caramel coloring in whiskey causes nightmares,
& an ingredient in beer produces hemorrhoids. Glycerol
in vodka causes anal seepage, & when girls enter puberty,
the growth of their left ventricles slows down for about a year.
Box-office receipts plummeted this week. Retail sales are sluggish.
The price of wheat rose. Soybeans sank. The Dow is up thirty points.
A man named Alan Gerry has bought Woodstock & plans
to build a theme park, a sort of combo Williamsburg-Disneyland
for graying hippies. The weather report predicts a batch of showers
preceding a cold front down on the Middle Atlantic Coast—
you aren't missing much. Day after day at the Ford research labs
in Dearborn, Michigan, an engineer in charge of hood latches
labors, measuring the weight of a hood, calculating the resistance
of the latch, coming up with the perfect closure, the perfect snapping
sound, while the shadow of Jupiter's moon, Io, races across cloud tops
at 10.5 miles a second, and a star is born in the Eagle Nebula.

Molecular hydrogen and dust condenses into lumps that contract
and ignite under their own gravity. In today's paper four girls
in a photo appear to be tied, as if by invisible threads, to five
soap bubbles floating along the street against the black wall
of the Park Avenue underpass. Nothing earthshattering. The girls
are simply there. They've blown the bubbles & are following them
up the street. That's the plot. A life. Any life. I turn the page
and there's Charlie Brown. He's saying, "Sometimes I lie awake
at night & ask, Does anyone remember me? Then a voice
comes to me out of the dark—'Sure, Frank, we remember you.'"

Marcia Southwick

first published in *The Gettysburg Review*, vol. 11, no. 3, Autumn 1998

OCTOBER 21

II. San Francisco

From Five Urban Love Songs

Pierced tongue. Do-it-yourself lisp.
What is this? Penitence? Native wisdom?
Mutilation? or signal: *I'll do anything*.
Was it a dare? or a careful plan? Did it sting—
or ache—and does the food get caught—
and should such a person *work* in a restaurant?
Customers' stomachs can turn—or does desire
turn to *her*—to wish—to feel the fire
glide over the silver (or is it gold?) pin?
And you, my darling, with your end-
less speculation: *Is he—is she—gay?*
Does he or she want you—or me—or either way?
Why do you need to know? I am *here*.
This is my body: eat. Unwrap. Disappear.

Kate Light
from *The Laws of Falling Bodies*

OCTOBER 22

Celan

There,
the whisper:

gradual breath
fattens

a word, bud
of stem form—

never before
this one,

the return of
the recognizable.

James Brasfield
first published in *AGNI*, no. 55

The Bear on Main Street

What made the man kill this bear?
His truck, across which the bear's body lies,
tells me it wasn't to feed his family
or because his children were cold.

The bear has beautiful black feet, delicate
almost, like the soles of patent leather slippers,
and the wind riffles the surface of its fur
with the sheen of water in the autumn sun.

The bear looks as if it might only be sleeping,
but its tongue lags from its mouth, and the man
has wrapped it with stout twine and bound it
to the bed of his truck,
as if he were afraid it might speak.

Three teenage boys pull their pickup to the curb,
One of the boys guesses what the bear must weigh.
Another wants to know how many shots it took,
and the third boy climbs down. He strokes its nose and forehead.
He traces the bear's no longer living skull
with the living bones of his fingers
and wonders by what impossible road
he will come to his father's country.

Dan Gerber
from *Trying to Catch the Horses*

Flood

This had happened before: rain that began
as mist—thick and windless, slow to fall.
In the bottomland, bloated spiders
caught fog and bound it; the webs sagged,
white and wet.

        The second day, the creek
argued with the rain, grew bolder before
losing itself, overcoming the banks
that had defined it. Its current cut,
the water grew still, intent on rising.
This changed everything.

        The third day, skeletal
corn-balk was lost. The trees waded in, waist-deep.
Boundaries drowned—the wire dead. I had
moved the cows to higher ground, and, puzzled,
they looked down on that placid other
that was not lake or pond.

        The rain abated
midday, and I knew the next morning
I would see the field reappear as if rising.
I would see the fenceline discovered,
and, more, some ancestral bone, white now
as a root, would appear in the storm-gore
that would gag the creek, sagging in its bed.
I would find crows, those disbelievers, drowned
in their sleep, feathers strewn in the cattails,
their mouths filled with mud.

        But long before
dawn, I would be there as before, at the edge
of what could not be sailed or sounded, watching
moonlight move over the body of that
black depthlessness—and I would be lost
as if I were in some distant place.

Claudia Emerson
from *Pinion: An Elegy*

Death Stayed

It feels like creation,
walking in on dogs
in their caged life and

pointing, that spark
ordained, "God
and man joined as animals,"

when we pick. Clouds
roll up and down the lot,
enchantment really,

as the dog jumps at my wrist
to kiss or tear. You open up
and tell me what it feels,

the third that makes the drama,
the queer addition
animals offer, our motion

of picking life off a seesaw
up now above the clouds,
the car climbing home,

our corporal selves
writ again
with death stayed in a dog.

Terese Svoboda
first published in *The Yale Review*, vol. 89, no. 1, January 2001
also from *Treason*

OCTOBER 26

Doubt

Virginia Woolf committed suicide in 1941 when the German bombing campaign against England was at its peak and when she was reading Freud whom she had staved off until then.

Edith Stein, recently and controversially beatified by the Pope, who had successfully worked to transform an existential vocabulary into a theological one, was taken to Auschwitz in August, 1942.

Two years later Simone Weil died in a hospital in England—of illness and depression—determined to know what it is to know. She, as much as Woolf, sought salvation in a choice of words.

But multitudes succumb to the sorrow induced by an inexact vocabulary.

While a whole change in discourse is a sign of conversion, the alteration of a single word only signals a kind of doubt about the value of the surrounding words.

Poets tend to hover over words in this troubled state of mind. What holds them poised in this position is the occasional eruption of happiness.

While we would all like to know if the individual person is a phenomenon either culturally or spiritually conceived and why everyone doesn't kill everyone else, including themselves, since they can—poets act out the problem with their words.

Why not say "heart-sick" instead of "despairing"?
Why not say "despairing" instead of "depressed"?

Is there, perhaps, a quality in each person—hidden like a laugh inside a sob—that loves even more than it loves to live? If there is, can it be expressed in the form of the lyric line?

Dostoevsky defended his later religious belief, saying of his work, "Even in Europe there have never been atheistic expressions of such power. My hosannah has gone through a great furnace of doubt."

According to certain friends, Simone Weil would have given everything she wrote to be a poet. It was an ideal but she was wary of charm and the inauthentic. She saw herself as stuck in fact with a rational prose line for her surgery on modern thought. She might be the archetypal doubter but the language of the lyric was perhaps too uncertain.

As far as we know she wrote a play and some poems and one little prose poem called "Prelude."

Yet Weil could be called a poet, if Wittgenstein could, despite her own estimation of her writing, because of the longing for a transformative insight dominating her word choices.

In "Prelude" the narrator is an uprooted seeker who still hopes that a conversion will come to her from the outside. The desired teacher arrives bearing the best of everything, including delicious wine and bread, affection, tolerance, solidarity (people come and go) and authority. This is a man who even has faith and loves truth.

She is happy. Then suddenly, without any cause, he tells her it's over. She is out on the streets without direction, without memory. Indeed she is unable to remember even what he told her without his presence there to repeat it, this amnesia being the ultimate dereliction.

If memory fails, then the mind is air in a skull.
This loss of memory forces her to abandon hope for either rescue or certainty.

And now is the moment where doubt—as an active function—emerges and magnifies the world. It eliminates memory. And it turns eyesight so far outwards, the vision expands. A person feels as if she is the figure inside a mirror, looking outwards for her moves. She is a forgery.

When all the structures granted by common agreement fall away and that "reliable chain of cause and effect" that Hannah Arendt talks about—breaks—then a person's inner logic also collapses. She moves and sees at the same time, which is terrifying.

Yet strangely it is in this moment that doubt shows itself to be the physical double to belief; it is the quality that nourishes willpower, and the one that is the invisible engine behind every step taken.

Doubt is what allows a single gesture to have a heart.

In this prose poem Weil's narrator recovers her balance after a series of reactive revulsions to the surrounding culture by confessing to the most palpable human wish: that whoever he was, he loved her.

Hope seems to resist extermination as much as a roach does.

Hannah Arendt talks about the "abyss of nothingness that opens up before any deed that cannot be accounted for." Consciousness of this abyss is the source of belief for most converts. Weil's conviction that evil proves the existence of God is cut out of this consciousness.

Her Terrible Prayer—that she be reduced to a paralyzed nobody—desires an obedience to that moment where coming and going intersect before annihilation.

And her desire: "To be only an intermediary between the blank page and the poem" is a desire for a whole-heartedness that eliminates personality.

Virginia Woolf, a maestro of lyric resistance, was frightened by Freud's claustrophobic determinism since she had no ground of defense against it. The hideous vocabulary of mental science crushed her dazzling star-thoughts into powder and brought her latent despair into the open air.

Born into a family devoted to skepticism and experiment, she had made a superhuman effort at creating a prose-world where doubt was a mesmerizing and glorious force.

Anyone who tries, as she did, out of a systematic training in secularism, to forge a rhetoric of belief is fighting against the odds. Disappointments are everywhere waiting to catch you, and an ironic realism is so convincing.

Simone Weil's family was skeptical too, secular and attentive to the development of the mind. Her older brother fed her early sense of inferiority with his condescending intellectual putdowns. Later, her notebooks chart a superhuman effort at conversion to a belief in affliction as a sign of God's presence.

Her prose itself is tense with effort. After all, to convert by choice (that is, without a blast of revelation or a personal disaster) requires that you shift the names for things, and force a new language out of your mind onto the page.

You have to make yourself believe. Is this possible? Can you turn "void" into "God" by switching the words over and over again?

Any act of self-salvation is a problem because of death which always has the last laugh, and if there has been a dramatic and continual despair hanging over childhood, then it may even be impossible.

After all, can you call "doubt" "bewilderment" and suddenly be relieved?

Not if your mind has been fatally poisoned...But even then, it seems, the dream of having no doubt continues, finding its way into love and work where choices matter exactly as much as they don't matter—when history's things are working in your favor.

Fanny Howe
first published in *Seneca Review*, vol. XXX, no. 2, Fall 2000
also from *Gone*

Sinister

As if a distinction might be drawn at the edge of a
    continuum.
As if this might shake us by the teeth.

You know that vagrant at hogkilling time he goes
farm to farm collecting dried bladders.
This is the bone he stuck in your gate.

As if the salted beer foam and boiled egg were
repercussions of our own feeling,
as if the barn swallows told us nothing.

He burns a scent into his clothes
to cover the hogstink, he chews on cloves.

As if this sentence were a cliff
and a witness, that dry birdnote its postulate.

Shows up at The Triangle one Saturday a month,
sits across from the mirror.

As if transformation came
from the isomorphic pressure
of close attention. As if, tenting his fingers,
his beauty were purified by restraint.

Outside the package store, with that Polaroid
you gave me, I took his photograph.
I've had these sooty paw prints under my eyes,
he said, *since time out of mind.*

As if the sadness of pictures
had to do with our exclusion,
even from those in which we appear.

As though our theories unfit us for wholeness,
and the surfaces were crazed,
and there were not time
to recover the yolk of ourselves.

He admired his likeness. *My wife's blind,*
he told me. *Last night in the yard,*
fireflies come out. Fireflies, I said.
She nodded yes. Then I heard, far off,
what she heard, horseshoes clanging.

Forrest Gander
from *Science & Steepleflower*

Prince of the Powers of the Air

O alienate from God, O spirit accurst,
Forsaken of all good; I see thy fall
—Paradise Lost

In Florida, where these things can happen,
I was driving south in the dead of winter—
that is to say, a day scrubbed of cloud,
only the sycamores brown and sullen
against a sky from a fresco centuries old.
In the blue gone chalky but still luciferous,
a dark scream of wings arced like stone.
Black feathers fell to the grassy median.
A vulture, feeding on the center line,
hit by a car...I had spun over my life

like that once, when I was six.
The classroom had grown too close, the lesson long,
recess rewarded only after purgatory.
I laid my head on the desk and closed my eyes,
only to feel myself whirled into the Void,
though I didn't know the word.
I was the null to keep it company.
Who would bear me up if I fell? Oh, fall
from that high state of loneliness! Far below,
a tiny nun was busy, improving on a Bible story—

and now here you were, dark angel,
just the way she said you'd fallen from heaven.
Had you tired of the Alone never being home?
Did you want the dead for your own?
I circled back. How to approach a hurt vulture?
But your wings were neatly folded.
Your bald nun's head was up, as if you were through
with prayer to a higher power—or was it real,
that whiff you caught again of flattened 'possum?
For he was afterward an hungred.

When I fell out of love, I would remember this.

Debora Greger
first published in *The Yale Review*, vol. 88, no. 3, July 2000

The Dogs in Dutch Paintings

How shall I not love them, snoozing
right through the Annunciation? They inhabit
the outskirts of every importance, sprawl
dead center in each oblivious household.

They're digging at fleas or snapping at scraps,
dozing with noble abandon while a boy
bells their tails. Often they present their rumps
in the foreground of some martyrdom.

What Christ could lean so unconcernedly
against a table leg, the feast above continuing?
Could the Virgin in her joy match this grace
as a hound sagely ponders an upturned turtle?

No scholar at his huge book will capture
my eye so well as the skinny haunches,
the frazzled tails and serene optimism
of the least of these mutts, curled

in the corners of the world's dazzlement.

David Graham
first published in *Poetry International*, issue II
also from *Stutter Monk*

october 3 0

An Ideal Woman

I know a man who put together an ideal woman
from all his desires: the hair
he took from a woman in the window of a passing bus,
the forehead from a cousin who died young, the hands
from a teacher he had as a kid, the cheeks from a little girl,
his childhood love, the mouth from a woman he noticed
in a phone booth, the thighs
from a young woman lying on the beach,
the alluring gaze from this one, the eyes from that one,
the waistline from a newspaper ad.
From all these he put together
a woman he truly loved. And when he died, they came,
all the women—legs chopped off, eyes plucked out, faces slashed in half,
severed hands, hair ripped out, a gash where a mouth used to be,
and demanded what was theirs, theirs, theirs,
dismembered his body, tore his flesh, and left him
only his long-lost soul.

Yehuda Amichai
first published in *The Marlboro Review*, no. 7, Winter/Spring 1999
translated by Chana Bloch and Chana Kronfeld
also from *Open Closed Open*

Ghosts in the Stacks

You know the signs: the sweet flower's
Scent in the bare alcove, the chilling
Cold corner by the unused desk,
The damp that seeps like sour water
Into each bone's marrow, lights
That circle a sleeping reader's head
Like a wreath in motion, the thud
On the roof on a windless day,
Or the familiar shadowy form that slips
From a carrel and floats to the floor,
The shy figure that always moves
Around the corner just as you look,
The one in the derby and the tattered
Sleeve, the beckoning fair one
That weighs you down like a low cloud
On a day when the hills are shrouded
And the trees are silent through
Hanging fog, the tinkle of crystal
Sprinkling the back staircase as from
A shattered chandelier, whispers
Of printed syllables turning on themselves
In sibilant discussion late in the day,

A groan as of bending heavy steel
When the last light is turned off
Just before the locking of the door,
The giggle that follows, patter
Of pages, and the blue glow of electrical
Screens searching themselves for answers
That cannot be found, and row on row on row
The books where dreams are bound and stamped
And stored, where all together, letter, mark,
And letter, the word we have always sought
May finally be written for all who see to see.

In memoriam, Richard Kirkwood,
1927–1993

R. H. W. Dillard
from *Sallies*

november 1

Saints' Logic

Love the drill, confound the dentist.
Love the fever that carries me home.
Meat of exile. Salt of grief.
This much, indifferent

affliction might yield. But how
when the table is God's own board
and grace must be said in company?
If hatred were honey, as even

the psalmist persuaded himself,
then Agatha might be holding
her breasts on the plate for reproach.
The plate is decidedly

ornamental, and who shall say that pity's
not, at this remove? Her gown
would be stiff with embroidery whatever
the shape of the body beneath.

Perhaps in heaven God can't hide
his face. So the wounded
are given these gowns to wear
and duties that teach them the leverage

of pain. Agatha listens with special
regard to the barren, the dry,
to those with tumors where milk
should be, to those who nurse

for hire. Let me swell,
let me not swell. Remember the child,
how its fingers go blind as it sucks.
Bartholomew, flayed, intervenes

for the tanners. Catherine for millers,
whose wheels are of stone. Sebastian
protects the arrowsmiths, and John
the chandlers, because he was boiled

in oil. We borrow our light
where we can, here's begging the pardon
of tallow and wick. And if, as we've tried
to extract from the prospect, we'll each

have a sign to be known by at last—
a knife, a floursack, a hammer, a pot—
the saints can stay,
the earth won't entirely have given us up.

Linda Gregerson
from *The Woman Who Died in Her Sleep*

november 2

The Downtown Bus

Out through the neighborhood with nothing more
Than home in mind, as the circling dog
Scuffs leaves along the curb, turns, sniffs, salutes,
Then races back then races off again,
Past Mrs. West who will not take the bus
But watches from her side yard where she waves
The passengers "good-bye" at seven-ten
And then "hello, hello" at five-fifteen,
When they unfold, walk forward, and step down,
Wait for the bus to clear, then eddy off
In twos and threes, take corners out of sight
As Mr. Probasco, who also waves,
Stands in his garden tying up the vine
That should have quit him weeks before, he says,
But keeps producing at its August best,

And the plain-faced houses lining the sidewalks
In shingled, bricked, and clapboard evidence,
And the half-bare oaks, colorful and gaunt,
As the street runs on, tunneling its limbs,
Or opening mid-block before the house
Where Wiggins sits, earmuffed in headphones,
Hunched with tuning his shortwave radio,
While next door Hooper's son honks through his sax
So the whole scale solos down into one
Long-complaining half-flat failing middle C
Which Wiggins hears through every frequency...
World News a monotone, Hooper's middle C,
Probasco standing halfway down his vine,
And Mrs. West, who knows its cancer, waving
The split infinitive of coming home.

Crosstown, home edges, creeps, and idles in
The evening traffic's legislative stop;
Indoors, it haunts from room to room as though
It were the echo, smell, uneven floor
Of parents primed and dressed for dinner out;
Side yard, it is the small self in the hedge
Half hidden like a lookout or a stray
Arrested in the quiet watchfulness
By which all cars slow to the one that stops,
Opens and admits into the sealed
Particular of simply going on;
        And now the downtown bus again, turning,
Slowing, braking to a door-wide rocking halt
With no one stepping off, only the driver,
Half cigarette and gravely bored,

Who checks his mirrors, elbows-in the door,
Then gazing absently, leans forward and shifts
Into the diesel's blue-smoke rag and wheeze
Throating its pleuritic, emphysemic sax
In hoarse successive half notes down the street—
So Hooper's middle C blends in, dissolves,
Then surfaces again, the bus rounding
A corner where its brake-lights wink from sight,
As Mrs. West now drops her wave, turns back,
Probasco watching, whistling "Hi ho,"
She charting careful headway toward her porch
Till both hands pumping one-twos up the steps
She leans into the front door and it gives
As though the entire balance of the house
Angled where she fumbles for the light.

Inside's a speculation down one hall
Into another, then three connecting rooms
As one, two, three—three lights go on,
While up the street a gradual of yards
Filters the long, arterially fine light
Through back-stitched, overlapping twig and branch
Stripped to a half-leaf, clinging, patchwork spread
By which the many little depths of field,
The planes and verticals of home recede
Into the mild coagulum of now
Where sun and afternoon are going down
Into the brief remissions of four names—
Probasco, Hooper, Wiggins, Mrs. West,
Till even Hooper's son gives up his sax
In time for what already's happened next:

There was the downtown bus again, unscheduled,
Barging and bulking box-high down the street,
Ragged and loud, start-chug-stall-stop, start-stop,
Until the driver braked, climbed down, walked round,
And holding up the hood, "Flat dead," he said,
Next turned, eased five steps off, lit up; looked back:
But then Probasco there, toolbox in hand,
And the dog tugging, barking, and wagging,
And Wiggins, Hooper, Hooper's son, under-
neath, and their eight legs sprawling randomly,
Four flashlights winking up through wires and hoses,
Each elbowing tools, all handing them round,
All talking in the tribal memory
Of how things work when they no longer work.

And then some loose wire tightened, the driver
Tried the door. Locked. Tried again; then looked
    instead,
Then waved the others over,
                        who from the curb
Saw posture perfect, large-hatted and gloved
At ease behind the wheel and eyes ahead
Like Hepburn at the apex of her art,
Mrs. West, key in hand—who starting up,
Cocked her head, listened, touched the brake, sat tall,
Shoved into gear, then staring eagles through
The bug-pocked windshield's upright tinted glass
Accelerated hard, braked, cornered hard,
Wound the diesel tight again, circled back,
Slowing, waving, grinding gears, hitting the horn,
Block-round and waving and the horn going,
Dog barking, we five watching. Drove that way.
Drove all the late fall light from sight that way.

Wyatt Prunty
first published in *Five Points*, vol. III, no. 3,
    Spring/Summer 1999
also from *Unarmed and Dangerous*

The Prodigal Son considers
a diplomatic career

Out of respect for the elders of the village where he finds himself sober for the first time in years, he shows reverence for their gods and doesn't laugh at their icons. They believe him and make him a holy man. Fearing that the villagers might be contagious, and thinking only of himself, he seals their wounds and concocts potions for their pains. They trust him and make him a healer. To show his vulnerability, he bathes in a small pond with the men, eats from their unwashed plates, sleeps with their women. As they parade by his bed, the villagers dry the cold sweat from his forehead and call him a martyr. He tells them that his condition is temporary. When he regains his strength and gets up, they call him a prophet. He predicts that from time to time, in their sleep, the women will hear the voices of the gods. The elders tell him that the women have always heard the voices of the gods. They call him a fraud and make him chief.

Dionisio D. Martínez
from *Climbing Back*

november 4

In the House

I am attracted by the dust
and silence of an upper shelf,
the strange air

that causes linoleum
to bulge in the cellar.
I know the walls come to hug

like grizzlies
if you stare at them too long,
and the kitchen knife

wants to be held.
I sense the aromas of sex,
the delicate, stale drift

of arguments and spite
no amount of cleaning will solve.
I know when love goes

it slips through all insulation,
forgets your name,
becomes sky.

Stephen Dunn
from *New and Selected Poems, 1974–1994*

november 5

My Husband Discovers Poetry

Because my husband would not read my poems,
I wrote one about how I did not love him.
In lines of strict iambic pentameter,
I detailed his coldness, his lack of humor.
It felt good to do this.

Stanza by stanza, I grew bolder and bolder.
Towards the end, struck by inspiration,
I wrote about my old boyfriend,
a boy I had not loved enough to marry
but who could make me laugh and laugh.
I wrote about a night years after we parted
when my husband's coldness drove me from the house
and back to my old boyfriend.
I even included the name of a seedy motel
well-known for hosting quickies.
I have a talent for verisimilitude.

In sensuous images, I described
how my boyfriend and I stripped off our clothes,
got into bed, and kissed and kissed,
then spent half the night telling jokes,
many of them about my husband.
I left the ending deliberately ambiguous.
Then I hid the poem away
in an old trunk in the basement.

You know how this story ends,
how my husband one day loses something,
goes down into the basement,
and rummages through the old trunk,
how he uncovers the hidden poem
and sits down to read it.

But do you hear the strange sounds
that floated up the stairs that day,
the sounds of an animal, its paw caught
in one of those traps with teeth of steel?
Do you see the wounded creature
at the bottom of the stairs,
his shoulders hunched over and shaking,
his fist in his mouth and choking back sobs?
It was my husband paying tribute to my art.

Diane Lockward
from *Against Perfection*
also from *Eve's Red Dress*

november 6

Dusk and the Wife

                 in with the child
who drops like a weighted lure,
flashes down, down to sleep.
The husband suburban, pulls up
a bright folder called Taxes
in the coming dark (his young
coworker in Baja, her unfettered
surface away on vacation).

In the coming dark the grey
squirrel ripples across outside
time-lapse.

So many leaves to the trees
this many   this many.

                What is it then?

He opens to the red head, her
sheer bra pulled down
lush strap hard pressed
to the fullest curve of her breast.
She slightly bites her lip
while the wife half a dream away
is pressed by his good friend
against a building. They could be
in Florence—all these angels.

A. V. Christie
first published in Quarterly West, no. 54, Spring/Summer 2002

My Other Life

1.

He owns a smoke shop, the bastard.
He reads books that take months to get through.
He says, Go ahead, live a little, to strangers
when they sniff an expensive cigar.
This is the man who lives my other life.
A master of smoke and other disguises.

2.

A miserable failure, he covets nothing
I envy: Not the women or the money,
not the hot thigh of success.
He admires my persistence, the leather of my skin.
He admires my insistence on answers.
A man with a future, he says with a smile.

3.

I ask if I can help, mix the burleys and virginias,
sort the meerschaums and the briars.
I ask if I can sleep with his wife,
steal the love of his children,
drink the last of his brandy.
He laughs as if I'd made a joke.
He hands me the keys to his empty house.

Peter Serchuk
first published in *Mid-American Review*, vol. XIX, no. 2, Spring 1999

Dawn, With Cardinals

After separating from Penelope, Ulysses
takes a smallish cottage out of town,
bounded by deep woods on one side, a golf course
on the other where children sled or startle frogs,
depending on the season.

Crows strut their turf beneath the plum trees,
furl their capes and bob like drunks.
Of the night birds, owls map the taller pines
with their iridescent eyes and moon hens
peck at drops of evening dew.

When the divorce is done, he'll move
to an island some miles out,
where he may settle on a narrow road
beside a spit of sand—beyond that, sea.
He could earn a modest pension
crafting bird feeders from mill scraps,
keep a brace of hunting dogs for company
and rake the silt for clams and oysters at low tide.

For now, he contents himself
recording local bird calls,
but forgets them quickly as he learns, save
the cardinal's song, a slight and mournful chirping
heard each morning just outside his porch.

And always the same two birds—
she quarrelsome, he quiet or detached or maybe
    mystified
at his helplessness to make a difference. Or, cocksure
he does, you see it in the ebony beak, crimson breast.
Look, the birdbath is full of cool clear water and still
she carries on like that, sharp
staccato chirps, high pitched, unwavering.
He with flutters but no sound, something holding on
inside him, something faintly chipped.
Not that Ulysses planned to wake so early
every morning. Sometimes you don't believe
in ritual for days or weeks, until it's a proven thing,
but here it is, persistent and regular.

Ulysses lets dawn filter through the screened porch.
First no light, then light.
First no birds, then song.
No wind; wind.

Jeffrey Levine
first published in *The Missouri Review*, vol. XXII, no. 1,
    1999
also from *Mortal, Everlasting*

A Misunderstanding

I thought Zen poems
were supposed to sound wise.

Now I'm going to buy
as much beer as five dollars

can buy and drink it
right here on the sofa.

Maggie Nelson
from *Shiner*

Voices

When I hear my lover singing, I sing, too.
   The tune? Something I make up in my head.
Words come and go—wind, mood, mode—
   listening and loving, I sing her what Henry
     said:
   No one else got music like you do.

The sound of music tells us who is who—
   a patterned mind, shapenotes in the dark,
rhythms (the thunder) pounding down the air...
   By pairs we populate imaginary arks
   and climb great mountains to paint a grander
     view.

Brash and raw like crows in morning rain,
   Achilles' war cry and mad Ajax's lament
pierce my dry heart. When Virgil sings for Rome
   (sings of arms and the man who founded a
     new race)
   I think of Troy in ashes and of Dido left to burn.

Time lies on the dead as they sleep in each
     other's arms.
   The celestial harmonies play on unheard.
Here is the day like a warm stone in my hand,
   the earth going round and round on its
     carousel
   as if, after life, the singing goes on and on.

F. D. Reeve
first published in *The Hudson Review*, vol. LII, no. 1,
   Spring 1999

november 11

Across the River

              a bull moose waits
    (for something)
to cross the river. Finally it crosses.
    You want to link the moose
to the pain in your chest
    but to compare
a moose's efforts to ascend a riverbank
    at dusk, in the heat,
to your own life

so you watch it go, and let the impulse go
    with it, over and out
of view of the zero stars
    governing a sky
increasingly savage in its clearness.

Brian Henry

first published in *The Kenyon Review,* New Series, vol. XXIV, no. 3/4, Summer/Fall 2002

NOVEMBER 12

The Perch

There is a fork in a branch
of an ancient, enormous maple,
one of a grove of such trees,
where I climb sometimes and sit and look out
over miles of valleys and low hills.
Today on skis I took a friend
to show her the trees. We set out
down the road, turned in at
the lane which a few weeks ago,
when the trees were almost empty
and the November snows had not yet come,
lay thickly covered in bright red
and yellow leaves, crossed the swamp,
passed the cellar hole holding
the remains of the 1850s farmhouse
that had slid down into it by stages
in the thirties and forties, followed
the overgrown logging road
and came to the trees. I climbed up
to the perch, and this time looked
not into the distance but at
the tree itself, its trunk
contorted by the terrible struggle
of that time when it had its hard time.
After the trauma it grows less solid.
It may be some such time now comes upon me.

It would have to do with the unaccomplished,
and with the attempted marriage
of solitude and happiness. Then a rifle
sounded, several times, quite loud,
from across the valley, percussions
of the custom of male mastery
over the earth—the most graceful,
most alert of the animals
being chosen to die. I looked
to see if my friend had heard,
but she was stepping about on her skis,
studying the trees, smiling to herself,
her lips still filled, for all
we had drained them, with hundreds
and thousands of kisses. Just then
she looked up—the way, from low
to high, the god blesses—and the blue
of her eyes shone out of the black
and white of bark and snow, as lovers
who are walking on a freezing day
touch icy cheek to icy cheek,
kiss, then shudder to discover
the heat waiting inside their mouths.

Galway Kinnell
from *A New Selected Poems*

november 13

A Man May Change

As simply as a self-effacing bar of soap
escaping by indiscernible degrees in the wash water
is how a man may change
and still hour by hour continue in his job.
There in the mirror he appears to be on fire
but here at the office he is dust.
So long as there remains a little moisture in the stains,
he stands easily on the pavement
and moves fluidly through the corridors. If only one
cloud can be seen, it is enough to know of others,
and life stands on the brink. It rains
or it doesn't, or it rains and it rains again.
But let it go on raining for forty days and nights
or let the sun bake the ground for as long,
and it isn't life, just life, anymore, it's living.
In the meantime, in the regular weather of ordinary days,
it sometimes happens that a man has changed
so slowly that he slips away
before anyone notices
and lives and dies before anyone can find out.

Marvin Bell
from *Nightworks: Poems 1962–2000*

Pieces

The queen moves with unbounded liberty.
Slant-eyed, a bishop offers up a prayer,
A horse-faced gallant full of chivalry
Enters the family trade, an officer.

A rook, high as a silo, lets fire fall,
Then ends its run behind a remnant pawn.
The king strolls past his garden's rose-grown wall
To issue statements from the castle lawn.

Only the pawns, bald-domed as army ants,
Urged to the common good by stripes and prayers,
Regard the board, cursed with their consciousness
Of all the horror of those empty squares.

Paul Lake
from *Walking Backward*

november 15

Your Hands

I.

In your hands
I fuse wheat
and the sky's edge.
Look at them, they thin out
before my hands
and blindly break the darkness of the dawn.

II.

Love comes to a house ablaze
and celebrated by the spirits of winter.

In your hands
I find refuges and mills
in them, the birds make their nests
of imaginary migrations.

In your hands
the first threads of rain
emerge
the fragrance of grass
after the daring
nights of love.
I paint in the peace of all the
spaces
and you at my side like the
sound of that which returns.

Marjorie Agosín
from *Starry Night*
translated from Spanish by Mary G. Berg

NOVEMBER 16

On a Stanza by Rilke

Difficult, isn't it?, to love these high-topped
foul-mouthed teens, this baggy threesome
in shorts and T-shirts—a torn one screaming,

as though it were informative or funny, Eat Me!
Sure, each was somebody's baby once—
this Beavis roughhousing with his Butt-head

buddies: chunky look-alikes, wanting
nothing more in the world right now
than to kick some ass in a game of fast-

break Two-on-One. Sometimes energy
has an odor and takes up a lot of space.
Thunk: somebody hits one. And immediately

a single gut-propelled syllable—Yes!—
spins through the gym, then echoes upward,
as if this voice meant to swallow the ceiling

that's higher than a steeple's. Next door,
in fact, they're actually building one—
or trying to. There's a half-done shell

and, on the grass, a huge bell by a sign
that says: Future Home of Grace Church.
Curiously, the makers are also believers:

I overheard one of them at a garage sale,
telling how he'd brought his family from Texas
to give his "brethren" a hand. They're not

the only ones, either; when I see them all
out there, during the day, measuring or carrying
or pounding on something, the parking lot's

crowded with silver trailers and cars
with out-of-state plates. Yes, the man said,
they were happy here thus far. So in that

they're like these boys: still strangers
to their grown-almost-to-adult-size bodies,
but pleased, why not?, with what

they've learned. Like the best way to hang
from a rim without snapping it, to slap the creaking
backboard as they test their newfound strength.

Do they feel like Supermen? Well, good for them—
but something still urges me to invoke the rules,
report them on the sly the way I did some-

times at practice: how else to get back at the one
who bullied me, the one who threatened
to piss in my mouth during showers?

Well, life's vulgar, I hear my eighth-grade coach say.
And isn't it? In the training room,
I put on the headphones that sing to me:

relax, and later, *pump up!*, and then a group
of preschoolers wanders into the gym,
assembled under watchful eyes. Whose?

—Camp-leader's? Baby-sitter's? Teacher's?
The hoops to these kids are higher than heaven,
so they roll a ball on the floor. And the teens

go off hungry to raid the machines,
to bang on the TV stashed under a counter
in the so-called supervisor's office: it's hard

not to judge them harshly, though my own son's
almost their age. There are too many people
in the world. As for the faithful, raising the church—

who'll struggle soon with that bell it takes
a two-story crane to lift—is it true what we
like to believe? That *for them existence*

is still enchanted. Still beginning
in a hundred places. A playing of pure powers
no one can touch and not kneel to and marvel.

Thomas Swiss
from *Rough Cut*

november 17

Those Graves in Rome

There are places where the eye can starve,
But not here. Here, for example, is
The Piazza Navona, & here is his narrow room
Overlooking the Steps & the crowds of sunbathing
Tourists. And here is the Protestant Cemetery
Where Keats & Joseph Severn join hands
Forever under a little shawl of grass
And where Keats's name isn't even on
His gravestone, because it is on Severn's,
And Joseph Severn's infant son is buried
Two modest, grassy steps behind them both.
But you'd have to know the story—how bedridden
Keats wanted the inscription to be
Simple, & unbearable: "Here lies one
Whose name is writ in water." On a warm day,
I stood here with my two oldest friends.
I thought, then, that the three of us would be
Indissoluble at the end, & also that
We would all die, of course. And not die.
And maybe we should have joined hands at that
Moment. We didn't. All we did was follow
A lame man in a rumpled suit who climbed
A slight incline of graves blurring into
The passing marble of other graves to visit
The vacant home of whatever is not left
Of Shelley & Trelawney. That walk uphill must
Be hard if you can't walk. At the top, the man
Wheezed for breath; sweat beaded his face,
And his wife wore a look of concern so
Habitual it seemed more like the way
Our bodies, someday, will have to wear stone.

Later that night, the three of us strolled,
Our arms around each other, through the Via
Del Corso & toward the Piazza di Espagna
As each street grew quieter until
Finally we heard nothing at the end
Except the occasional scrape of our own steps,
And so said good-bye. Among such friends,
Who never allowed anything, still alive,
To die, I'd almost forgotten that what
Most people leave behind them disappears.
Three days later, staying alone in a cheap
Hotel in Naples, I noticed a child's smeared
Fingerprint on a bannister. It
Had been indifferently preserved beneath
A patina of varnish applied, I guessed, after
The last war. It seemed I could almost hear
His shout, years later, on that street. But this
Is speculation, & no doubt the simplest fact
Could shame me. Perhaps the child was from
Calabria, & went back to it with
A mother who failed to find work, & perhaps
The child died there, twenty years ago,
Of malaria. It was so common then—
The children crying to the doctors for quinine.
And to the tourists, who looked like doctors, for quinine.

It was so common you did not expect an aria,
And not much on a gravestone, either—although
His name is on it, & weathered stone still wears
His name—not the way a girl might wear
The too large, faded blue workshirt of
A lover as she walks thoughtfully through
The Via Fratelli to buy bread, shrimp,
And wine for the evening meal with candles &
The laughter of her friends, & later the sweet
Enkindling of desire; but something else, something
Cut simply in stone by hand & meant to last
Because of the way a name, any name,
Is empty. And not empty. And almost enough.

Larry Levis
from *The Selected Levis*

Daphne and Laura and So Forth

He was the one who saw me
just before I changed,
before bark/fur/snow closed over
my mouth, before my eyes grew eyes.

I should not have shown fear,
or so much leg.

His look of disbelief—
I didn't mean to!
Just, her neck was so much more
fragile than I thought.

The gods don't listen to reason,
they need what they need—
that suntan line at the bottom
of the spine, those teeth like mouthwash,
that drop of sweat pearling
the upper lip—
or that's what gets said in court.

Why talk when you can whisper?
Rustle, like dried leaves.
Under the bed.

It's ugly here, but safer.
I have eight fingers
and a shell, and live in corners.
I'm free to stay up all night.
I'm working on
these ideas of my own:
venom, a web, a hat,
some last resort.

He was running,
he was asking something,
he wanted something or other.

Margaret Atwood
from *Morning in the Burned House*

November 19

for Beth Ann Fennelly

Do I still like to think
of myself in the third
person? I do, I mean,
he does. He liked, too,
to read the paper on
the couch with a cup
of coffee in his robe
daydreaming of a girl
he hadn't met who
liked doing a pirouette
in an ankle-length
silvery gray skirt
that flares in a full
circle when she does so.
Not that she planned
to do so onstage, but
it was nice to know
she could. She thought
of herself as a fair warrior
on the strand hearing
the warring voices
of the sea, and he was
her demon lover, who
liked sitting around
dreaming of the things
he liked, like the girl
who shoplifted lipstick
because she liked
the sound of its name.

David Lehman
from *The Daily Mirror*

Ballad

(after the Spanish)

forgive me if i laugh
you are so sure of love
you are so young
and i too old to learn of love.

the rain exploding
in the air is love
the grass excreting her
green wax is love
and stones remembering
past steps is love,
but you. you are too young
for love
and i too old.

once. what does it matter
when or who, i knew
of love.
i fixed my body
under his and went
to sleep in love
all trace of me
was wiped away

forgive me if i smile
young heiress of a naked dream
you are so young
and i too old to learn to love.

Sonia Sanchez
from *Shake Loose My Skin: New and Selected Poems*
also from *Homegirls and Handgrenades*

The Sausage Parade

When the Roman Empire, like an overcooked
kielbasa, began to shrivel up, Christians made them

illegal. Peperone, Calabrese, Sanguinaccio:
from speakeasy kitchens, butter, lard and onion

hissed. Holsteiner, Genoa, Cervelats:
20 centuries later, the High-Production

Pickle Injector ensures a steady supply.
Presskopf, Figatelli, Jagdwurst:

could it be their names? That each must form
to its casing? Whose nose hasn't longed

for the scent of fennel and pork?
Who can say *sausage* isn't onomatopoeic?

"Cook them slowly," *Dishes of the World*
insists. "To keep from bursting, prick."

Robert was my first: red pepper, pimento
pinch. Chorizo de Lomo. Taught me

sizzle, avoidance of smokehouse shrink. Never
would I settle for less. Byron Speer—oatmeal, vinegar,

thyme—loved to go shirtless March to November.
Skin silken gravy, oven-baked. Chuck, a Drisheen—

running ox, tansy-tinged; two parts blood
to one part cream. Helmut, all-hands-in-the-pot

simmering shallots, 6'2," 220; sweetness
soaked (lawyer by day, Braunschweiger

by night); Dylan a Rotwurst, *keeping sausage—*
sage, chestnut purée, lemon, Muscadet—

would have kept and kept....

The man I love doesn't love my bread-crumb-soaked,
sputtering-pork-and-chipolata past—

salsiccie, budini, zamponi.
But the past is long as Italy's boot.

It is made of leeks, red wine,
crushed garlic, whole peppercorns.

There is plenty of room at the table.

Martha Silano
from *What the Truth Tastes Like*

The Music We Dance To

Winnowed along the earth or whirled along the sky,
Life lives on. It is the lives, the lives, the lives that die.
Lucretius

For instance, the last time I saw my friend
alive—though I didn't know it was the last
time, or I would have said something, put a wedge
in the revolving door, to stop its panes
from breaking up her sandy hair, turning
her reflection out into the New York City street.
But perhaps not, for I have always liked the apocryphal
St. Francis who, asked how he would spend his last day,
answered "keep on hoeing the garden."
So, perhaps, knowingly, I would still have given
Beth the flowers that others had given me—
an over-generous bouquet, mingling the blooms
of summer, and of spring, their conflicting
fragrances, odd lengths of stem, falling over
into the porcelain box full of water.
I didn't know what to do with them; I was leaving
for Seattle and couldn't imagine carrying
that severed field, sloshing, to the other side
of the continent. Beth's arms were empty,
she had helped pick the flowers, was,
in a sense, transporting them back
to their origins, back to the impulse
that had first sent them to me,
and she gathered them up gladly,
maneuvering their fragile coronas
through the narrowness of the glass door.

I don't mean to suggest her going
was anything like Persephone being swept out
of view, the flowers falling back
to earth, dissevered, dying.
It was a real cab she got into,
not the one we invented the night before
to escape a boring crowd. When we talked
about this habit people have of disappearing,
we meant how our chums from college had wanted to go home
too early, though it wasn't to "home," but some hotel
or friend's apartment; we had all been able to meet, precisely,
because we were away from 'home,' had vacated its premises,
assumed a somewhere else, 'behind' or 'ahead' of us—
where we would be awaited with longing,
like those small grains Demeter hoarded
to outlast the winter. In my hotel room, we kept on talking
while I packed. Then, a moment of quiet—like the wound
that uprooting leaves in the earth—began eroding
into canyons, abysmal rifts. Much later,
I was to connect the ease with which she had slipped away
to the cancer, its blood red seed beginning to sprout,
as it must have been possible, so long ago,
to hear the grasses being crushed,
beneath the rim of that black chariot wheel,
as the Lord of the Underworld coasted into view.

I kept packing, cramming everything
into my suitcase—reminded of how Unamuno said
we were all travelers who stuffed whatever
we could into our luggage, then trimmed away what
did not fit—though it was the night itself
that the clock's fluorescent hands were pruning
down to nothing. In the morning, when she ran
toward a cab, pulled away forever from the curb,
I remembered how, in college, we always danced together
to *I Heard It Through The Grapevine,*—the same way
I would hear of her death, called
from a warm bath to the phone,
thinking it was a joke, as the chilling water
dripped and pooled on the floor around me.
The last time I danced with her,
we were holding hands, twenty of so of us,
in a line of bodies, whirling through a darkened student union,
the Charlie Chaplin movie flickering
on the opposite wall, mingling our hands, our faces,
with bits of the tramp's twirling cane, his sad expression.
I followed Beth's white blouse, an ordinary white blouse,
as we rushed ahead, but she didn't pull me along;
it was the momentum of the circle itself, the force
of those leaping bodies, a merry-go-round of flesh, linked
hand to hand to the one before and the one after—a wheel
like that other wheel, black spokes, rim of iron, moving
faster and faster until the velocity, the whip effect
at the end of the line, began to snap us off,
one by one, flying into the darkness.

Rebecca Seiferle
from *The Music We Dance To*

november 23

The Last Picture

"This is the last picture of me
standing," my friend says, pointing
into the album during my visit
to his apartment where everything's
within easy reach for someone in a chair,
the center of the floor open
as if for a dance, and all I can do
is nod and stare, caught
in the headlights of those words
as simple as ice on a road's
curve, as penetrating as the sound of metal
rolling over on itself like tickets
in a thunderous drum of chance.

In the photo he's a lanky twenty,
more than half a life ago, his legs
slightly spread, taking the measure
of the earth, a smile that speaks
the sun at noon, though he does not look down
to see himself shadow-free
in every direction.
Simplified to black-and-white,
Leo isn't looking anywhere that day except
out at me, who's been exposed,
the one sitting by choice.

Afterwards I will imagine other
last pictures, for other lives—
this is the last picture of me
believing in God, this is the last picture
of me making love, this is the last
picture of me writing a poem—
and albums will collect and fill
with last pictures, a great and drifting snow,
while the photographers of last pictures,
those self-renunciatory saints,
work in obscurity and the knowledge
that a last picture's never
a last picture until it's too late.

For now, though I'm still marveling at how
the plainest English—quiet, matter-of-fact,
a mild disturbance of sound waves
between pictures of parents and sisters,
farm-scenes—can shrapnel through the air
and make spines anywhere send a blizzard
of electrical information up and down
their long and living strands.

I am afraid to stand up, or try to.
I start taking pictures in my head, fast.
I pose with Leo for a picture
we both know is already developing.

Philip Dacey
first published in *Shenandoah*, vol. 47, no. 3, Fall 1997

NOVEMBER 24

In Hilo Hospital

Mr. Yamaguchi is washing his wife's *yukata*.
I hear the water gushing from the faucet
on the other side of the hospital wall.

He washes and rinses then rinses again
to be sure all scum is gone.
Then the water gurgles down the drainpipe.

Each night he washes. I listen from behind
the metal patch over my right eye
which sees nothing, my ears

just beginning to hear again
after the air bag's explosion.
Mr. Yamaguchi sleeps all night

on the hospital floor beside his wife's dying.
Because the nurses tell me this,
I know when I hear the tap water flow

his tears mix in the slosh. He scrubs
his own underwear too. Percocet
does not drown the sound of his shirtsleeves'

tangle or the coming of morning
when he must once more rise to greet her
with cheer, kiss her brow, gather

the dark blue and white of her favorite garment
to cover her shoulders, begin cooking.
I smell the pungence of his pure

attention. I hear the feet of the sun climbing.
Did I say that I cannot see?
I would like to see him washing her *yukata*.

Joan Swift
from *The Tiger Iris*

The God Who Loves You

It must be troubling for the god who loves you
To ponder how much happier you'd be today
Had you been able to glimpse your many futures.
It must be painful for him to watch you on Friday evenings
Driving home from the office, content with your week—
Three fine houses sold to deserving families—
Knowing as he does exactly what would have happened
Had you gone to your second choice for college,
Knowing the roommate you'd have been allotted
Whose ardent opinions on painting and music
Would have kindled in you a lifelong passion.
A life thirty points above the life you're living
On any scale of satisfaction. And every point
A thorn in the side of the god who loves you.
You don't want that, a large-souled man like you
Who tries to withhold from your wife the day's disappointments
So she can save her empathy for the children.
And would you want this god to compare your wife
With the woman you were destined to meet on the other campus?
It hurts you to think of him ranking the conversation
You'd have enjoyed over there higher in insight
Than the conversation you're used to.

And think how this loving god would feel
Knowing that the man next in line for your wife
Would have pleased her more than you ever will
Even on your best days, when you really try.
Can you sleep at night believing a god like that
Is pacing his cloudy bedroom, harassed by alternatives
You're spared by ignorance? The difference between what is
And what could have been will remain alive for him
Even after you cease existing, after you catch a chill
Running out in the snow for the morning paper,
Losing eleven years that the god who loves you
Will feel compelled to imagine scene by scene
Unless you come to the rescue by imagining him
No wiser than you are, no god at all, only a friend
No closer than the actual friend you made at college,
The one you haven't written in months. Sit down tonight
And write him about the life you can talk about
With a claim to authority, the life you've witnessed,
Which for all you know is the life you've chosen.

Carl Dennis
from *Practical Gods*

November 26, 1992:
Thanksgiving at the Sea Ranch,
Contemplating Metempsychosis

You tried coming back as a spider
I was too fast for you. As you
climbed my ankle, I swept you off, I ground you

to powder under my winter boot.
Shall I cherish the black widow,
I asked, because he is you?

You were cunning: you became
the young, the darkly masked
raccoon that haunts my deck.

Each night for weeks you tiptoed
toward the sliding doors, your paws
imploring, eyes aglow. *Let me in,*

Let me back in, you hissed,
swaying beside the tubbed fuchsia,
shadowing the fancy cabbage in its Aztec pot.

And you've been creatures of the air and sea,
the hawk that sees into my skull, the seal that
    barks
a few yards from the picnic on the shore.

Today you chose a different life, today
you're trying to stumble
through the tons of dirt that hold you down:

you're a little grove of mushrooms,
rising from the forest floor you loved.
Bob saw you in the windbreak—

November mushrooms, he said,
off-white and probably poisonous.
Shall I slice you for the feast?

If I eat you will I die back into your arms?
Shall I give thanks for God's wonders
because they all are you, and you are them?

The meadow's silent, its dead grasses
ignore each other and the evening walkers
who trample them. What will you be,

I wonder, when the night wind rises?
Come back as yourself, in your blue parka,
your plaid flannel shirt with the missing button.

These fields that hum and churn with life
are empty. There is nowhere
you are not, nowhere

you are not not.

Sandra M. Gilbert
from *Ghost Volcano*

Famous Poems of the Past Explained

Imagine how much I hope, imagine
what a fan I am, how I want to read
wisdom, yes, and applaud such confidence.
I was about to step when I noticed
there was no world there, so I turned
quickly searching for foot-sized solidity
to enhance my belief in the future.
Then I noticed the little yellow flowers
that sprang timely in my footprints

impressions graceful and slender as a past.
Another time you were with me and we
were young it had to do with sex
we breathed heavily the hard air
and saw our own internal shapes turn white
in front of us then fade into the borrowed
dusk of the room. It was perhaps
our first time, and I was in love
with your bravery, how you fearlessly

gave yourself into yourself, so I gathered
a small nosegay of yellow violets
that were the color of the bed
and of the dust floating languorous.
And then the barest small foot of you
kept creeping into my memory, as if
I had seen you naked and unafraid, as
each tiny foot of yours impressed itself
in the snow and the white nativity

of the season turned itself sorrowful
but so attractively. No one knew better
than you the look of the afternoon,
and how the foot is slim and of a shape
to win a woman's greatest ease and note that
the memory fades, and I pay my bill

and walk home past the flower shops.
Orpheus tracing his steps back to the surface
to make music again; how the instrument

is a body of wood breathing, a wisdom of
will and carpentry given voice; how he knew
tunes to turn trees into audience. Anyway,
the little family in the church held their dirty hymnals
and sang the old songs to the wheezing
box behind them. Nobody thought about anything
much: hunger, horror, the grand harmonies
of the light, the night where nothing
but blossoms of stars would crowd

and tumultuous clouds come pouring
over the rim from Canada
tendering the shiny coin of rain upon the plain:
Let not the darke thee cumber;
What though the Moon do's slumber?
   the starres of the night
   will lend thee their light,
like Tapers cleare without number.

—for Linda

Bin Ramke
from *Wake*

A Few Words on the Soul

We have a soul at times.
No one's got it non-stop,
for keeps.

Day after day,
year after year
may pass without it.

Sometimes
it will settle for awhile
only in childhood's fears and raptures.
Sometimes only in astonishment
that we are old.

It rarely lends a hand
in uphill tasks,
like moving furniture,
or lifting luggage,
or going miles in shoes that pinch.

It usually steps out
whenever meat needs chopping
or forms have to be filled.

For every thousand conversations
it participates in one,
if even that,
since it prefers silence.

Just when our body goes from ache to pain,
it slips off-duty.

It's picky:
it doesn't like seeing us in crowds,
our hustling for a dubious advantage
and creaky machinations make it sick.

Joy and sorrow
aren't two different feelings for it.
It attends us
only when the two are joined.

We can count on it
when we're sure of nothing
and curious about everything.

Among the material objects
it favors clocks with pendulums
and mirrors, which keep on working
even when no one is looking.

It won't say where it comes from
or when it's taking off again,
though it's clearly expecting such questions.

We need it
but apparently
it needs us
for some reason too.

Wislawa Szymborska
first published in *AGNI*, no. 54
translated from Polish by Stanislaw Baranczak and
        Clare Cavanagh

The Sudden Tug of the Familiar

The raised grain of golden oak in sunlight
is richer for scars
made beautiful with the caress of lemon oil
on a soft cloth gathering dust,

the patina of use,
the comings and goings of hands
in touch after touch after touch
for which years are as necessary

as the astringent lemon oil
scenting the room
to the slow pulse of the radio.
Ziggy Elman's horn, exquisitely visceral,

the bittersweet pull,
the segue to Ekstine and Vaughan,
to the muss and rumple of body and soul
in the old untidy life.

This is my room. It is peaceful.
Yet, it accommodates much of the past,
entertains lies,
makes boredom welcome.

The smooth plane of the coverlet
defines my bed. It is single.
Naked as a needle I slide in,
sleep the sleep of a nun.

I've a gift for arranging things
in a very small space.
My prayers would fit on a pin.
The dogwood at the window keeps nothing

but the bones of this November.
Warmth shrinks in its brittle grasp.
A shadow swallows the room,
folds me into myself.

Faye George
first published in *Poetry*, December 1996
also from *A Wound On Stone*

november 3 0

Coach Class Seats

Each has a foot-square paper napkin stuck
to the headrest: a bow to budget travelers' sensibilities.
Too bad each square evokes a paper toilet seat:
a 747 full of people shuffling in, then settling down to reek.

At least my hair won't pick up grease
from God-knows-whom. At least I won't be colonized
by roaming lice, or forced to lie, in effect, cheek-to-cheek
with a stranger (though his brain contains the same serotonin,

dopamine, and endorphins as mine, that mediate
the same trembling at takeoff, same intake of breath,
same slow relaxing of the hands on the armrests
as the plane climbs and the earth opens its green Atlas below).

No other head has ever been here, the squares state.
This experience is fresh, reserved for you.
The waiter changing the tablecloth before seating new
lovebirds where you've just proposed—

the nurse tearing a length of paper from the doctor's
table on which you bled and writhed—no,
you're not interchangeable, these gestures say. The way
that two-pound brookie sipped your Wooly Bugger,

then wrapped your line around a jutting root has never
in fishing history occurred before today.
Your fingerprints: unique as snowflakes. Your lover's
kiss: nonpareil. You were the first, stepping onto your lanai

in Kona, ever to say, "Whoa, honey, look at that view!"
How cheap the thrill if everybody felt that way.
Of course they don't, these napkins say. In all the miles
this plane will fly, there'll never be a passenger to rival you.

Charles Harper Webb
from *Liver*

december 1

December 1, 1994

I put the pyracantha in a blue vase
and spread the coneflower over my kitchen table.
I had to make sure they could bear the noise
and catch the benefits of my small radio
as if they were more than flowers—glass frogs at
    least,
or metal quail, their ears amazed, their small heads
nodding with the music. As far as the changes
in government, as far as *that* noise, the frog
presides over that, he is a kind of congressman
anyhow with his huge mouth open to catch
the flies and beetles; he has turned green from
    money
sticking to his skin. As far as the coneflower,
as far as the rays, they were already gone
and only the wood was left, only the naked
beautiful heads. As far as my love was concerned
I picked them before the snow came, before the ice
filled up the cavities and the cold leaves
turned thin and curled themselves around the stem.
As far as the pyracantha, as far as the vase,
as far as the metal quail, their eyes turned up,
their tiny beaks in the air, I turned the knob
from music to religion and let it rest
on wisdom, two or three voices, an English, a
    German,
discussing rape in Asia, discussing starvation, the
quail nodded, even the pyracantha nodded,
and I, a little furious, I turned to Canada
to see what the French were doing. That day I ate
soba, with parsley; I ate standing up; I fed
the quail; I fed the plants, though they were dead,
I listened to the forecast, I shaved in the dark,

making sure I got both cheeks and the hair
above the bullet. Afterwards I opened
a 1970 *New York Times*, something
about the new mayor, something about a murder
behind a bush, something about a dump
on fire, either a bomb or a match, a heartless
speech by a Georgia senator, a horoscope,
a kidnapping, a stock decline. I sang
first to the cloves but I whispered to the garlic
and ate two pounds of grapes. The frog lay down,
as far as I know, with the pyracantha, it was
something like bestiality, the coneflower
wrapped itself around the vase and I
lay down on the sofa; but first I put my glasses
in my right shoe and dropped my keys in the delicate
acorn bowl, then turned my leg so the wallet
wouldn't cut my buttocks. As I recall I thought of
the quail before I went to sleep, one of them
is tall and straight, he is the watchdog, the other
bends down to eat. I have to lie just so
with my head like that and my feet like that, it is
a little small for a bed, although my sleep,
of all my happy sleeps, is happiest there
on that white silk. I had a word with the frog
and one with the pyracantha, I had to school them
considering the date; all the holidays
were happening at once and it would be
disaster if they didn't get ready. "America
may not have room for you," I said. We giggled
and turned the lights out; even a little light
can ruin your sleep, no matter how much Mozart
flows over you, no matter how much Fats Waller.

Darkness is what we love. "Darkness, darkness,"
they sang; the frog was a tenor—what a shock!—
the pyracantha was a pipe, the coneflower
a wheeze or two. I was an alto—after
all those years a measly alto with only
a little range: "Oh put us all to sleep,
it's 1994, put us to sleep,
darkness, darkness!" A little tin shout from the lower
two registers, a little rusty gasp from the upper.

Gerald Stern
from *This Time: New and Selected Poems*

december 2

Well, You Needn't

In discord this incipience, disregard.
You are unhappy with the slant of the windows.
You eat an egg for breakfast, and are ungrateful.
Your hair is a black and gray wing that could be clipped.

I'm not the necessary angel.
My coffee is hot and bitter and so I like it.
Hunter-red your jacket, visible rube.
You know one, two, three, five things and like to sing them.

A mattress on the floor, a cork beneath the chair.
What do you know about comings and goings?
Speak to me sweetly of the smoothness of skins.
No light, no moon, no morning asks our opinion.

Spruce tree, white pine, where do you list?
What am I doing and whom do I move?
One, two, three blue blankets warm my darling.
Ten, twenty, thirty red kisses send him home.

I'm beginning to wonder if love's just a blunder.
Split moon, preacher, of an evening, in a mist.
My coat, bruise-purple, is a visible ruse.
Spruce tree, vagrant, where do you list?

Karen Volkman
first published in *The Paris Review*, vol. 42, no. 155, Summer 2000

december 3

Umbra

We share a habit of accepting hospitality.
Mix, Bless, Count, Drink—instant indispensability.
You are (you stir) relaxed, on novel number three.

English major, accent minor.
Trace. Ohio crossed with stroke of luck—
to other manners born.

It smells like heaven here.
Clover mown, clever man.
O kept bohemian—come walk with me.

See, on the potato fields, a haze.
They're up for sale by Sotheby's.
Estates already named: Duplex Oblige, Feigned Ease.

At night, the floodlights silver
These new-minted trees.
White ash. Prefabricated legacies.
Not bad for weekend company.

Dana Goodyear
first published in *The Yale Review*, vol. 90, no. 3, July 2002

december 4

My Test Market

Let's fly off to Finland, far
from the long arm of Olestra. There

in bog, arctic fen, and sand
are others who may understand

our epic innocence. Oh, how many
names for snow! and none

with growing market share. Where
are the snows that make no sense

so early in the morning, when the snow
is blue and blowing on the steppes?

Where is the *qanisqineq*,
the "snow floating on water"?

We may ask Vigdís Finnbogadóttir,
who's not a Finn. She may not know,

but she may point us toward
the northern lights. Her aim is true,

her snowshoes always full of snow.
We won't come back. You come too.

Rachel Loden
from *Hotel Imperium*

december 5

In Particular

Recognition in the body
moves like a swarm of bees: you know all
over at once. Your place
in history has not been betrayed
as you find what you really feel follows
no language: wild stir
of insects, flurry of birds, one bone
of the earth shows through, night root
tightened within its ground.
Can we be hypnotized by the primitive?
I heard a *tick, tick, tick*
once, turned and stared with the light
thinking about nothing.
But I noticed the fine grain of sink wood
like waves, weaving, the real bending
of trees against wind, over—how beautiful it was.
This is
what it is like before sudden disaster, before
the inhospitable truth:
our other brain, the one
which cannot speak, the one who sleeps incipient
on the job, walks the dog, erasure,
and gives in, hears
the *tick, tick, tick*, turns
toward it with the light
and makes us look—whether for the first
or last time, we look.

Elena Karina Byrne
from *The Flammable Bird*

DECEMBER 6

A Feeling

However far
I'd gone,
it was still
where it had all begun.

What stayed
was a feeling of difference,
the imagination
of adamant distance.

Some time,
place,
some other way it was,
the turned face

one loved,
remembered,
had looked for
wherever,

it was all now
outside
and in
was oneself again

except there too
seemed nowhere,
no air,
nothing left clear.

Robert Creeley
from *Life & Death*

DECEMBER 7

Vast Problem Still Obscure

Most of the mass of the universe
may be contained in dark matter.
No one knows what that may be.

Astronomers say we could be
dealing with planetary objects
unable to produce luminosity;

some believe we are looking
at black holes or other things
formed when stars are born or die.

(For physicists, the heart
of dark matter lies in axions,
strings, magnetic monopoles.)

If related to stars, dark matter
presumably will be found where
stars are. If indeed exotic,

it won't react with matter
as we know it nor, likely,
with itself; and surely

it will, in any case,
have nothing at all to do
with everyday matter.

Siri von Reis
from *The Love-Suicides at Sonezaki*

december 8

Clever and Poor

She has always been clever and poor,
    especially here off the Yugoslav train

on a crowded platform of dust. Clever was
    her breakfast of nutmeg ground in water

in place of rationed tea. Poor was the cracked
    cup, the missing bread. Clever are the six

handkerchiefs stitched to the size of a scarf
    and knotted at her throat. Poor is the thin coat

patched with cloth from the pockets
    she then sewed shut. Clever is the lipstick,

Petunia Pink, she rubbed with a rag on her nails.
    Poor nails, blue with the cold. Posed

in a cape to hide her waist, her photograph
    was clever. Poor then was what she called

the last bills twisted in her wallet. Letter
    after letter she was clever and more

clever, for months she wrote a newspaper man
    who liked her in the picture. The poor

saved spoons of sugar, she traded them
    for stamps. He wanted a clever wife. She was poor

so he sent a ticket: now she could come to her wedding
    by train. Poor, the baby left with the nuns.

Because she is clever, on the platform to meet him
    she thinks *Be generous with your eyes*. What is poor

is what she sees. Cracks stop the station clock,
    girls with candle grease to sell. Clever, poor,

clever and poor, her husband, more nervous
    than his picture, his shined shoes tied with twine.

V. Penelope Pelizzon
from *Nostos*

december 9

The Oration

after Cavafy

The boldest thing I ever did was to save a savior.
I reached heights of eloquence never achieved before
Or since. My speech turned the mob around!
They lifted the rood from his back, they dropped to the ground
Their nails and flails. But the whole time I spoke
(It's a wonder it didn't throw me off my stride)
The prophet or seer or savior, whatever you care to call him,
Kept groaning and muttering, telling me to be silent.
He was mad of course, so I simply ignored him. Poor fellow,
The beating they had given him must have turned his wits.

Every ounce of persuasion it took to convince the crowd
in the powerful sun, including the priests and his followers,
Exhausted me utterly. When I was sure he was safe,
The ungrateful fellow! I took my way home and collapsed
On my cushions with chilled wine. Then, I heard later,
The savior harangued the mob with outrageous statements
That roused them to fury anew: he denounced the priesthood
As corrupt; he pronounced himself king of the world;
He said God was his father. So they strung him up again.

A violent thunderstorm woke me to a sky full of lightning
So I rushed out in the rain, forgetting my cloak,
And found him dead and alone except for a handful of women
Weeping and carrying on. Well, it taught me a lesson,
To mind my own business—Why, the crowd might have turned on me!
Still, I have to be proud of my eloquence.
                    It was the speech of my life.

Carolyn Kizer
first published in *The Threepenny Review*, 78, vol. XX, no. 2, Summer 1999
also from *Cool, Calm & Collected: Poems 1960–2000*

december 10

Last Night

When the sun sets, and he isn't home, she walks
Not to be waiting, but she leaves a note:
Back soon, her only message, only wish.

After all, she didn't think he'd stay;
No plans, so no surprises when it ends.
The dishes wait unwashed. Bitter stains

Stretch out like shadows on the tablecloth.
Once you believe in finding gods in mortal men
You understand their restlessness as faith;

The way she feels his truth against her skin,
The rough edge of a matchbook, while she grieves
To see her saviors lost, and lost again.

God save the church that she takes refuge in,
The sanctuary given fools and thieves,
This silent girl who loves a man who leaves.

Chryss Yost
first published in *The Hudson Review*, vol. 54, no. 2, Summer 2001

Elegy for Jane Kenyon (2)

Jane is big
with death, Don
sad and kind—Jane
though she's dying
is full of mind

We talk about the table
the little walnut one
how it's like
Emily Dickinson's

But Don says No
Dickinson's
was made of iron. No
said Jane
Of flesh.

Jean Valentine
from *The Cradle of the Real Life*

december 12

Bachelor Song

It's Saturday night and Lisa
is burying her husband
and me in Scrabble, long
words coming out of her
like children—theirs
are upstairs, finally asleep
at 9 o'clock, when Lisa's
speech slurs from exhaustion
and Arthur calls me Honey
by mistake. They wrestle
on the carpet in hysterics,
roll into a kiss.

The window in the guest room
douses the bed with moonlight.
I close my eyes picturing
Susan Sarandon in *Atlantic City*
bathing her chest with lemons.
Last night Nina phoned.
She's decided to stop dating.
She hasn't gotten over
Howard, and her hands
are full with her 5-year-old.
She asked about work, about
my poetry. I said, Listen
I feel fine: you're not dating
and I'm glad I was the man
who helped clear that up
for you. I'll never

get to sleep in this light.
Now I remember, it's the last
night of the new comet.
Hale-Bopp, two guys
who spent their lives looking
at the sky, found it.
They say it won't be back
for 2000 years. I don't
understand how a chunk of ice
holds together for that long,
leaving its comb of light
like a whistled song.

Douglas Goetsch
from *Nobody's Hell*

DECEMBER 13

You Could Have Been Me

Just you walk out from that hospital air into the rasp edge of winter
when trees look fresh as a black lace hem
frayed in somebody's backseat.

Just walk out of the hospital, where grief is stripped and intricate
as winter trees.

I was fresh out of the sonogram room where they tilted a sensor
over and over a place in my breast.
You could have been me there—
a jacklighted deer
hearkening.

Ultrasound, imperceptible to anyone but bats,
will pass through liquid and bounce off solid
as sonar reveals a torpedo.
As it sees a malignant mass.

Doctors are whispering.

One looks over: *You mind us talking?*
Talk, I said. *Sing, if you feel like it.*

I walked straight out of that hospital
the moment the just-set-sun was casting a pearl shell over the city.

A man asked for change.
I told him the truth. I was out of work.

God bless you, he said, *come back tomorrow, I'll have money.*

My sonogram film now stood packed in with a thousand others.
When you rejoice, you forget the unspared ones.

You just watch that godlike blue between sunset and night,
blue laced with underlight curving around the shoulders of the earth
until it falls like a veil teased off—

and as a Chevy full of folks creaks down the way,
headlights swagging down the alley,
something shifts—inside me again is a perfectness.

No harm will come to us.
The street will not swallow us, the night not oppress us.

Something opens inside my chest—
a flower from a pellet in a glass of water, a toy
for a child so dumb with delight she's forgotten the difference
between herself and the one to be thanked
and the thanks, the very thanks.

Belle Waring
from *Dark Blonde*

DECEMBER 14

Natural

The leaves are coming down in huge bunches now
   (all I can think is hair after chemo), and we're to believe
      the death around the corner of December is natural—
because it happens unstoppably, because it unhappens
   when earth tires of being stone, when liquid comes alive
      in the heartwood, the topsoil, so we've got to swallow
our medicine now, break out the scrapers and mittens
   and salute the natural order, which will mean at least
      one ice storm per county, racking up 4.5 highway deaths
whether or not highways are natural, or the jaws of life,
   for that matter, which is what's got its teeth around my
      mother's wrist, holding on, her soul meanwhile
stalled out on the dark road right there in her living room
   where her feet dig in, her knees unlock, she must be
      dragged to her chair, she must be as tired of this
as her dragger, who is informed at monthly appointments
   that this is a natural progression, even the newest
      wrinkle: his sweetheart's wordless refusal
of the muffin he offers up to her clenched mouth,
   just as for years he offered his parishioners grape juice,
      little squares of white bread, the promise of eternal life.

Ellen Doré Watson
from *Ladder Music*

december 15

What I Remember the Writers Telling Me When I Was Young

For Muriel Rukeyser

Look hard at the world, they said—
generously, if you can
manage that, but hard. To see
the extraordinary data, you
have to distance yourself a
little, utterly. Learn the
right words for the umpteen kinds
of trouble that you'll see,
avoiding elevated
generics like *misery*,
wretchedness. And find yourself
a like spectrum of exact
terms for joy, some of them
archaic, but all useful.

Sometimes when they spoke to me I
could feel their own purposes
gathering. Language, the dark-
haired woman said once, is like
watercolor, it blots easily,
you've got to know what you're
after, and get it on quickly.
Everything gets watered
sooner or later with tears,
she said, your own or other
people's. The contrasts want to
run together and must not be
allowed to. They're what you
see with. Keep your word-hoard dry.

William Meredith
from *Effort at Speech: New and Selected Poems*

Olives

They are, we know, an acquired taste—
something for adults, just like martinis,
truffles, caviar, asparagus, or sweet and thoughtful
sex. Imagine someone who has never seen
or eaten one: where to begin? With a taxonomy
by shapes or size, or color, ripeness, flavor,
oiliness, consistency? ("... and darker

than a Muscat grape when they are ripe;
when green, looking a bit like alligator pears,
but smaller, although ovoid, like a pebble
or a robin's egg—smooth in the Spanish
style, wrinkled as a prune in Greece.") And then
there are the place of origin, the age of groves;
one could evoke the ancient art

of growing them, the holy trees of Palestine,
the rocky hillsides of Provence
(and say how trunks are sculpted, almost into stone,
as van Gogh saw them in the fields near Arles).
Or one could tell the name of the estate,
and gesture toward imagined slopes,
or sound the wind that soughs among the leaves

at evening when the fruit is taking shape,
and paint the moon as honeyed
as it hangs at harvesttime. Or should one classify—
explaining, first, the part about the seed, and how
the olive may be pitted, filled
for further flavor—classify the things, I say,
by stuffings: anchovy, pimiento, pearly

onion, almond bits? And what about their uses—
surely what we make of things
is what they are? Describe Italian salads,
canard aux olives, a relish dish with radishes
and celery and olives, stuffed? and then
back to martinis, which I started with, when you
stirred up a pitcher, cold and rolling suave

upon the tongue, and kissed me with a hint of brine,
because, while you were mixing,
you had cheated, finding that a pickled olive,
plump, savory, and salubrious (do not forget
the good cholesterol), could wait
no longer to be tasted—so, enticed it and the latent
aspects of its being from a bottle,

out into the actual—a bite, a crunch, another bite,
a pleasure on the palate. But I found you out,
a prestidigitator and a surreptitious
hedonist, now trying to amend
the matter with an extra olive for me, also. Is this
the essence of an olive, of a man—
best when surprised, when serendipitous, with salt?

Catharine Savage Brosman
from *Places in Mind*

december 17

Mediterranean Cooking for Two

Octopus in one hand, cookbook in the other, he nearly
loses his focus over the black print, the famous chef's direction
to dash the small body against the sink's steel—"vigorously,"
according to the recipe, in imitation of Greek women
tenderizing the new catch right on the shore's wet rocks.
Here in his kitchen the sound of that flesh landing again and again,
flaccid and unmusical, troubles him. "Fifteen or six-
teen times," read the instructions! But something of his own
body sings in that dull sound, mortal and precarious. He
would serve the dish later that afternoon with a fine sherry,
the house already redolent of garlic and olives. *Nine. Ten.*
It *is* love: the small creature pitched and retrieved again
from the stainless cold (*thirteen*), sliced, sautéed, and oil-
drizzled: *Fifteen.* It must be. *Sixteen.* All he can handle...

Janet Holmes
from *Humanophone*

december 18

The Vines

Vines Cottage, Wales, 1996

This year we've lived in stone,
in what our Welsh friend calls
a cowshed, watched the vine
or vines that climb along the walls
and hang above the doors
go gold, with purple grapes,
then bare, then green.
Mornings brought the sheen
of spider webs, dew on the lovespoon
scrollery of trellised roses,
the carpet stitched with silver
traceries of snails,
in frost the filigree of garden hose
about to coil, suspended by its tail.

We thought we knew
exactly where we were, until
we woke, the breadcrumbs gone,
you blaming me, me blaming you,
in a forest dark where ways
we thought we had by heart
diverged or crossed, a maze,
until we nearly came apart.
As good as lost, almost alone,
our single sorrows met and turned
into a footpath doubling back to home,
this cottage, where we've learned
how vines that tangle also twine—
have to, to crush and come to wine.

William Greenway
from *Simmer Dim*

december 19

American Pylons

Spreading their legs between the rows
  of stubble wheat or corn,
they stand their ground against the lash
  and icy sting of storms.

While all the country lies asleep,
  they brace beneath cold stars,
gripping their buzzing cables, stiff
  and faithful in the dark.

When light returns, their ribs allow
  blown leaves an easy passage
while they convey, without a pause,
  all power and no message.

Kevin Durkin

first published in *The Yale Review,* vol. 88, no. 1, January 2000

DECEMBER 20

Neanderthal, with Help from Cave and Bear, Invents the Flute

In the dark cave of Slovenia,
     40,000 years of utter silence.
No one to lift this leg bone of bear.

Two finger-holes punched through
     to take the mortal breath away,
end open to let out the skein

of tones closer to human moan
     than human moan, hoot of moon
wind-honed, horned, fervid scents,

fevered puddles of bison blood, beak
     and breath of Gray Father, steam
of Mother Milk. We didn't know

Neanderthals had an ear.
     We didn't know they beatified
their dead with color. In petal,

pistil, stamen they invented
     prayer, and on the first flute
the closer-to-beastly unkin of us

worked, out of starless dark,
     the melodies of bear, and birds
lifting off at dawn. The cave

is a flute, the skull is a flute
     for wish to move through, true,
eye and nose hole waiting for

the skill to finger out our voices.
     From the bones of our parents
we tease out the music of us.

David Citino
first published in *American Literary Review*, vol. X,
     no. 2, Fall 1999
also from *The News and Other Poems*

december 21

Her Purse, at the Winter Solstice

The needled red tea roses were distorted
by the quilt in the fabric of the cheap cotton
bag she carried through the filth
of snow to the transfusions

and back again to her bed
where she fanned herself
into the soft pink blankets and then closed
into them like a small item,
lost. Sometimes I couldn't find her—

a swansdown powder puff,
misplaced. All night

I'd dream of black taffeta, locked inside
a day bag of white painted metal plaques
or an evening clutch of lacquered brass,
covered with ash, ribbed silk. Her purse

had too deep a background,
where blossoms were pinned down
—stitch to stitch—
with never a hope they could climb off
and into the coming spring air, join

the others. I'd dream of a framed
French carryall, pale blue silk
and silver thread worked into
a pattern of a spiderweb, finished

with a tassel of carved steel
beads, my fingers constantly being cut
by handles decorated with flowered urns
and the cold heads of the sphinxes.

Susan Hahn
from *Holiday*

Embertide in Advent

for J.R.W

They waited beneath the cold December snows,
Late flowers of the fall, the folded rose,
The angels'-trumpet crumpled in the mold,
Daisies of Michaelmas, the hidden lily curled
In dust of goldenrod and marigold,
Old matter's liturgy, a pregnant world
Out of whose star-of-Bethlehem arose
A Roman hyacinth, sweet-olive of the snows.

David Middleton
from *Beyond the Chandeleurs*

The Unstrung Lyre

With what can I string this antique lyre:
A snowy contrail? A trace of ether?
A little belt of stars the morning veils?

The wet end of a sounding line that drips
Souvenirs from the wintry depth's calm?
These unaccompanied words, *a capella*,

May as well be words in an empty chapel:
Fire-gutted, cellar-cold, shadows gathered
In the pews instead of parishioners.

What are words spoken to no one but prayer,
But the restless gibber of the heart,
Frantic, willing to say anything,

To beg mercy of what might silence it?
As bright as an Annuciation lily,
As a bowstring shimmering to stillness,

The Word is what I heard and cannot replicate.
This unstrung frame may as well be a loom
Upon which no tomorrow is woven,

Upon which no tomorrow is postponed.

Eric Pankey
first published in *New England Review*, vol. 20, no. 1, Winter 1999

Entrance

Whoever you are: step out of doors tonight,
Out of the room that lets you feel secure.
Infinity is open to your sight.
Whoever you are.
With eyes that have forgotten how to see
From viewing things already too well-known,
Lift up into the dark a huge, black tree
And put it in the heavens: tall, alone.
And you have made the world and all you see.
It ripens like the words still in your mouth.
And when at last you comprehend its truth,
Then close your eyes and gently set it free.

Rainer Maria Rilke
first published in *The Formalist, a Journal of Metrical Poetry,* vol. 13, issue 1, 2002
translated by Dana Gioia

december 25

Processional

Think what the demotic droplet felt,
Translated by a polar wand to keen
Six-pointed Mandarin—
All singularity, its Welt—
Anschauung of a hitherto untold
Flakiness, gemlike, nevermore to melt!

But melt it would, and—look—become
Now birdglance, now the gingko leaf's fanlight,
To that same tune whereby immensely old
Slabs of dogma and opprobrium,
Exchanging ions under pressure, bred
A spar of burnt-black anchorite,

Or in three lucky strokes of word golf LEAD
Once again turns (LOAD, GOAD) to GOLD.

James Merrill
edited by J. D. McClatchy and Stephen Yenser
from *Collected Poems*

december 2 6

History

Even Eve, the only soul in all of time
to never have to wait for love,
must have leaned some sleepless nights
alone against the garden wall
and wailed, cold, stupefied, and wild
and wished to trade-in all of Eden
to have but been a child.

In fact, I gather that is why she leapt and fell from grace,
that she might have a story of herself to tell
in some other place.

Jennifer Michael Hecht
from *The Next Ancient World*

Mother of Us All

Mother of the long silences
that pinned us to our chairs,
where were you in your body
if not here with us?

Mother of the stolen roses
that faded like kisses,
why so pale by the window,
peering in at us?

Mother of the prayer beads
that pooled on our pillows,
what were you murmuring,
hands like paper pressed from us?

Mother of the snakes
that coiled around each wrist,
did it ever occur to you to poison us?

Mother of the mirrors
that disassembled the walls,
how many times did we see you look beyond us?

Mother of the incessant purges
that sent our beautiful books and toys to charity,
what perfect world had you not already given us?

Mother of the busy hands
that tore at the spiked tongues,
what were you pulling, hiding at dusk from us?

Mother of the white hair
that sprouted overnight,
what made you skittish,
lock every door behind us?

Mother of the diminishing voice
that broke into chalk,
how could we have known there were things
you had wanted to tell us?

Mother of the disappearance
that shadowed Father's face,
when did you decide you had to leave us.

Cathy Song
first published in *Shenandoah*, vol. 49, no. 2,
    Summer 1999
also from *The Land of Bliss*

Evening in the Country

I am still completely happy.
My resolve to win further I have
Thrown out, and am charged by the thrill
Of the sun coming up. Birds and trees, houses,
These are but the stations for the new sign of being
In me that is to close late, long
After the sun has set and darkness come
To the surrounding fields and hills.
But if breath could kill, then there would not be
Such an easy time of it, with men locked back there
In the smokestacks and corruption of the city.
Now as my questioning but admiring gaze expands
To magnificent outposts, I am not so much at home
With these memorabilia of vision as on a tour
Of my remotest properties, and the eidolon
Sinks into the effective "being" of each thing,
Stump or shrub, and they carry me inside
On motionless explorations of how dense a thing can be,
How light, and these are finished before they have begun
Leaving me refreshed and somehow younger.
Night has deployed rather awesome forces
Against this state of affairs: ten thousand helmeted footsoldiers,
A Spanish armada stretching to the horizon, all
Absolutely motionless until the hour to strike
But I think there is not too much to be said or be done
And that these things eventually take care of themselves
With rest and fresh air and the outdoors, and a good view of things.
So we might pass over this to the real
Subject of our concern, and that is
Have you begun to be in the context you feel
Now that the danger has been removed?

Light falls on your shoulders, as is its way,
And the process of purification continues happily,
Unimpeded, but has the motion started
That is to quiver your head, send anxious beams
Into the dusty corners of the rooms
Eventually shoot out over the landscape
In stars and bursts? For other than this we know nothing
And space is a coffin, and the sky will put out the light.
I see you eager in your wishing it the way
We may join it, if it passes close enough:
This sets the seal of distinction on the success or failure of your attempt.
There is growing in that knowledge
We may perhaps remain here, cautious yet free
On the edge, as it rolls its unblinking chariot
Into the vast open, the incredible violence and yielding
Turmoil that is to be our route.

John Ashbery
first published in *The Mooring of Starting Out: The First Five Books of Poetry*

To Two of My Characters

Emily, as I entered a real greenhouse,
I feared I failed to do you justice, to see
with Teddy's eyes, to smell as he would have
the cyclamens, the mums, the pithy tilth
and near-obscene sweet richness of it all,
which he ascribed to you, despite
your gimpy leg and spiky manner—
you were his hothouse houri, dizzying.

And Essie, did I make it clear enough
just how your face combined the Wilmot cool
precision, the clean Presbyterian cut,
hellbent on election, with the something
soft your mother brought to the blend, the petals
of her willing to unfold at a touch?
I wanted you to be beautiful, the both of you,
and, here among real flowers, fear I failed.

John Updike
first published in *Poetry*, vol. CLXXVI, no. 5, August 2000
also from *Americana and Other Poems*

december 30

After the Poem Who Knows

After the poem who knows
What the vandals will do.

For now they have been sighted
At the mall, at the bank, down by

The fire station, everywhere
Myth revises history.

I want I want I want I want!
The vandals have been heard to chant,

Their chant a chant heard far away.
(Ear to the ground, finger in the air.)

Above, a cloud,
A gull, another cloud,

Capriciousness. In the tree
At the edge of the stanza, the ghosts

Of two squirrels chase each other up
And up and up and up

Then downdowndown!
(The stanza ends.)

And you and I? Who knows
What we might do

Once the poem concludes, the vandals gone,
Our words remembered as...

Recidivist! screeches a screech owl.
And the vandals stomp onto

The scene, picking their teeth clean
With the chipped tips of dullèd knives.

And you and I, and you and I?
We ready ourselves for death

(O yes the poem has taught us to)
Pack up our little picnic, close the book,

And step into the future:
Hello? We're here. Is anybody home?

Alan Michael Parker
first published in *Boulevard*, vol. 13, nos. 1 and 2, Fall 1997
also from *Vandals*

Learning the Angels

Waiting up, he's deep in Angels & Archangels:
lion-bodied Cherubim, Principalities
six-winged, translucent as cathedral windows,
heavily armored Archangels, and the usual

angels for the dirty work, recording, hand-
delivering, and as he now learns, placing a finger
on the lips of every newborn, leaving the cleft
imposing silence concerning clouds of glory.

Now she breezes in, douses the light, wants
to cuddle, undoes, runs a finger along the cleft
that gives the tip of his sex its face of a heart.
It's devil's work, he knows.

At dawn he's in the dew-damp garden, picking
strawberries for her,
turning the leaves pale-side-up to uncover
the heart-shaped fruit,

and finds the garden snake,
a hog-nose, head up, neck flared and glistening.
Oh you above, from the simplest two-wingers
to complicated wheels of fire, be vigilant,

he thinks, and returns
full of Powers and Dominions. She yawns,
half-rises on her divan, plumps a pillow,
pours cream on the berries. Its blush

deepens. He finds himself
sliding a hand beneath her robe,
along the nape, the shoulders, the spine,
the small, that valley lightly downed—

which leads to what comes over him,
her shoulder blades working the air, her finger
on his lips.

Rennie McQuilkin
first published in *The Gettysburg Review,* vol. 12, no. 4,
    Winter 1999
also from *Learning the Angels*

CreDITS

All poems reproduced by Poetry Daily with permission.

JANUARY

"V, x" copyright © 1995 by William Matthews. Reprinted from *The Mortal City: 100 Epigrams of Martial,* Ohio Review Books, with the permission of Sebastian Matthews. All rights reserved.

"An Attempt" copyright © 1998 by Emerson College. Reprinted with the permission of Angela Ball. All rights reserved.

"Forget How to Remember How to Forget" from *Figurehead* by John Hollander, copyright © 1999 by John Hollander. Used by permission of Alfred A. Knopf, a division of Random House, Inc. All rights reserved.

"How the Demons Were Assimilated & Became Productive Citizens" copyright © 1999 by A.E. Stallings. Reprinted from *Archaic Smile,* University of Evansville Press, 1999 by permission of the University of Evansville. All rights reserved.

"The Silence of the Stars" copyright © 1999 by David Wagoner. Reprinted from *Traveling Light: Collected and New Poems*, University of Illinois Press, 1999 with the permission of the University of Illinois Press. All rights reserved.

Dorianne Laux, "The Nurse" from *Awake.* Copyright © 1988 by Dorianne Laux. Reprinted with the permission of BOA Editions, Ltd. All rights reserved.

"Pine" from *Mosquito & Ant* by Kimiko Hahn. Copyright © 1999 by Kimiko Hahn. Used by permission of W. W. Norton & Company, Inc. All rights reserved.

Bob Hicok, "Absence" from *Plus Shipping.* Copyright © 1998 by Bob Hicok. Reprinted with the permission of BOA Editions, Ltd. All rights reserved.

Kim Addonizio, "What Do Women Want?" from *Tell Me.* Copyright © 2000 by Kim Addonizio. Reprinted with the permission of BOA Editions, Ltd. All rights reserved.

"Fetch" copyright © 2002 by Jeffrey Skinner. Reprinted from *Gender Studies*, Miami University Press Poetry Series, 2002 with the permission of Miami University Press. All rights reserved.

"How Came What Came Alas" copyright © 1999 by Pleiades Press. Reprinted with the permission of HeidiLynn Nilsson. All rights reserved.

"Nothing in That Drawer" copyright © 1995 by Ron Padgett. Reprinted from *New & Selected Poems,* David R. Godine, Publisher, Inc., 1995 with the permission of David R. Godine, Publisher, Inc. All rights reserved.

"A Dog's Grave" copyright © 2001 by Witness. Reprinted with the permission of Ted Kooser. All rights reserved.

"Old Man Leaves Party" from *Blizzard of One* by Mark Strand, copyright © 1998 by Mark Strand. Used by permission of Alfred A. Knopf, a division of Random House, Inc. All rights reserved.

"What the Living Do" from *What the Living Do* by Marie Howe. Copyright © 1998 by Marie Howe. Used by permission of W. W. Norton & Company, Inc. All rights reserved.

"*from* Unholy Sonnets" copyright © 1997 by Mark Jarman. Reprinted from *Questions for Ecclesiastes,* Story Line Press, 1997 with the permission of Story Line Press. All rights reserved.

"A '49 Merc" copyright © 2002 by Kurt Brown. Reprinted from *More Things in Heaven and Earth,* Four Way Books, 2002 with the permission of Four Way Books. All rights reserved.

"Nearly a Valediction" from *Winter Numbers* by Marilyn Hacker. Copyright © 1994 by Marilyn Hacker. Used by permission of the author and W. W. Norton & Company, Inc. All rights reserved.

"On a Portrait of Two Beauties" copyright © 2000 by John Balaban. Reprinted from *Spring Essence: The Poetry of Ho Xuan Kong,* Copper Canyon Press, 2000 with the permission of Copper Canyon Press. All rights reserved.

"Landing Under Water, I See Roots" copyright © 1999 by Partisan Review, Inc. Reprinted from *Calendars*, Tupelo Press, 2003 with the permission of Tupelo Press. All rights reserved.

"Best" copyright © 2002 by Gregory Orr. Reprinted from *The Caged Owl: New and Selected Poems*, Copper Canyon Press, 2002 with the permission of Copper Canyon Press. All rights reserved.

"Gravelly Run". Copyright © 1960 by A.R. Ammons, from *Collected Poems 1951-1971* by A.R. Ammons. Used by permission of W.W. Norton & Company, Inc. All rights reserved.

"Why Fool Around?" from *Pallbearers Envying the One*

FEBRUARY

MARCH

APRIL

MAY

JUNE

SEPTEMBER

OCTOBER

DECEMBER

TITLE INDEX

author index